ISBN 10: 0-9985055-0-1
ISBN-13: 978-0-9985055-0-3

DEDICATION

To the original <u>Story of Kennett</u> by Bayard Taylor
that brought recognition and life of the community to the greater world in 1866.
And to our spouses, Bob Holliday and Jane George,
who supported us through the many hours that went into this book.

ACKNOWLEDGMENTS

It takes a village like Kennett to receive the cooperation for writing our story. Our thanks go out to nearly fifty community members. We had no one refuse an interview, but, instead, we received gracious acceptances and dedication of time, not only for the interview, but time given to editing the final write-up. Thank you, interviewees! You are the essence and heart of this book.

We feel such gratitude to those who offered their time and expertise towards our project:

- **Wesley George and Lucas Freire**, our interns, who researched data and helped shape some of the thinking in the reflection chapters.
- **Kris Russomagno and Karen Ormstedt**, who volunteered their time and creativity to design and layout the cover and interior of our book. Their self-publishing skills and energetic spirit offered organization and artistic appeal, which brought this final product to fruition.
- **Mary Ann Piccard**, who volunteered to provide another round of editing, as she did this work in her previous job at DuPont Company.
- **Larry and Geoff Bosley**, co-owners of The Market at Liberty Place, for providing a welcoming community space for conducting interviews and developing the book, along with having a great cup of coffee and meals to enjoy.

Photography:

- **Chris Barber** from Historic Kennett Square, who provided the front and back cover photos in addition to photos within the book. She is a long-time Kennett news reporter and photographer and carries a genuine "feel" for the town.
- **Bob George**, who put away his computer and picked up his camera to capture images for the book.

Inheritance

"This little light of mine, I'm gonna let it shine."
— African American Spiritual —

Kennett's Inheritance
by Joan Holliday

Before we move into the interviews about the youth programs, along with the educational, business and grassroots leaders of the community, this preface on Kennett's Inheritance is intended to give the reader a backdrop to hold, while soaking up the stories. Inheritance is a gift that has come to us through the land we inhabit and the legacy that the residents, who lived before us, have left behind. Kennett's inheritance is central to many of us, who have been involved in our community work, and in listening to the stories, we are certain that you will hear the same resonance.

We all have in common living on the same inherited land. This is the smallest whole that is not divisible when working as a community. Reflecting on the spirit, the essential virtue of the land, a grassroots group came to see it as "peaceful progressive inclusivity" and took that as our living philosophy for overall guidance and meaning in our community work. Bridging the Community, came out of this and continues to be a grassroots leading process, a process which includes an openness to exercising choice, people choosing to step into the grassroots leading and volunteer process. You will marvel at the many ways initiatives have started and continue because of the living out of this philosophy.

Behind all this, Kennett Square has been nourished, fed and inspired by the Quaker Friends, who created a platform for peace, caring and inclusivity in the early 1800s. One can walk down East Linden Street and see the plaques on the homes that identify Quakers and run-away slaves, who lived side-by-side, essentially living out a higher order of humanity together. They saw the dignity in each human being, regardless of the dangers involved in feeding, clothing, protecting and aiding a run-away slave. The Quaker process has instructed and influenced what Kennett is today; the Quaker's way of being is behind the care and attention that is being given to each child through the variety of youth programs and the way the town faces and processes adversity and divisiveness.

Today, the dominant culture in this country looks at a problem and tries to solve it by generating causes to keep us energized. The infrastructures and costs involved then use up the resources of the community and through time often reduce any spirit that was present.

The people of Kennett start from the heart, stay on the potential-side, encourage and support grass-roots leaders and volunteers, and build community spirit from this foundation. It has been proven time and time again, that this way of living sustains us through hard times and brings inspiration at creative times.

We, the people of the Kennett community are committed to honoring our inheritance and leaving a personal and group legacy of advancing humanness and nourishing life for the next generation. It naturally follows that this underlies the secret of our community's ongoing progress in moving towards wholeness and oneness.

Bridging the
Community

CONTENTS

Interviews

*"UNLESS
Someone like you
cares a whole awful
lot, nothing is going to
get better. It's not."*
—The Lorax (1971)
by Dr. Seuss, American
writer and cartoonist

> ## *"Taking the time to build community, to get to know people, will have long-lasting benefits."*
> — Clifton Taulbert, American author —

INTRODUCTION

The Kennett Story
by Bob George

This is a story about Kennett Square, Pennsylvania. Don't get it confused with Bayard Taylor's <u>Story of Kennett</u> written in 1866, 150 years ago, which was a page turner of a novel about *his* Kennett Square with highwayman Sandy Flash and buried treasure. This is our attempt to explain this small town and the surrounding community today and, in doing so, possibly help bring an understanding of what is going on in the outside world. We want to show how all of us need to be part of the solution for addressing the challenges facing communities all over the country. We are hoping to portray in detail what makes up a great place to live and raise a family. Kennett and the local area are doing a variety of things well and we want to share those processes and strategies and recognize the folks that make them happen. One of the bonuses of analyzing the processes of a small town is that it is small enough to see how it works. While the cities are getting bigger and are key drivers in our nation's productivity and global competitiveness, the small town is more transparent.

The United States is not winning in the global race in a number of ways. The reason our country helped win World War II and had such a great growth spurt in the 1950s was arguably because we had the best educated citizens in the world. American 15-year-olds have fallen from 15th in the world in the subject of English in the year 2000 to 26th and from 19th in math to 36th, in just twelve years. There are some gathering clouds in the future, and we would like to identify them and anticipate how to address them.

What we found were the heroes that made this country great, like Alexander Hamilton and Rosa Parks, are alive and well in the people today; they just work at different places in the process. Men, women and kids are making sacrifices every day to help this community thrive. There are also a number of negative trends, some captured by the recent 2016 election cycle, for example, that may be better understood when we see them firsthand. We want to recognize and build contingencies to respond to these forces so that we can maintain the resources needed to keep being a great place to live and raise a family. There is also the simple fact that we need to understand what works and what doesn't, so that we can maximize our resources for a future that ensures all of our citizens, rich and poor, have the potential to achieve the American dream and live a good life in this great experiment in democracy called America.

Kennett is a small borough with about 6,000 inhabitants, nestled between a number of townships like Kennett and New Garden in southeastern Pennsylvania. Specifically, it is located in southern Chester County, an area where 100,000 of the county's population of 500,000 live. Chester County is the richest county in Pennsylvania with a medium income of $100,000. However, Kennett Square's median income is closer to $63,000. 42% of the Kennett School children are disadvantaged and eligible for free or reduced lunches. The national average of public school children coming from homes that are under-resourced is over 50%. By looking at a small sample size of the USA you may get a better idea of what works and what doesn't, and what resources need to be enhanced (early childhood) and where we can find economies (leveraged and shared resources) that improve process efficiency.

The idea for this book came from a 2015 national conference on poverty in Cincinnati where leaders of the local Kennett food cupboard went to share their ideas around how an organization goes from providing fish to teaching fishing. The Kennett Area Community Services (KACS), our local food cupboard, has been giving out turkeys for Christmas and Thanksgiving for over 60 years. But in the Great Recession of 2007, their client base grew to over 500 families and they started to deal with deeper resource issues such as housing and finances. KACS started asking about the root causes of these issues and how they could make their clients more resilient.

One of the hot topics at that conference was immigration and some folks from Houston, Texas were writing a book about immigrants. After talking with us, they asked if they could include Kennett in their book. The Kennett school system has the 4th highest level of immigrants in the 500 school districts of Pennsylvania and while it doesn't have all the answers, it certainly has some ideas about what works. The school district of York, Pennsylvania, which is ranked first in Pennsylvania for their English as a Second Language (ESL) program, has 22% ESL kids and Kennett has 14% (the Houston school system has 17%). Kennett is like a lot of towns in the United States where immigrants have been a significant part of the population for the entire life of the town. William Penn's Quaker descendants started growing mushrooms over a hundred years ago and they brought in Germans, who brought in Italians who now have mostly

Mexican Americans doing the hard work for not much more than $8 an hour. The cycle continues as now almost twenty of the smaller mushroom farms are owned or at least run by Mexican Americans and other South American workers are moving in. This history has led to a culture of generally being tolerant of immigration. But there are expectations of the immigrants, expectations about language, for example. I remember at a Rotary Club meeting one senior member of the community told me how, in the 1950s, his two uncles had a bet that if one of them spoke Italian on the job, he would owe the other a pack of cigarettes.

So, we came back from the conference in Cincinnati and I volunteered to organize and collect the information about Kennett. I soon discovered the story of Kennett was about a lot more than immigration. I needed someone to partner with who really knew the current Kennett. Finding just the right person to pull the story of Kennett together was much easier than I imagined. I asked the executive director of Kennett Area Community Services (KACS) Melanie Weiler who she thought I should ask, and she answered without even thinking; "Joan Holliday." I asked a number of other folks and they all came up with the same name.

In Chapter 7, we provide a stress test for Kennett using the James Fallows report on the "11 Signs a City Will Succeed". In this stress test, the second sign that a city will succeed is knowing how to pick out the local patriots. Fallows would ask the question, "Who makes this town go?" And, it was a good sign when everyone in the town had the same answer. And that is what I found, when I asked the question, everyone said that the best person to do this job is Joan Holliday. She was the public health nurse for more than thirty years and leads the Bridging the Community effort (a meeting that brings volunteers and resources together for the town) and has done more for first-time moms than anyone. I knew Joan, and to me she was always the Florence Nightingale of Kennett Square. But someone who knows her better than I do says that she and her husband Bob are the best examples you will ever find of two angels set down upon earth. There isn't much she doesn't know about Kennett and everyone knows and trusts her. Plus, it's not bad to have an angel on your team. I asked her and she said, "Yes." I'm not sure what I would have done if she said "no," but there is a good chance this book wouldn't have made it into print.

As we interviewed the community we quickly realized that much of the focus of the various resources in Kennett was on the kids. My family tends to interpret life through movies and I flashed back to one of my favorite movies *Back to the Future*. At the very end Doc Brown comes back from the future and surprises Marty and says; "Marty! You've gotta come back with me!...Back to the future!"; Marty asked: "Wait a minute, Doc. What are you talkin' about? What happens to us in the future? Do we become as@!#$%^ or somethin'?" And Doc says: "No, no, no, no, no, Marty. Both you and Jennifer turn out fine. It's your kids, Marty! Something's gotta be done about your kids!" And that tends to be the focus in Kennett. There is also a sense that the parents want better for their kids, or at least as good. In the movie *Breaking Away*, Dave Stoller (Dennis Christopher) was being given "the talk" by his dad (Paul Dooley) about what his life was like growing up in the college town of Bloomington, Indiana. They were called "Cutters". They were looked down on by the university as they worked in the quarries with their hands and came home dirty and exhausted every night. Dave said, "Dad, I'm proud of being a Cutter." And his father said, "Son, you're not a Cutter, I'm a Cutter." And we found it in the interviews with the kids. Their parents didn't want them to go into the mushroom houses, they wanted them to make a life for themselves with an education.

So the title of the book became <u>The Story of Kennett: Shaping Our Future One Child at a Time.</u> And to shape the future we have certain goals for our kids: to feel safe, to be healthy, to be resilient, to be knowledgeable (i.e. working to grade level or above), to be skillful (i.e. proficient in music, sports, volunteering and/or the outdoors), to know themselves (i.e. what they love, how they learn, what are their hot buttons), to embrace diversity, and to feel successful and confident so they can take on the world. To attain these goals, we touch both the home and the school environments to provide support to the parents and teachers in raising and teaching the kids.

As we thought about why kids are so important to the Kennett model we referred to the Kennett dream and parsed it, "Kennett is a great place to live and raise a family." And that means for everyone, not just the rich and middle class. On the spectrum of life, we want to end up on the "healthy and happy" end, not the "sick and sad" one. So what do you need to live well and raise a family? There is security. The family needs to feel safe and Kennett Township was recognized as the safest municipality in Pennsylvania in 2015. And of course, you need your family not to go hungry. Our food cupboard served 500 families during the Great Recession of 2007. (It is down closer to 400 families now, which is still close to 2,000 individuals.) Thirty years ago, there was pretty much one Acme grocery store to cover the whole area, though it was one of the largest in the chain. Today, we have 5 grocery stores serving the area plus a number of farmer's markets. Then there is a need for a roof over your head, and KACS now has two full-time case managers keeping people in their homes and off the streets. There is some low cost housing available. Even so, the Kennett area, still has the highest level of homelessness in the county after the city of Coatesville. There is always the need for health care for everyone and that is getting better, although still too expensive and in flux. Finally, you need a system that has the kids' kindergarten-ready. Only a third of the high risk kids are getting help with early education preparation, and performing at grade level all through school until they go off to college or some other form of higher education. The area is improving in kindergarten-readiness, but will be one issue that we will need to address to continue excelling in the Kennett model.

That's our belief, and we will make the case that Kennett is doing a very good job of being a place where we can all live well together. It was reinforced by the interviews, but the crux of this model is the kids. When I helped start the Kennett Education Foundation in 2000 with the presiding School Superintendent Rudy Karkosak and a school board member Skip Reynolds, none of the 100 ESL kids that graduated that year from

Kennett High were going to college. The first generation Hispanic immigrant's accomplishment of far surpassing their parents with a high school diploma was a great start, but to truly capture their potential we needed to provide programs that would enable them to go on to further education after high school. The key to all of the programs that make up the Kennett model is the will to make Kennett better and the availability of the needed resources: United Way donations, great teachers, generous foundations, dedicated public and private social workers, and most of all volunteers. Over 100 volunteers are needed to support 4 to 6 families with housing through our homeless program, Family Promise. It takes well over 2,000 volunteers to cover all the programs that support the Kennett area.

The Dr. Seuss quote at the beginning of this chapter has become part of the theme of this book. I encourage everyone to take it to heart. Without these resources, Kennett could follow the path of Wilmington, Delaware, which was referred to as Murder Town USA in *Newsweek*. There, but for the grace of God, go our communities. According to the best places to live website, the violent crime rate in the United States is 31. In Chicago the rate is 59, and in Wilmington, Delaware it's 94. Chester County is half the national average. On the *Parenting Magazine* website, they list the top ten most dangerous cities in the United States. Baltimore was 6th and Wilmington, Delaware, just 15 miles from Kennett, was number one. It can happen.

We really can make a difference in the quality of life in our hometown. Today, sixteen years later, the Kennett Education Foundation sees more than a quarter of the ESL kids going off to college. And this last year Christian Cordova was moving into his dorm for his sophomore year at Harvard, his mother is a custodian for the high school, which always came in handy so he could stay late after school. He told the story recently of how he was checking into his new dorm room and then caught up with his friend Miranda and her parents asked him to join them for dinner. Everyone who has taken their kid to college will know this experience and be thankful that another family included your child for the last family meal before school starts. But this time Miranda's father just happened to be the great Astro Physicist, Neal Degrasse Tyson. Now that would make the dinner conversation interesting. Christian is a unicorn, an exceptionally talented young man that worked harder than anyone else in school to get where he is. He provides all of us great hope, but he is not the norm. There are hundreds of young men and women in Kennett that won't get the chance that Christian got. Some won't even finish high school, and we need to be the community that is there for them too.

Only measuring the difference that these programs have made on the ESL kids each year who are leaving Kennett for college and getting a degree, you see the creation of $45,000,000 worth of wealth over their lifetime in added income. They will pay taxes and help ensure that their kids get that opportunity to achieve the American dream—a real chance at the pursuit of happiness. So, enjoy what is hopefully a roadmap to success and the American dream.

Children

"Each child is designed with capability of becoming fully and truly human—of becoming a perfect vessel for the entry and flow of love into the whole of creation"
— Terry Anderson and Sandra Maslow, philosophers —

FORWARD

It's All About the Kids
by Joan Holliday, community organizer

When Bob George asked me if I would be interested in writing a book about Kennett, we both agreed that one prominent element of our community was programs focused on children and youth. We started counting the number of youth programs serving the Kennett area, and we were amazed. Bob graduated from the Kennett schools and is one of the founding fathers of the Kennett Education Foundation. For thirty-two years I have served Kennett area children and youth as a public health nurse, working in concert with most of the youth programs. We decided we were the right partners to write this book, The Story of Kennett: Shaping Our Future One Child at a Time. As an affirmation, Bob amusingly remembered a line in the movie *Back to the Future*, when Doc responded to Marty, who had concerns after returning from the future, by telling him, "It's all about the kids, Marty! It's all about the kids!" As we've conducted nearly fifty interviews in the Kennett community, Bob and I are resoundingly saying, "It's all about the kids!" Beyond the historic accounts about our town, the new Kennett story for the past twenty years is one in which the community has focused on developing our kids' potential and giving them equal opportunity.

In the following chapters, you will read about the many ways Kennett community members, schools and nonprofit agencies have wrapped their arms around the children in the Kennett area. They have been taking it upon themselves to start and implement children and youth programs, which cover the gamut of child life phases from prenatal through high school. Bob George and I carried out nearly fifty one-on-one interviews with the directors or managers of these children and youth programs. We also interviewed the leaders of Kennett, as we believe that they provide the surround that supports the safety for our youth's growth and development. From December 2015 through November 2016, Bob George and I conducted one-hour interviews with a series of questions (included at the end of this chapter.) I took notes from our individual sessions and created a summary paper for each interview. The director or leader was then offered the opportunity to edit, delete or add to the summary story, and speak in the first person voice. While the individual stories are inspiring and instructive, the collective story also offers some food for reflection. Common themes, characteristics and challenges will be discussed later.

In 1997, the Kennett Episcopal Church of the Advent led a town "Listening Project" to assess the needs of the community. It was this process that identified the void in community youth programs. The leaders of the survey developed **After-The-Bell,** an after-school enrichment program for Kennett Middle School students, leading the way for the formation of many other community youth programs. After-The-Bell received national recognition through a *TIME* magazine article and continues to be a shining example of a school and community partnership.

At the same time, the **Bridging the Community** process was being developed. With the changes that were happening around town, such as the corporate headquarters of Genesis Health Care Ventures moving to the center of town and more Latino children entering the schools**,** a small group of committed and concerned citizens met to explore what the community could create and lead to assure a healthy town evolution. They promoted the living philosophy of *peaceful, progressive, inclusivity* and held Bridging the Community meetings to generate new ideas, leaders and volunteerism. These bi-monthly gatherings held at different town sites, continue to create the inspiration and arena for community members to become more broadly involved as volunteers and focused on matching our town's resources with its needs to work towards a healthy evolution.

Study Buddies after-school tutoring programs "mushroomed" out of the Bridging the Community effort. With five after-school programs held on consecutive days in a different town church, a template was created for the town. The volunteer leaders who brought their hearts and commitment to the process were Anna Anderson, Ruth Williams, Marcia Malchione, Bob Walton, and Joan Holliday. The intent of Study Buddies was to walk side-by-side with the vulnerable elementary children who needed homework support and enrichment. The community was in this together and understood the reciprocal benefit of working with the child. There would be no more "them and us," as we were all teachers and students. Today, Carter CDC has developed a nonprofit neighborhood association on the street where Study Buddies started and their central effort is providing three days of Study Buddies after-school tutoring and enrichment. Carter CDC sees this effort as a pivotal neighborhood grassroots process for breaking the cycle of poverty. Their motto is: "It takes a child to raise a village."

During this time, the idea of "bridging" caring adults with elementary children was started through Mentoring Youth in Kennett Elementary. This effort was intentional about "bridging" the seniors from the Kendal and Crosslands's communities with the kids, demonstrating the benefit of intergenerational relationships in a town community. Today, there is an InterGen Coalition, which continues to develop new processes to bring together all generations, capitalizing on the assets of each age group. As for evolving the process of mentoring youth, the **Together for Education** program for elementary and middle school students was developed in 2007 and received its nonprofit status. As an expansive element, this program has corporate employee involvement and support, which demonstrates the benefit of business as a "partner" in a town community.

In 2007, the **Walk In kNowledge (WIN)** program targeted high-school Latino students, who needed more support navigating the path to higher education. Today the program is open to all students who desire academic support. In 2009, **Path Stone Migrant Head Start** arrived in the area and with their focus on migrant early childhood education, they have added to the efforts of the long-standing Migrant Education Program and to the existing **Head Start Program**.

The Garage Community and Youth Center has become an established place in the center of town since 2001. The mission statement on the front door announces the intent of developing our youth's potential. This is making a statement to the town that we care about our kids and we have a physical space for them to gather, study, be mentored and tutored and to be given the opportunities to become contributing citizens today and in the future. This has been so successful that another center has been established in the neighboring community of West Grove.

The establishment of the **Kennett Area YMCA**, which attracts families and youth to wholesome physical and character development, has been another town symbol of caring for our kids. In the interview with the director of the YMCA, you will read how the leadership and its members continue to explore how to meet the next emerging need to help raise a healthy child. Housing a Montessori school has been one of these successful ventures, which developed from an initiative by a community member.

Camp Dreamcatcher was included in this story because it is one nonprofit agency that has chosen to work with a group that is probably the most isolated and faces the greatest stigma; these are children and families affected by HIV/AIDS. The "therapeutic camp community" has become not only a haven for Kennett area HIV/AIDS affected families, but it serves other eastern states. Volunteers from Kennett support this effort, which in turn has a community ripple effect on our "care for all kids."

Opportunities for youth to spread their wings and make a contribution to the community are offered by the **Good Neighbors** nonprofit organization. Every summer, a group of youths give up a week of vacation to provide housing repairs for low-income seniors and other local residents. The youths learn invaluable lessons about life while developing in home repair skills and, best of all, joining the circle of community volunteers.

And, top this off with the approach of a longtime **Boy Scout** leader's story of how the organization approached a problem from the potential side. The successful outcome took time to see the underlying needs and values and addresses them from a different philosophy.

As the elementary, middle and high school youths are supported through strong programs, the Kennett community has also been providing services for the prenatal, postpartum, and early childhood periods. The interventions of the **Chester County Health Department Public Health Nurses, YoungMoms, the Maternal Child Health Consortium, Family Center, La Comunidad Hispana, Kennett Area Community Services, Tick Tock Early Learning Center and Family Literacy** will all be highlighted as significant contributors to healthy beginnings.

Let's remember that, at the helm, the schools and their direct partners play a fundamental role in preparing our kids for becoming our future. Three superintendents (our current and two former) will share their experiences as leaders and the impact they had and continue to have on our present school system; we are now one of the top rated school districts in Pennsylvania. The **Kennett Education Foundation** and **Chester County Futures** will share how they partner with the schools towards higher education and an education consultant and a local high school teacher will reflect on what comprises a good education.

The town surround story of having an effective community-minded **Kennett Police Department** will be told. The **Honorable Magisterial District Judge** will share his experience with the Kennett youth during his long-time appointment. We will get a glimpse of the town's economic status as the stories are told by the **Historic Kennett Square,** the **Kennett Borough Council, the current and former mayors**, and a leading **mushroom farm owner**.

For the past two years, an open forum for different generations to interact and to get to know each other continues to take place at the **InterGen Kennett Community Coffee Klatch**. The coffee klatch has established an identity in town, and you will read about what goes on in this dynamic communing process.

Funding is a subject and concern in every one of the interviews. The executive director of the **United Way of Southern Chester County** shares insight into current and future funding. This agency is the steward of the whole community and provides base funding for most of the programs whose leaders we interviewed.

To bring to life the effect of the many youth programs, you will be reading **Stories from the Youth.**. These first person accounts interspersed through-out the book will best demonstrate what it means to be a child growing up in Kennett Square.

A recent *New York Times* bestseller entitled, <u>Our Kids: The American Dream in Crisis</u> by Robert D.

Putnam, focuses on how the promise of the American Dream has a disturbing "opportunity gap" between the have and the have-not backgrounds. He explores this issue through a body of research about the current state of affairs and what can be done. The good news is that he promotes community youth programs beyond the schools. Putnam writes, *"At the permeable boundary between schools and community are after-school activities, mentors, and above all, extracurricular activities. America invented extracurricular activities precisely to foster equal opportunity, and we know from dozens of research studies that this strategy works."* p. 258.

The Kennett Square community is discovering the benefit of working with the kids, not only because they need us, but also because they provide the hope for our community by being the "seeds for creating world peace."

Interview Guide

Introduction: We are interviewing the different organizations, youth programs and leaders that make Kennett such a strong community. You are one of these. First tell us about your background and your role in the organization.

1. Tell us about your organization, how big is it, what does it do and how did it get started?
2. What was it like before you came around?
3. What gap did you fill and what value did/do you provide?
4. How are you doing?
5. What are the challenges that you are facing? How are you addressing them? Do you have adequate resources?
6. How is it evolving?
7. What are your goals?
8. What gaps still exist in your programs and services to achieve your goals? What would you do with more resources?
9. How do you measure your success? What data do you have and can you share that with us?
10. Going forward, what are the trends that you have to deal with? How will you keep the organization sustainable?

Interviews

"It takes a village to raise a child."
— African Proverb —

After-The-Bell
Kathy Do, executive director

01/14/2016. I filled the executive director role at After-The-Bell about eighteen months ago. I had served on the Unionville Chadds-Ford School Board, where I developed a deeper understanding of students and their needs, which led me to this position.

Most Kennett residents know the history of After-The-Bell, an after-school program for middle school students; but it is worth repeating. In 1997, the Episcopal Church of the Advent presented the results of "A Time to Listen" project. This was a bottom-up report on the quality of life in Kennett Square. Over one hundred community members were interviewed, and the study identified a serious gap in the care and supervision of middle school children between the ages of twelve and fourteen. The community felt that the elementary school kids were fairly well supervised, and the high school students had many activities that vied for their attention such as sports, extracurricular activities and jobs. Starting in middle school, however, many kids were left to fend for themselves between 2:30 pm when school let out and 5:00 pm when the working parents started coming home. Too young for employment and with limited afterschool activities to engage in, the middle school students had difficulty filling their time and avoiding boredom. The study concluded that these "latch-key" children were vulnerable to the consequences of risky behaviors and exploitation. By tapping into the caring spirit and generosity of the Kennett area community, After-The-Bell provides the solution to ensure that these kids have a safe and engaging place to go to after school.

John and Denise Wood and Marshall Newton were the visionaries that recognized the problem, determined a solution, and set about to turn their idea into a successful program. They created the Kennett After-School Association (KASA) in 1998 to fulfill this need with the help of the Kennett Consolidated School District Superintendent Dr. Larry Bosley, followed by Superintendent Dr. Rudy Karkosak. With hard work, dedication, and love for the youth of the Kennett area, the community developed this unique program called After-The-Bell, which continues today, even after the passing on of the founders.

- **Vision Statement:** All middle school children will have a safe, enriching environment to go to after school.
- **Values:** Respect for self and others, caring relationships with adults, improved interpersonal & social behaviors, an appreciation for volunteerism, and an exploration of varied opportunities.

Key principles of After-The-Bell were set up at the formation of the program. No student or family will pay for the program activities. Each child is welcome, and there are no barriers for any child to participate at an appropriate level. It is a language safe zone, a place where English language learners are encouraged to practice their English. It is a bully-free zone. Bullying is not tolerated, and students who engage in bullying will be asked to leave the program. The staff of After-The-Bell reinforces the importance of respect and tolerance, and ensures that students know that participation in the program is a privilege that should not be abused.

KASA's After-The-Bell program is a collaboration of many. KASA enjoys a strong partnership with the Kennett Consolidated School District, which offers invaluable support by providing the use of Kennett Middle School for the After-The-Bell program. In addition, the faculty and administration support the program with their volunteer contributions of their time and efforts to ensure that middle school children take full advantage of the program.

KASA is a 501(c)(3) nonprofit organization supported by individual donations, community gifts, foundation grants, and the United Way of Southern Chester County (UWSCC). After-The-Bell is free to the students and comes at no direct cost to the taxpayer or the school district. After-The-Bell collaborates with many community organizations, local businesses, and other nonprofits for activities, volunteers, and program space. The annual budget for 2015-2016 is $215,252. In regards to funders, United Way of Southern Chester County makes up 15% of the funding, donations comprise 40% and grants are 45%.

After-The-Bell relies on approximately 200 volunteers each year teaching between 50 and 60 classes a week, of which about half are full to capacity, to serve more than 300 students per year. We run six-week cycles in the fall, winter and spring on Tuesday, Wednesday and Thursday afternoons. The classes are designed to draw on the talents and hobbies of the community volunteers and then offered to the middle-school students as activity choices. The following are examples of the activities offered by After-The-Bell:

- **Creative Activities** include Landscape Drawing, Pottery, Photography, Jewelry Design, Fun with Flowers, Knitting, Guitar, Glee Club/Chorale, Arts & Crafts, Calligraphy, and Scrapbooking.
- **Health & Physical Activities** include Tennis, Basketball, Bowling, Running Club, Yoga, Glamour Girls, Martial Arts, Soccer, Outdoor Fun + Games, Swim Club, Kickball, and Golf.
- **Science, Nature and Engineering Activities** include Science Experiments; Junior Engineers; Lego Robotics; Animal Handling; Pony Partners; The Land Conservancy; Animals Inside and Out; Outdoor Adventure; Farm Animal Helpers; Astronomy; Outdoor Survival Skills; and Hands On, Boots in the Water (at the Stroud Water Research Center.)
- **Leadership & Service Activities** include Sweet Shop (learn about selling your own products), Adventures in Babysitting, Cops, Project Alert, and Warm Heads, Hands & Hearts.
- **Cultural Activities** include Around the World, International Cooking, Zumba (Latin dance and aerobics), Día de los Muertos, and Take a Look at Italy.

Kennett Middle School has received recognition as a *School to Watch* by the National Forum for Middle-Grades Reform. This designation was bestowed upon 341 public middle schools from the 13,000 school districts in the United States. The Forum cited After-The-Bell as one of the top reasons for this prestigious designation for Kennett. (For more information, see the After-The-Bell website.)

KASA is proud of the fact that no child has ever had to pay to participate in After-The-Bell and has never received taxpayer support. It is a uniquely successful model that relies on the strong, long-standing support of the Kennett area community.

Volunteers are truly the lifeblood of After-The-Bell and are the key to the program's success and sustainability. A tremendous asset to After-The-Bell in its efforts to recruit new volunteers is the community-networking gathering called Bridging the Community. (Bridging the Community is discussed in a later chapter.) These bi-monthly "bridging" meetings provide an opportunity to introduce the After-The-Bell program and bring to light the essential importance of the volunteers. It is at these bi-monthly meetings where the need for volunteers is announced; and it is at these meetings that community members, "coming from their heart," are led to volunteer.

∞

There are, of course, many challenges that are encountered on the road to sustainable success. One recurring challenge is the need to recruit new volunteers beyond those who step forward at the Bridging the Community meetings. After-The-Bell volunteers include current and retired educators, business professionals, scientists, therapists, nutritionists, musicians, artists, college interns, and high school students. Many of our high school volunteers are former After-The-Bell participants who want to give back to the program that gave so much to them. And a significant number of volunteers come from the Kendal-Crosslands retirement community and the Episcopal Church of the Advent. All three of the founders had been members of the church, and two of them had lived at Kendal. The majority of After-The-Bell volunteers return year after year, but many, including high school and college students as well as busy adults, volunteer for a limited amount of time and then move on.

The costs of any program always threaten its sustainability. After-The-Bell relies on funds donated by local businesses, community members, and foundations such as the United Way of Southern Chester County to cover all program expenses. Procuring adequate funding for the effective operation of the program is an ongoing priority for KASA's board and staff. A significant cost factor is staffing. A staff of five is responsible for the day-to-day operation of After-The-Bell: two full-time staff members – the executive director and the program director, and three part-time employees – the program associate, the activities manager, and the attendance specialist/translator. Bus transportation home from After-The-Bell is another considerable expense, second only to salaries. Fortunately, the school district generously provides the middle school building to house After-The-Bell thus saving the program quite a bit of money.

Another continuing challenge is the ever-changing technology, and the need to maintain and regularly update a current and efficient database of students, activities, and volunteers.

After-The-Bell attracts a diverse population of students. In 2014-15, 45% of After-The-Bell students were English as a Second Language (ESL) students, and 61% were on the government-subsidized Free and Reduced Lunch Program. A large number of Kennett middle school aged students with special needs actively took part in After-The-Bell and approximately half of the students in the program were enrolled in the 6th Grade. Two reasons exist for the reduced attendance of the older middle school students. First, the 7th and 8th graders are eligible to participate in the middle school sports program and second, as students get older, they are often required to care for younger siblings after school.

At the end of each program cycle, students are surveyed to determine if they had a positive experience at After-The-Bell. In addition, students who participate in the program's "Brain Base" homework help laboratory are asked if the activity has helped them to complete their homework on time and improve their overall school performance. The results of these surveys consistently show that After-The-Bell has provided a positive and beneficial experience to all students and volunteers.

Whenever I meet someone who is not familiar with After-The-Bell, I love to tell them that for the last 17 years, we have provided more than 4,500 middle school students with safe, structured and engaging after-school activities at no cost to any child or family, and at no cost to taxpayers. And when they ask me how this is possible, I answer with one word: *community*.

In summary, the Kennett area is second to none when it comes to volunteers; people who care about children, and who are willing to give their time, energy and resources to improve and enhance their community. At After-The-Bell, it really does "take a village."

"Music is a more potent instrument than any other for education."

— Plato, Greek philosopher —

Youth Story
Christina Liu, Kennett High School student

12/06/2016. I am a freshman at Kennett High School. My father came to the United States in 1995 from Fuzhou, China to learn English and to see if he could find work and like living here. He took a job in a restaurant of a friend and worked himself up in different restaurant jobs. He eventually became a chef and learned how to make sushi. My mother came to the United States 6 years later, took English classes, and helped my father in the restaurant business. I was born in 2002 in New York City and my sister, Lina, was born in New York City in 2007. In 2010, our family came to Kennett Square and became the proud owners of Lily Asian Restaurant, 104 W. State St., Kennett Square, PA, where we live and work today.

When I was one month old, my parents sent me back to China, and I stayed with my paternal grandmother. I spoke only Chinese (Mandarin) until I was 8 years old, so I was challenged learning English when I arrived back in the United States. I attended Mary D. Lang School in Kennett for 3rd grade and Greenwood Elementary for 4th and 5th grades, followed by Kennett Middle School.

Even though my parents are very involved in the restaurant business, my father wants me to go to college and experience what the world is like. As I grow up, he does not want me to work in the restaurant, because he wants me to study and plan for the future. Right now, I would like to go to college to study music. I have been playing the piano for 2 ½ years with a private teacher named Rose. I really like the piano and enjoy playing "smooth" music. I practice thirty minutes a day and if I had a recital I would play, "Marriage D'Amour" by memory. It would be my dream to receive a scholarship and be able to attend Curtis School of Music in Philadelphia.

I am happy to be attending school in the United States. It seems that I feel more free to be myself. Education in China is very strict with lots of homework. They always are striving to be perfect, and this can be very stressful. Developing friends in this country has also worked out for me here in Kennett. When I was in middle school, before I started to make the first invitation, friends started to choose me. They started to call me "Cookie" because I like eating cookies. I have three close girlfriends, and we do many things together.

I attended After-The-Bell all three years of middle school. One of my favorite sessions was "Smoothies and Movies". We made smoothies with fruit and yogurt and then watched movies; my favorite movie was "Frozen." I also enjoyed the double session of cooking classes. After-The-Bell was a great place to go to after school, and I really enjoyed going three days a week. My parents were happy because I had bus transportation home. It was a rewarding experience, so now I am thinking of giving back and becoming a volunteer with the After-The-Bell program next year.

Another group that I am part of is called Hermanitas; it means "sisters." (Although we have two boys that are participating now.) Being in this group exposes us to many new things. I learned how to make and sell "handmade crafts" such as earrings, and, then with these earnings, I was able to help pay for the costs of field trips; for instance, to New York City to see a play.

I also attend the WIN program on Tuesdays and Thursdays after school. (Note: Please refer to Walk In kNowledge chapter). Loretta Perna heads up both the Hermanitas and WIN programs and is like a "counselor friend" helping me with so many things.

Sometimes I also go to The Garage Community and Youth Center when school is over. I like to help out there and, when I need homework assistance, they have tutors to assist me. I especially like the subject of music right now and listening to songs. The only sport that I am involved in at this time is tennis.

Kennett Square is a nice town, and I like living here. Our home is upstairs from the restaurant, which is on the main street. Being in the center of town, I get to participate in all the parades and activities going on, either from my upstairs window or in person. Yes, I did like going to the Mushroom Drop on New Year's Eve this past year. Sometimes the sirens can get noisy and my Dad sometimes doesn't like it, but it isn't a big problem. Most of all, my family and I feel safe and secure living here.

When you ask me what else Kennett could offer students, I would say more help is needed for students who enter the school system in later grades and are unable to speak English. My English is improving, but I started learning English in the 3rd grade and I still am in an ESL class. My sister, Lina, has been in Kennett school system since kindergarten and is now in the 4th grade. Lina only attended an ESL class for one year, and she speaks and understands English better than I do. We speak Chinese (Mandarin) at home. I also speak a little Spanish.

My dream for the future is to go to college, get a nice job and have a family. I have many people helping me in the community to stay on this path. I don't know, but someday I could still live in Kennett Square after this all happens.

"Humanity has only scratched the surface of its real potential."
— African Proverb —

One Kennett Story: Bridging the Kennett Community
Joan Holliday, community organizer

As a public health nurse, who has worked within the boundaries of Kennett Square, PA for thirty-two years and walked in and out of all facets of the community, I have a Kennett story to share. My story will highlight how a small group of caring, committed citizens, by leading from a living philosophy, has activated an energy field that inspires volunteerism and the spirit of working together towards "Bridging the Community!"

Walking the streets in Kennett in 1982, I experienced a comfortable, quiet town that was comprised of residents who had lived in the community for quite some time. The town square had a 5 & 10 store with a lunch counter, a pharmacy, a mercantile goods store, a couple of diners, a sub shop, an historic inn and restaurant, a jewelry store, and a men's clothing store. There was a grocery store at the edge of the town square where most residents shopped. In addition to the commercial stores, there were the lawyers, accountants and medical clinics. The town cared for the local residents, and only a couple of the places drew customers from beyond the Kennett area. The town residents would say that it was a great place to raise a family.

During this time, I visited mushroom camps and provided preventive health care services to the Mexican men who had recently migrated to the area to work in the mushroom industry. Many of the men were housed on the mushroom farm property, so they were not very visible in the town of Kennett. The community didn't seem to be impacted by the immigration that was taking place at that time.

In 1986, amnesty was granted for the undocumented worker through the Immigration and Reform Control Act (IRCA): *"A blanket amnesty for some 2.7 million undocumented immigrants."* This was the first dramatic change that the town of Kennett experienced. Mexican families were now joining their husband/father in the United States and settling into the town of Kennett and its surrounding area. It took a couple of years before I started to receive referrals for prenatal Mexican women, who were living the dream of having a child born a United States citizen. However, by the time I retired from my public health nursing job in 2014, my caseload of thirty-five plus families was mostly Mexican women.

Housing and health care became two of the major issues related to this change. Landlords came into the area and filled their apartments quickly. Realtors found opportunities for home ownership. All of this helped serve the new population entering the town community, yet rents and mortgages were high, and doubling up family habitation was the trend. The pay for a mushroom picker was paid by "piece" or volume, which still left the Mexican worker with a low salary despite long work hours for seven days a week.

∞

I recall one event, when a neighborhood was concerned by the large number of cars that were being parked in a driveway on their street. A long-time resident led a procession accompanied by other long-time residents, placing yellow ribbons on the mailboxes of the over-populated residences. The aim was to draw the attention of the code enforcement officer about the doubling up of housing and the impact that this may have on the value of their home properties. This led to educating the residents about town safety and zone rules, but only through a formal process. There was no neighbor-to-neighbor communication since there was a language and cultural barrier. Obviously, we had a lot of work to do to become a vibrant, interactive, harmonious community. It wasn't until the early 2000s that a team of community advocates organized neighborhood meetings, and held these meetings in the very neighborhood where the yellow ribbons had been placed. During these meetings, the code enforcement officer, the landlord, and a group of apartment residents accompanied by an interpreter discussed what the roles and responsibilities needed to be for each group. This communication appeared to bring some new neighborhood interaction between the permanent residents and the Mexican immigrants. The best part was that a local group of bilingual youth assumed the role of walking around the affected neighborhoods and spoke to each household about Kennett's housing codes in the spirit of inclusivity. Later that year, Nancy Ayllon received the Chester County Outstanding Youth Citizen award for this volunteer leadership.

Provision of health care was the other issue that had to be faced with the new influx of Mexican immigrants. A couple of years before amnesty, a bilingual and culturally competent public health nurse and practitioner had left the traditional public health government agency and joined with La Comunidad Hispana, a social service agency, to bring a nurse managed health center to the community. Peg Harris understood the need for preventive health care, as well as the importance of basic medical care for the vulnerable, and took this on as a mission. The model of a nurse managed health clinic was a fairly new concept, and one that matched the Mexican culture and could be operated at a lower cost. The immigrants arrived in the United States healthy and with few medical issues. Over time, performing the back-breaking agricultural work, eating the American fast food diet and having less opportunities for walking than in Mexico, brought about a need for medical care that addressed more orthopedic, diabetic, arthritic and high blood pressure issues. Prenatal care came later, and to date, the infant morbidity rate remains above the national average. Through Peg's leadership and others, the health clinic today is a federally qualified health center (FQHC), which receives federal funds for the underserved and sees over 4,000 patients a year.

∞

The story of Kennett Square's current revitalization begins in 1998, when my public health nursing hours were reduced due to budget cuts. My experience as a home visitor helped me realize that many resources were needed in the vulnerable Mexican community and African American neighborhoods, and when I engaged the larger community, I experienced the potential for providing those resources. I decided to activate the idea of volunteerism community-wide, and also volunteer my time to take on a community leadership role. It was at this time that the corporate headquarters of Genesis Health Ventures was relocating to this conventional community. Also, there was the development of the Kennett Square Revitalization Task Force that received a Main Street PA grant to develop the economic/business side of Kennett Square. There was a voiced concern that the town would lose its unique "small town" culture with "big business" coming to town. In concert with this major town change, the number of Mexican family residents was growing, and it was clear that the Mexican people had moved to Kennett for a better life and planned to stay. The mushroom industry was in need of dependable workers, and the Mexican culture considered agricultural work "honorable." The mushroom industry was unique because it called for agricultural workers year around, as the mushrooms were grown in small buildings with a controlled temperature. The Mexican youth also started to fill the schools and the parents expressed high hopes for their children to have a better life in regards to higher education and employment in the United States.

With the help of my friends, Terry Anderson and Sandra Maslow who were working in organizational development, I gathered a diverse cross-section of community members to discuss how we could deal with the community changes in a positive way, especially the changing structure of the town and the ongoing influx of migrants. We spent several sessions reflecting on the history of Kennett and what brought settlers to the area. We drew on the wisdom of the Lenape Indian, who responded to the energy of the land, as their way to build a home that matched the tribe's nature. The Lenape Indian was peaceful and was drawn to southern Chester County's peaceful land that included an immense variety of flora and fauna over rolling hills. This grassroots group decided to create a phrase that described the energy that drew the Lenape Indian to settle in this area, as well as the peacemaking Quaker settlers. We came up with the phrase – *peaceful, progressive inclusivity*, which we then started to promote as our town's living philosophy. This was the birth of the "current Kennett" – an awakening of the spirit and nature of our town that was calling the early settlers way back when. The nature of the land is something that belongs to all of us; thus it is an obvious starting point that could serve as an all-encompassing unifier for the residents of Kennett Square area.

In looking for a forum that brings people together to learn about our inspiring roots, we came up with the concept of Bridging the Community bi-monthly meetings led by guiding principles.

- Come from the heart, not a task
- Keep our community efforts a process, not a program
- Focus on potential, not problem
- Work for community, not personal agenda
- Add no infrastructural burden; which means no officers, membership or dues
- Each person discovers a role to play, not only delegated officials

The original plan of scheduling the meetings at different locations around town continues to this day, and reminders of each meeting are advertised in the newspapers and recounted via word-of-mouth. By traveling around town, we enter neighborhoods where many residents haven't entered. We meet at mushroom farms where many residents have never visited. In the near future, we are gathering at La Comunidad Hispana, which will be the first visit for many. We hold meetings at local businesses where many have never shopped. It is a *peaceful, progressive, inclusive* way to introduce community members to the broader community. In fact, the Each and All Dialogue Group formed at the same time with an open invitation to any interested community member. We joined in a reflective dialogue process to deepen our understanding of how to live by our town's philosophy.

As a public health home visiting nurse, I served mostly minorities. Through time, I experienced and respected the core values and talents that this minority group offered the broader community. The community forum (i.e. Bridging the Community) encourages each person to see that there is a place for each and all. I might add that each community member is needed in creating a thriving community.

Bridging the Community has been a vibrant and community life-giving process since its birth in September 1997. (Previous meetings had been held and called Community Bridging Generations.) Bridging the Community is an ongoing, bi-monthly gathering of between 35 and 70 persons of all ages, creeds, economic levels, and cultures; always with old and new attendees. Never has the Bridging the Community gathering been cancelled due to weather or other events and proudly celebrated its 100th meeting on March 11, 2015. When the tragic terroristic attacks of September 11, 2001 occurred and everyone was in total despair and disbelief, Bridging the Community went on with a group of about fifty community members gathering together to affirm commUNITY!

∞

Coming together to share resources and needs and to bring new ideas while providing an arena for anyone to step into is progressively changing the Kennett Square culture. In the documentation of the meetings, we can see that there is a gradual entry of the Latino residents into the community circle. First the providers of Latino services attended and continue to attend, then there were ESL students who attended with their teacher to practice English and join in, and recently in 2015, two new Mexican residents came to "Bridging" and announced that they wanted to learn more about volunteerism because this concept was unfamiliar in Mexico. The meetings have a bi-lingual co-facilitator, who can interpret for anyone that needs help. There are also certain Mexican residents who attend meetings regularly and bring information back to their friends and family. The same progression of participation in Bridging the Community meetings occurred with the town's African American minority group. First, the African Methodist Episcopal Church representatives attended the meetings; then some of the local leaders showed up, followed by the clients who received services from local agencies.

One of the most stunning examples of how the African American community took leadership, as the result of the empowerment that came out of engaging Bridging the Community was reported in a local newspaper.

The Wilmington News Journal   POSTED: 09/03/09

Joan Holliday has been employed for 28 years by the Chester County Health Department as a public health visiting nurse. One day in October 2003, she was chatting with longtime resident Theresa Bass, 52 years old.

"Theresa was complaining about the conditions of the neighborhood, that it was really going downhill, and no one seemed to do anything or care about it," Holliday recounted. "I told her that it was her street, and if she wanted change, the people who live there were the only ones who could do it."

Bass teamed with longtime residents Donnie and Laura Jackson, and with Holliday's guidance sought the assistance of the Alliance for Better Housing. That led to two five-year grants: $686,000 from the Pennsylvania Department of Community and Economic Development for improvements to secondary downtown streets, and $450,000 from the Wachovia Regional Foundation to develop tutoring, computer and financial planning programs for residents.

"At the beginning of the project, people thought they could not make a difference," said Holliday. "Now they know they are the only ones who can do it. East Linden is a vital street, with a lot of spirit."

∞

The Bridging the Community process continually promotes working with our youth. When we speak about potential, it is a no-brainer to focus on the youth, who are our future. "Come from the heart" and "No infrastructural burden" are two additional principles that have guided the community youth efforts such as:

1. After-The-Bell, an after-school program for middle school students in partnership with the schools and staffed mostly by volunteers.

2. Study Buddies, which provided after-school tutoring for elementary churches in four town church basements and was totally operated with volunteers for over eight years. Currently, one program has become its own neighborhood nonprofit and holds Study Buddies all four nights.

3. Mentoring Youth in Kennett Elementary, which provided mentoring to the town elementary school students by retirement community volunteers for over eight years. Together for Education, a nonprofit organization staffed entirely by community volunteers except for the coordinator position, continues mentoring the elementary school students.

4. The Garage Community and Youth Center, which provides after-school tutoring and mentoring for middle school and high school students and is now a nonprofit.

5. Migrant Education, which organized after-school tutoring at the Kennett Area YMCA for Latino youth using volunteers.

6. KHS youth-led street fairs to make REAL the living philosophy of Bridging the Community with the themes of "Chip and Dip Festival" (promotion of volunteerism), "We are Family," and "Colors of Kennett."

Picture for the Future: In my heart of hearts, I believe that Bridging the Community is now part of the Kennett community culture and will continue, even when I and other regular attendees are gone. Bridging the Community is an ongoing volunteer process and not a funded program. The only formality is one of assuring that there are two facilitators at the meeting to share the Bridging vision and philosophy along with its guiding principles and the structuring of time for the meeting. On leaving a Bridging gathering, Tom Hoehle, a volunteer Bridging leader would say, "I feel like I have been shot out of a cannon!" or "We accomplished more community work tonight than a board of directors in a year!" There is a bonding and joining together that can't be measured. There is an affirmation of one's role in the community, and the good work that is being done. There is a refueling of one's mission, and when everyone experiences that, we ultimately are on the same page. There is a crossing of boundaries with new ideas offered and new volunteers signing-up for efforts. It is a great place to be for one and one-half hours bi-monthly, yet more importantly, one that carries the message out into time and space beyond the meetings.

"It is easier to build strong children than to repair broken men."
— Frederick Douglass, abolitionist and statesman —

Study Buddies Program on East Linden Street
Joan Holliday, community organizer

01/06/2016. *Study Buddies is a concept and a community process that came out of Bridging the Community. In 1998, when a group of concerned citizens joined to talk about the Kennett community and the potential that was untapped, Marcia Malchione pointed out that there were many elementary school-aged children in the borough of Kennett who were out on the streets after school, and that many of them would flourish if they had some help with their schoolwork. She approached her church, The Kennett Presbyterian Church, to start an after-school tutoring/mentoring process on Monday nights. The name Study Buddies came out of the idea that there is no higher or lower here when it comes to learning. Tutor and student can join in a reciprocal process, whereby each is learning something new.*

With the bi-monthly meetings of Bridging the Community, additional women leaders came to the foreground and decided that other town churches could provide Study Buddies the other nights of the week. Mrs. Ruth Williams opened the doors of 2nd Baptist Church for Study Buddies on Tuesdays, Joan Holliday and Sharon Garrett, community nurses, started the Study Buddies at Bethel AME on Wednesday nights. Originally they started the program at New Garden AME, but the site was difficult to enter so they moved to the basement space at Bethel. And Anna Anderson from Christ Temple (Greater Works Ministries) started Study Buddies on Thursday nights. To top things off, Bob Walton from Kennett Presbyterian Church cooked a healthy meal every Friday night and opened the doors to all the children for a shared meal and games.

∞

This community-wide process went on for over seven years with no funding, no infrastructure and was totally staffed by volunteers. The leaders of each Study Buddies program were committed to this good work, and Anna Anderson even drove the church van around to pick up the youth for Thursday night Study Buddies. Volunteers were generated from Unionville High School, Kennett High School, Lincoln University, Bridging the Community meetings, church members, as well as from the broader community. Many of the Unionville students started the volunteering to gain community volunteer hours for National Honor Society, but after their hours were completed, they continued participating because there had developed a mutual love and caring among the Study Buddies. There were several field trips set-up to visit Lincoln University, Wilmington Blue Rocks games (funded by a local business), Longwood Gardens and Brandywine River Museum. The beauty of all this was that the community responded to be chaperones and provide transportation. The students contributed their $1 per students for their investment.

At that time, there was a simple permission slip signed by the parents with an emergency contact number. Speakers on nutrition, police work, prevention of drugs and smoking were also invited in to educate the children about a healthy lifestyle. There were community meals, which were held around Black History month and the end of the year. Parents were invited to the student presentations and joined in celebrating the success of their students. Basic rules for behavior were set-up and if there was a problem, the student would be brought home and held out of Study Buddies for one session. The leaders had interactions with Mary D. Lang teachers, and the principal at one point would show up on Wednesday night to encourage the students and tutor. Notes from the teachers would be sent to the Study Buddies leaders about what areas of schoolwork needed support.

Study Buddies became a place where the broader community could enter. Church of the Advent offered funding for school supplies while Operation Warm provided coats and KACS Thanksgiving turkeys and YMCA Angel Tree gifts were passed out at Study Buddies. The Longwood Rotary provided book bags for many years. The idea that we all are Study Buddies, and "you do your part" and "we do our part" was a guiding principle. There were no "giveaways," but a community relationship that was established.

As the volunteer leaders decided to close Study Buddies at their respective churches, Study Buddies at Bethel AME on East Linden Street continued to be offered. Joan Holliday and Esther Rochester (Linden

Street resident) co-led the process until 2008. When Joan left, Esther Rochester and Theresa Bass continued the one-day a week Study Buddies until Historic East Linden Street (Joseph Carter CDC) volunteers took over the process in 2011. Today, there is an active three days-a-week Study Buddies after-school program.

"Children see magic because they look for it."
— Christopher Moore, writer —

Joseph Carter CDC
LaToya Myers, executive director and Ethan Cramer, board member

03/03/2016. ***Background of LaToya M. Myers:*** *I graduated with a Bachelor of Science in Pre-Med, Psychology and Business Management from the University of Pittsburgh and received my Master's Degree in Public Health from the University at Albany. I worked as a community outreach coordinator for Maternal Child Health Consortium for three years, and currently am working in Philadelphia with the Maternity Care Coalition as director of Family Support Programs. I have been involved in Study Buddies since I was a high school student, and I'm currently running the program until a full-time teacher is hired.*

Background of Ethan Cramer: *I received a bachelor of science from Swarthmore College in philosophy. I am an activist for neighborhoods, and founded and ran a community organizing nonprofit in Wilmington, Delaware. I have held a variety of positions at public gardens in the Delaware Valley and worked in the community greening programs at the Delaware Center for Horticulture.*

LaToya: I became actively involved with Study Buddies when I moved back to the neighborhood after receiving my Master's Degree in Public Health. From the time my mother, Theresa Bass, took on a leadership role on East Linden Street in 2003, I have been involved in some support functions.

Study Buddies is part of the strategy that the Carter CDC has adopted to achieve our mission. We are focused on positive change through resident-planned programs. We believe that if we focus on the kids, helping them to reach their potential, then we will also break the cycle of poverty. We have turned around the famous quote in the Historic East Linden Neighborhood – "It takes the children to raise a village."

In 2009, we changed the Study Buddies model to three days a week. We meet from 4:00 pm to 6:00 pm. We offer a healthy snack when the children first enter, and then at 5:00pm a healthy meal that has been provided by the Catholic Archdiocese of Philadelphia, which manages the United States Department of Agriculture distributions. We started a summer lunch program from this same source in 2003, and this continues today with as many as fifty youth attending five days a week in the summer. The Meal Program, started by my grandmother, Ophelia Bass, was passed on to my mother, Theresa Bass, and myself. My daughter, Payton now helps out.

Our Study Buddies enrollment stands around sixty students from kindergarten through 6th grade. On an average, we have 17 youth attending on a daily basis. We believe that to make the most change in a young person's life, we need to reach them early.

About four years ago, the Kennett school district donated fifteen computers that they were replacing with new computers. This has been very helpful to the students, but we are getting to the point where we will need to buy new ones and we are currently applying for a grant.

East Linden Street, which runs parallel to State Street in Kennett Square is one of the most diverse neighborhoods in the Kennett Borough. Theresa Bass, the president of our board, makes it very clear that every student is welcome to attend Study Buddies. The children get along with each other and travel together to Greenwood Elementary. In addition, they attend monthly field trips together as a group. There is a sense of "family" and "community."

Our objective is to educate and care about the whole child – academically, physically, socially and emotionally. We are not just an education organization, but a grassroots effort that is rooted in the neighborhood. We have a relationship with each student's parent and partner with them around their child's learning. Our organization continues to address adverse street life to insure there is a safe environment for children and families to live, learn and engage.

We are very proud of our relationship with the Kennett police department. Chief Zunino is a board member. In collaboration with the police department, the Carter CDC has presented a National Night Out for the past five years. In preparation for the event, children gained an understanding of the role of law enforcement and developed positive relationships with local police officers through tours, walking with the officers on their beats, and interviews. National Night Out was the perfect opportunity to celebrate the peace created by the partnership between the neighborhood and the police department.

The Study Buddies group is challenging to work with at times, but we have the bottom line that no student will be "kicked out" of Study Buddies. We discipline the children by talking to their parents and giving them a break from the program for a day or two, but we never will give-up on a child. We also are willing to be an advocate for students in the school system. We have paid for additional tutoring so that students can advance.

One of our greatest challenges is finding a teacher who will work for a small stipend. Our thought is that we really need to hire a full-time teacher who will implement our innovative curriculum and be the advocate with the school system. It will take a person who is committed to these kids and who embraces our philosophy of caring for the whole child!

Ethan Cramer: Our organization has had the commitment of volunteers. LaToya Myers, Theresa Bass, previously Joan Holliday, and I put in the extra mile. At the same time, we need to think of sustainability and this involves finding the stable funding sources to hire our first employee.

We know that we need to start collecting data about our success. We see many of the student's report cards, and this is testimony to improvements. At the same time, we observe the fantastic leadership development that occurs among the older students; this merits measurement and articulation. Students have a strong role in National Night Out; they participate in our fundraisers, and they organize and lead the Annual Community Block Party.

We have developed meaningful partnerships throughout the region. In the past three years, LaToya, Theresa and I have gone out to meet with many community members. Our goal is to get the word out about Carter CDC and Study Buddies. We know that without the neighbors working together on East Linden Street and providing the comprehensive Study Buddies program, the street could lose the ground we have gained. We need to continue to engage the broader community to invest in the future of our kids.

**"All kids need is a little help,
a little hope and somebody who believes in them."**
— Earvin "Magic" Johnson; retired NBA player, philanthropist & entrepreneur —

Mentoring Youth in Kennett Elementary (M.Y.K.E.)
Dr. Gerry Zippilli, co-founder

04/18/2016. Dr. Gerry Zippilli, a retired dentist and previous resident of Chadds Ford, Pennsylvania, is one of the original founders of M.Y.K.E. He now lives in Florida and has provided the below history.

In 1997, I attended the first organizing meeting of Bridging the Community in Kennett Square. I had recently retired and was looking for something meaningful to do. While there, I met John Wood and Admiral Jim Wilson. The three of us decided to work together to help some of the vulnerable kids in Kennett. We were told by Joan Holliday that a gentleman by the name of Bob Casey developed a mentoring program in Wilmington, DE called Creative Grandparenting. We arranged a meeting with Mr. Casey after which the three of us decided to move forward and start a similar mentoring process within the Kennett school system. After several meetings, we decided we would call the effort M.Y.K.E, which stands for <u>M</u>entoring <u>Y</u>outh in <u>K</u>ennett <u>E</u>lementary. We also decided we would mentor students from kindergarten through fifth grade. We used the same tetrad model of Creative Grandparenting to guide the mentors' thinking during interactions between a child and a caring older adult, keeping in mind four focal points at all times: the purpose, the present moment, the roles/values, and unconditional love/acceptance.

We then went to the three elementary schools and spoke with the principals to find out if they were interested. All three principals were receptive and willing to have respective school counselors identify students that needed support. We then needed to go out and find mentors. John Wood and Admiral Wilson recruited mentors from the Kendal-Crosslands retirement communities since that is where they resided, while I recruited from the broader Kennett community. Our process began with each mentor being assigned a student to meet with for forty-five minutes once a week. We were not tutors, but mentors to help build their identity and self-esteem. I might add that the mentors got as much out of this relationship as the students. Before long we had signed up forty mentors.

Most importantly, our effort was totally a volunteer one with no funds attached. We closely followed the Bridging the Community principles: "No infrastructural burden" and "Coming from the heart." This gave us the freedom to go about our volunteer work, and not worry about fundraising. We three leaders met weekly, and I think we did a great job of organizing the effort, training the mentors and dealing with any other issues that came up. We also met with all the mentors once a month to receive input from them, which helped in motivating everyone by the success stories. In 2004, M.Y.K.E won a grant award from the Kennett Education Foundation. We were very happy to receive the recognition, but we turned down the grant money as we were pleased with what we were doing and had no need for money.

I personally mentored two students. It was gratifying to see the potential grow in these young boys and develop through our interactions and explorations. I moved to Florida in 2004 and M.Y.K.E slowed down. John Woods and Admiral Jim Wilson are now both deceased, but I am certain they would be as happy as I am to hear that Together for Education has picked up the ball and continues the mentoring process within the Kennett school system.

"Any child you encounter is a divine appointment."

— Wess Stafford, president emeritus of Compassion International —

Together for Education
Sam Heriegel, board member

04/18/2016. *I grew up and attended public school in Downingtown, P.A. I graduated from the Pennsylvania State University's College of Engineering with a degree in Engineering Science and Mechanics in 2000. After 5 years at Accenture, working in Philadelphia, Little Rock and New York City, I came to southern Chester County in 2005, where I accepted a job at Chatham Financial. The company was about 100 employees at that time, and today it has grown to over 450 employees. I live in Oxford with my wife and our two sons, who are eight and seven years old. From the time I started working at Chatham Financial, the CEO Michael Bontrager encouraged employees to get involved in the broader community and supported volunteering during the workday. Encouraging employee volunteerism supports Chatham's purposes, results in happier, more engaged employees, and recognizes the reciprocal relationship a company has with the broader community. For example, if we have good schools, we have a better chance of recruiting outstanding employees and having those employees not only work in the community but want to live here as well.*

One of Chatham's employees had a child in Andrea Rozsit's first grade class at Mary D. Lang Elementary School in Kennett. Andrea welcomed parents and members of the community to visit her class to read with the students. The effort started with a few volunteers from Chatham Financial who went for one hour a week to support reading students. Other teachers observed this effort and started identifying needs in their classrooms. As the requests grew, we realized the demand and saw it as an opportunity to become independent. Together for Education became a 501(c)(3) nonprofit in the fall of 2007. This opened the door to community volunteers, who now number over 50 every school year and who assist in about 50% of the elementary school classrooms in the Kennett Consolidated School District (KCSD).

Our Mission: Together for Education strengthens the partnership among educators, students, parents and the community in the Kennett Consolidated School District to help children reach their greatest potential. We connect volunteers and mentors to teachers and students, and foster a network of organizations supporting our educational community.

Together for Education is the embodiment of a deep respect for education and the responsibility of every community member to make it better. It is the concept of working together for both the common good, and for a cause greater than one's self. Just saying that education is important is not enough; our actions must prove it. We join together to coordinate community members as in-class volunteers and mentors, and we connect organizations that support the Kennett public schools.

With our nonprofit status, we grew to having a part-time executive director, who is our only employee. Our first director was Cathy Robine, then a recently retired principal from the KCSD. Cathy's knowledge of the district and staff helped to establish our foundation. Jen Augustine, who followed Cathy as the next executive director, expanded our relationships with the community. Since 2010, we are pleased to have Jennifer Lewis as executive director, who also brought tremendous experience as a former teacher with deep roots in Kennett Square. Jen Augustine continues to play an active role as a member of our board of directors, and is also the director of the Kennett Square Pre-School Cooperative.

We are currently sustainable with an annual budget of approximately $30,000. Our board of directors consists of Michael Bontrager, Jen Augustine, Joe Godek and myself; and we meet bi-monthly with Executive Director Jennifer Lewis. Craig Pflumm was a founding member of Together for Education as well, and he also was active with the Kennett Education Foundation.

Jen, as the executive director, works with the teachers and counselors to identify classroom needs, recruits volunteers, and manages the matches between the volunteer and the classroom. Our up-to-date web site at www.tfed.org is our way of communicating who we are and how to get involved.

Beyond classroom support with reading, we help to coordinate mentors as well as organize summer programs. Together for Education has understood the importance of filling a gap during the summer months, when students may fall behind on their studies. We have built a partnership with The Kennett Library to provide a summer reading program. There are six different sessions that are held on Tuesdays and Thursdays for first, second, and third graders. This year, we are starting a new program in partnership with the Kennett

Area YMCA entitled "Math and Motion." It will be composed of about twenty students in the fourth grade and meet one night a week for two hours; the first hour will be for studying math with volunteer tutors, and the second hour will be for swimming and/or participation in YMCA activities. The parents are invited use the YMCA facility while they are waiting for their students.

Together for Education strongly believes in partnerships and helping organizations unite to create a network for education for the Kennett Consolidated School District. We host a yearly Serving Education Together Conference to network and to have presentations on particular topics of interest to all of us. We have been partnering with After-The-Bell, Carter CDC, Chester County Futures, The Garage Community and Youth Center, Head Start, Kennett Area YMCA, Kennett Consolidated School District, Kennett Education Foundation, Kennett Kennect, The Kennett Library, La Comunidad Hispana, Migrant Education, and Parent/Teacher Organizations from the Kennett elementary and middle schools.

∞

The conference has helped build relationships beyond Together for Education. For example, thanks to Chatham Financial's great building space, Chester County Futures asked us to host an all-day middle school camp in November 2014. Chatham paired the hosting of the event with more than 30 Chatham Financial volunteers to help the students on a project to develop marketing approaches for the future students interested in the program, complete with a logo and tagline. This day-long camp continued at other locations in the county including Lockheed Martin and Longwood Gardens, and has expanded at Chatham Financial this past year into a series of monthly after-school sessions with 35 Kennett Middle School students and more than 20 Chatham Financial volunteers.

In addition to my role in founding Together for Education, I personally volunteer in a classroom, where I join a group of students around a table and work with them on gaining math and/or reading proficiency. For more than 7 years, I have been working with Joan Viscuso, who has taught both 3rd and 4th grade students in the Mary D. Lang, Bancroft and New Garden elementary schools. I have followed her path because we have developed a great working relationship, and I enjoy her classroom environment. Volunteering with the kids has been a very rewarding experience for me. If I am having a bad day at work, I walk in and the students warmly welcome me with a "Hi, Mr. Sam". This helps to reinforce the proper priorities in life; I get to witness our future first-hand. In addition to seeing the skill and care that teachers like Joan invest in the children, I believe that I am also offering the help that is needed to build the students' self-confidence and educational success. I hope to be serving as a role model who cares and genuinely shows each child that he or she is important. At the end of the year, I invite my wife and sons to join the class in an informal end-of-the-year celebration. My children, who were new readers last year, read to the students, representing a wonderful reversal of roles; it allowed the 4th graders to model success to my children.

I personally like to offer the frame of mind that if we work to being inclusionary, the diversity in our communities can be a special attribute rather than a challenge. We can embrace our local diversity to help the students grow into global citizenship!

"I continue to believe that if children are given the necessary tools to succeed, they will succeed beyond their wildest dreams!"

— David Vitter, United States senator —

Walk In kNowledge Program
Loretta Perna, coordinator

01/20/2016. *I have served as the Walk In kNowledge Program (WIN) Coordinator since its inception in 2007. The program began with a three-year 21ˢᵗ Century Community Learning Centers Grant. When the three-year grant ended, the Kennett Consolidated School District (KCSD) continued funding my salary with Title 1 funds. The remainder of the program continues to be largely supported by charitable donations from private individuals, community organizations and local businesses.*

I moved to Kennett Square from my home state of Texas in 1985, obtained a degree in fine arts from West Chester University, and thereafter worked as an actress, primarily in Philadelphia and New York.

My direct involvement with the Kennett Square community began in 1998 when the site director of the Migrant Education Program (MEP) inquired about my acting career. I informed him that I was pulling-back from acting to focus more on the visual arts, and also mentioned that I had been asked to mentor a student at New Garden Elementary School. He eventually offered me the opportunity to teach drama during the MEP summer program, which I accepted. I grew up in a Spanish-speaking household until I moved away when I was nine years old. After that, I rarely spoke Spanish. In addition to my desire to work with young people, I thought the MEP summer teaching position would give me an opportunity to refresh my Spanish. Soon after the summer program concluded, I was hired full-time as an MEP Student Support Specialist, where I worked for the next 10 years. Through my experience with MEP, I witnessed first-hand the importance of providing academic support to the Mexican migrant students. Because I understood Spanish, and could effectively communicate directly with students and families, I discovered I could be persuasive in helping them view academics as a priority.

My essential role over the last eighteen years has been to assist with the acculturation of the Mexican family. When a Mexican family arrives in Kennett Square, the parents typically possess the equivalent of a second grade education. In fact, the women usually have completed the second grade studies, however, the men often have no more than a first grade education. Perhaps one of the reasons for this is that in the Mexican State of Guanajuato and the city of Moroleon, the origin of most Kennett migrant families, education beyond sixth grade is fee-based.

Consequently, for Mexican families that migrate to the United States searching for more profitable work, higher education is not a priority. Attending college is not even an option for the families, due to the insurmountable cost of post-secondary education as well as the need for students to begin working during high school and immediately after graduation in order to help support their families both here and in Mexico. My job is to support these students and allow them to dream beyond the path already established for them. But, before I can fully advocate for the students, I must convince the parents that college is a good idea. In most cases, this is a hard sell.

∞

One example that I clearly remember involved a bright female student who told me that she was going to "leave home" because her father did not want her to attend college. He preferred that she instead "go to work" immediately after graduating from high school. I made a personal visit to this student's home. When I arrived, her mother, father and all of her siblings sat down to participate in the discussion. For about two hours, I listened to the father's concerns, while continuing to emphasize the importance of education in this country. The father finally, but reluctantly, agreed to allow his daughter to attend college—mostly because he could see that she was serious about leaving home if he did not agree. As I was leaving his home he stated, "so now she is your responsibility." I took this to heart, and impressed upon this student, the oldest daughter in the family, how important it was for her to become a role model for the rest of her siblings. I am happy to report that this student eventually graduated from college and presently works for a program funded by the Pennsylvania Department of Labor. All of her siblings later attended college: her younger sister is now a registered nurse at a local hospital, and her younger brothers are presently in college—one is now in his second year at Harvard University with a full scholarship, and the other is a freshman at Penn State University. But without that fateful meeting with this student's parents years ago, none of this would have been possible. This is the kind of cultural bridging that is essential if we are to integrate the Mexican community into our education system.

In addition to cost and parental resistance, other impediments to higher education for migrant students are the fear of the unknown and, most poignantly, the fear of failure. I try to acknowledge these fears, yet consistently reinforce the message that if they stay committed and focused these hesitant students will overcome their fears and find their paths to graduation. Our mantra is, "We do not give up!" I arrange for current college students and college graduates from our program to return to make presentations to help inspire the high school students. I also assist with identifying sources of much-needed funding. One high school student, who insisted at the beginning of the year that she didn't want to go to college, has now changed her mind. "I heard what these speakers said, and I now think I want to go to college."

∞

In 2007, the superintendent of Kennett schools applied for the 21st Century Community Learning Center (21st CCLC) grant for funding the Walk In kNowledge (WIN) Program. The grant was awarded to the school district, and the superintendent suggested that I administer the WIN program whose specific mission is to provide academic support with a focus on tutoring in mathematics, increased options for post-secondary education, and assistance with acculturation, mentoring, and delivery of information to parents concerning the American school system. Components of WIN include homework assistance for students, after-school tutoring, after-school transportation from program activities, provision of computer equipment and student workspace, weekly acting lessons, opportunities for community service, home visits, character workshops, and college preparatory activities for seniors. In addition, WIN includes community service with the intent of helping students to "make their community their home."

Although WIN initially targeted Latino students who needed more support navigating the path to higher education, today the program is open to all students who desire academic support. We still follow most of the original 21st CCLC grant objectives even though the grant has expired, and there is now an alternate funding source. This has resulted in a reduction in funding, which means there is no longer a summer program.

I believe that any successful program must bring about systematic and lasting change. From the beginning, I realized I must work closely with parents and supportive community agencies as key partners in this process. For example, it is important to have internships to expose students to multiple career alternatives, so toward this end I developed relationships with local businesses, agencies and service organizations, particularly Longwood Rotary and Exelon. It was also necessary to build relationships with colleges in order to encourage them to "take a chance" on some of our students. Presently I have a working relationship with many colleges including: Penn State University, Indiana University of PA, West Chester University, Marywood University, and Immaculata University. My expectation is that college options and scholarships will continue to expand. I routinely encourage students to get to know their school counselors in order to better understand academic and financial aid options.

We also assist non-college bound students with finding gainful employment as an interim step to college. For example, one student who wants to become a medical doctor is currently working to help pay-off a family land loan, after which we will step in and help her with college admission and funding alternatives.

∞

Once the three-year 21st CCLC grant ended in 2010, program funding became a significant challenge. In 2012, WIN was destined to close its doors, however, many Mexican families and their children persuaded the KCSD Board to continue the program with myself as director. Title 1 funds were used to cover my salary, although transportation was still limited which significantly curtailed our after-school programs. MEP provided assistance, but eventually MEP changed its program to Saturdays, bringing our collaboration on transportation to an end. Fortunately, the next year WIN found a generous donor who helped with the cost of transportation and other program activities. With additional help from many such donors, we have re-instated and expanded our after-school tutorials, which include seven teachers paid by the district on Tuesday and Thursday afternoons. We currently have 122 students in the program, which is about 30% of the Latino high school enrollment, and expect to graduate approximately 35 seniors in 2017.

As additional funding becomes available, my wish list would be to expand transportation services, increase the summer tutorials, and enhance the cultural adaptation programs. Building on existing KCSD summer programs would also be beneficial to the program.

One measure of success for WIN is the percentage of our students who graduate from high school. To ensure success in high school, we regularly look at the student's attendance and grades and then mentor from this base. Another measure of success is the number of program participants who attend, and graduate from, college. We are also beginning to monitor the job rate of our college graduates, and pay particular attention to whether those jobs are appropriate to the type of college degree. For example, we occasionally discover college graduates working in the mushroom industry as "pickers" or "packers." This may be because such work is readily available and familiar, and some students simply are hesitant to enter the broader professional world.

KCSD is the fourth largest ESL district in Pennsylvania. The superintendent currently holds monthly meetings with community businesses and agencies who serve the Latino population. The goal is to be on the same page and to give a united message to parents, "Be more engaged with your children's education."

After-The-Bell for Kennett Middle School students is a wonderful after-school program that offers many varied activities in a safe environment. It does not take much to encourage WIN juniors and seniors to volunteer as facilitator assistants. The older students thoroughly enjoy tutoring their middle school counterparts in a variety of subjects.

I believe WIN is sustainable, because it has community and district-wide support. Many talented individuals continue to volunteer their time to help these aspiring students. Of course, in order for this program to remain strong, its future leaders must view the position as a vocation rather than simply a job.

In the next decade, our challenges will grow along with the burgeoning migrant population. The current kindergarten population is approximately 50% Latino, suggesting that in just a few short years the high school must be prepared with greatly expanded programs. It is important to remember that by helping our Latino students embrace our way of life, we will be simultaneously be adding value to our American culture.

9

"Words of wisdom are spoken by children at least as often as scientists."
—James Newman, American astronaut —

Kennett Area Latino Youth
Sarahi Zamores

05/11/2016. *My story of living in the Kennett Square area starts at when I was twelve years old. My father had lived here since he was eighteen years old, working in the mushroom industry. He would travel back and forth to Mexico, and married my mother during one of his visits. I was born in a very small town in the state of Jalisco. I was the fourth child of five children and the only girl. My father had brought my two older brothers here when they were sixteen and seventeen years old, and they started working at Manfredi's cold storage. Two years after my brothers immigrated, my parents thought it was time that we all lived together; so I clearly remember the day of July 16, 2005. I came to live in a small trailer with three bedrooms and two bathrooms in Toughkenamon, PA.*

My first shock was the heat and humidity. I was accustomed to the heat in Mexico, but not the humidity. I remember that summer as very lonely and boring. We had no friends or neighbors, and Mom could not drive. My parents did not want me to go anywhere because they did not know the culture, and I could not speak the language. My dad and older brothers would come home sometimes for lunch and dinner, but their working hours were from 6am to 10 pm. Needless to say, we rarely saw anyone during the day.

The student support specialist of the Migrant Education Program (MEP) worked with my parents to get my brothers and I enrolled in Kennett Middle School (KMS). My brother, Lisandro, although a year older than me, was placed in seventh grade with me, but in a different classroom. I had one English as a Second Language (ESL) class, and all the rest were regular English speaking classrooms. I did not understand any of the assignments, and I felt powerless every time I went to school. I started to feel afraid and depressed. I would cry almost every day before going to school, on the way home from school, and at night. I just did not want to go to school! As time passed, I eventually was able to perform well in math because Mexico is ahead in this subject; also, for me the language was easier to understand in these classes. There were only a few Mexican students in my regular classes, and they tried to help me and explain the assignments or what the teachers were asking for, but it did not seem to be enough help.

∞

There was this one day that I clearly remember. I came late to school due to a doctor's appointment, and I had a written excuse from the physician. When I went into the main office to hand in the paper and to try and explain why I was late, the receptionist told me to sit down and not to talk. Because I could not find the English words to explain and because she gave me a harsh direction, I did as she said and sat there for four long hours. When school was being dismissed, the principal discovered that there was a misunderstanding and that I had been mistaken for another student who was in trouble in the classroom. Since that day, I started to notice that people made assumptions about me and about others, and I was angry with them. But I was also frustrated with myself because I knew that if I spoke the language I would be able to communicate well and not allow others to make assumptions about me. It was a very difficult time all the way around. I started to take my frustration out on everyone else, especially my parents and teachers. I was angry at everyone and I refused to do my homework. I would not follow the instructions in school, and I would argue with my parents often. My parents really did not know that I was in trouble at school because no one had explained it to them.

My parents did not allow me to take part in any sport because sports are for boys. And I was also not allowed to be a cheerleader because the skirts were too short. The only extracurricular activity that I was part of in eighth grade was After-The-Bell. It felt good to have something to do after classes were over because there was only the television at home. The Migrant Education Program (MEP) also provided classes in the summers, and this was a time when I started to learn more English and could catch up on classes that I fell behind in during middle school. The summer classes with the MEP were completely different from our regular school classes. I felt safe, and everyone there spoke Spanish which made me feel like there were other people like me.

That summer after eighth grade, I met Ms. Loretta Perna. The very first day I met her she challenged me and the other students in the classroom. She asked that we stand up and introduce ourselves in front of the classroom. I was not very confident, so this was a big challenge for me. She was very kind and understanding. She kept telling us that there was nothing to worry about, and that it was a judge-free zone. When I moved on to Kennett High school, I started to visit her and asked her for help with class homework. It was during one of my visits that she told me she was starting an after-school tutoring program called the "Walk In kNowledge" program (i.e. WIN). I was one of the first ten students to be identified for the WIN Program. I understood this as a privilege, so I accepted. From the beginning, Ms. Perna started to mention college and discuss how it would open many more doors in my future. I had no idea what she was talking about.

During my sophomore year at Kennett High School, Ms. Perna asked, "If I was a fairy godmother, and I could make you whatever you wanted to be in the future, without going to college right now, what would you choose to become?" "A lawyer," I responded. Ms. Perna then brought me back to reality and said that if I really wanted to be an attorney, I could become one if I was willing to work hard for it. She also said that she would continue to be there for me, guiding and assisting me in any way necessary. I still think she is really a fairy godmother or an angel. She has been a mentor, a friend, and a second mother to me. If it wasn't for her, I would have never even thought of college, let alone attend college.

∞

Eleventh grade was a very exciting year for me because I went to Penn State University (PSU) on a field trip with other students. I immediately loved the campus and started wondering how it would feel to live there. It jump-started my passion about attending college. It was in this year that I started to develop more self-confidence and the fear of rejection started to lessen. I was performing better in my classes and, through the WIN program, I began to love to serve my community. We did a lot of volunteer work. My favorite activity was to paint over gang-written graffiti. We were cleaning up the community and trying to overcome stereotypes. I also volunteered with the Kennett Rotary to pick up trash along Old Baltimore Pike, at the Kennett Area Senior Center and with the Kennett Run. Being involved in the community gave me a sense of belonging. My parents allowed me to participate, but many times they had no idea what I was doing.

I was also a member of the Hermanitas program that Ms. Perna coordinated every year since 2004. I learned many things about leadership, time management and goal setting. I was also invited to a Hermanitas leadership conference in San Diego, CA. This was such an amazing experience because it was my first time in California, and because I got to meet girls from all over the country. We also had the opportunity of staying in the dorms at San Diego University. It is such a beautiful campus, and I had a wonderful time.

One difficult time that I had in eleventh grade was when I spoke to my school counselor, who asked me what I wanted to do after high school graduation. When I said I wanted to go to Penn State Main Campus, he told me that a better choice for me would be to attend a community college, and that he could help me apply; but that PSU just was not suited for me. I was heartbroken. I immediately ran to Ms. Perna and asked her to be completely honest with me. I wanted to know if all along she was just trying to give me hope or was it really possible for me to go to PSU. She sat me down and told me that she would do all that she could to support me in my goal of attending PSU; and that we would work through all the steps together to help me overcome all obstacles that stood in my way. She felt that PSU was very possible for me if I was willing to work hard to make this dream come true. She also reminded me of all the other Latino students attending PSU, or that had graduated from it. Another obstacle closer to home was my parents and their friends from work. They told me that it was not safe for a girl to go away to school, and they were vehemently against my decision to go to PSU. After many weeks and months of arguing with my parents, they agreed to go on a trip for WIN parents and to learn more about the College Assistance Migrant Program (CAMP), a transitional program for migrant students and parents. This visit changed their mind, and they became more supportive of me going to a university that was three to four hours away.

∞

My first year at PSU was covered 100% by scholarships. The rest of the years, I continued to receive some financial help, but eventually had to take out Federal Student Aid loans and become employed. I was a receptionist at the Multi-Cultural Resource Center and an assistant to a research specialist. I lived in campus dorms for three years and then in an apartment with other students during my fourth year. I graduated with a Bachelor's Degree in Labor and Employee Relations. I do have some debt now, but I have no regrets and accept the responsibilities of paying off my loans. I am currently working at Longwood Gardens in the human resource department.

Regarding my siblings, my oldest brother never adjusted to the life in the United States. He did move back to Mexico, and he recently got married. My second oldest brother owns a spawning business and will be married soon. My third oldest brother graduated from high school and is still in the area. Lastly, my youngest brother, Fabian, received a full-ride to Penn State to study architectural engineering. He is a college sophomore, and I could not be more proud of him.

I am now living with my mother and two older brothers. Even though my mother and I had a difficult relationship when I was younger, I do admire her and understand how difficult it must have been for her to come to a new country. To this day she still has problems with the English language. However, I am very proud of her because she became a citizen after being a resident for only seven years, and she did everything in English.

One of my biggest dreams for the future is to buy a home for my mother. I want to give back to her because she gave so much to all of her children. I also wish she could find a job where she can contribute in a bigger way and feel respected and valued.

Since graduating from college, I have volunteered in the WIN program and search for ways to give back and help Ms. Perna with anything to ensure more students go to college. She continues to be a great support, and an inspiration in my life.

Beyond that, I haven't thought much further. I never grew up thinking I wanted to be married or be a mother, so I am not looking for that right now. I do want to continue to learn new things, to travel everywhere and to meet new people. I also enjoy engaging and bantering over interesting topics. I am always up for a good discussion and never opposed to debating. I want to also continue helping others in need and volunteering in my community. My life has just begun!

10

**"No other person or outside force
has a greater influence on a child than a parent."**

— Bob Keeshan, American television producer & actor (aka Captain Kangaroo) —

Migrant Head Start Program
Claudia Turner, education coordinator

03/31/2016. Since 2009, I have served as the early childhood education coordinator for Path Stone Migrant Head Start. My family history goes back to the first mushroom growers, so I have a long relationship with this area.

The Migrant Head Start Program is currently located at 421 McFarland Road in Kennett Square, and is federally funded by East Coast Migrant Head Start Project. We are under the umbrella of Path Stone, which, in addition to Head Start, has programs for employment, housing, and child & family services.

The mission of Migrant Head Start is to provide quality child care for children ages 6 weeks to 5 years as well as family services including education, training, disability, family literacy, nutritious meals and advocacy services. Our program serves low-income families from southern Chester County. We are open from 7am to 5pm from September through March with no charge to the families. To qualify for our services, one parent must work in the agricultural industry, which includes mushrooms, vineyards and landscaping in our southern Chester County area. Eligible families also must fit the criteria for migrant status, which means the family has changed their residence by moving within the last 24 months from one geographic location to another for the purpose of engaging in agricultural work. We also provide services for seasonal families who work in agriculture and live in the area but are not recent migrants. The definition of the term "agricultural industry" has been greatly expanded. It now includes categories and jobs that will increase the number of families that are eligible to enroll in the program.

We provide wrap-around family services and facilitate these services through our family service coordinator and our health and disabilities coordinator. This involves providing referrals to social service agencies; and supplying food, clothing, formula, and diapers to the families. We even try to arrange transportation to appointments if a staff member is available. We contract a bus service to pick up the child at his/her residence and return them home at the end of the day. This requires us to have our own car seats and adequate staff on the buses.

Currently, we have seven classrooms and a total of 24 employees. Two teachers are assigned to each classroom, and at least one must be bilingual. The pre-school curriculum for the three to five year olds is taught in both Spanish and English.

We are educating children who otherwise would never be ready for kindergarten without our services. We are required to provide data about our effectiveness to our funders. We have an entry assessment, Ages and Stages Questionnaire 3 (ASQ3), followed by two other skill-based assessments, Learning Accomplishment Profile 3 (LAP3) and Early Learning Accomplishment Profile (E-LAP) three times a year. Please refer to the glossary for a short description of these assessment tools. We have a review by our East Coast Migrant Head Start funders twice a year, and every two years we have a federal review. Our reviews have always been above satisfactory. We keep the parents informed by providing a report on each child's progress in addition to the overall outcomes for Kennett's Migrant Head Start program. We also provide the reports to the parent's employers.

∞

Recently, Path Stone has received state funding for Pre-K Counts, which serves low-income families in the area. There are no requirements for migrant status or length of time of residency in the area. We have seventeen children enrolled and are hoping to receive additional funding to expand. Statistics prove that one of the most strategic points for a child's success in formal education is based on kindergarten-readiness. Starting behind the line does not bid well for a child's self-esteem, his/her confidence, or the ability to build on his/her foundation. We need to be advocates for the children!

One of the strongest elements of the Migrant Head Start program is parental involvement. We have been on the forefront when it comes to understanding that the most effective child development occurs when our parents are supportive partners. A family enters our program with a home visit to determine what the parents' interests are and how to incorporate these interests into our curriculum. We conduct two conferences a year involving their child/children at our location and an additional home visit. For our program to be a success, it's critical that the parent feels included and is taking the helm with their child's development and education. We encourage reading at home and supply English and Spanish books if needed.

We also conduct parent education programs once a month, which emphasize the role of the parent and provide the information and tools and resource information for parents to become more actively involved. We encourage all participants to speak up at meetings and to ask questions, thus developing a sense of empowerment. We felt such satisfaction when, during a presentation on domestic violence, female participants found the courage to rise and ask the tough questions. During this past year, we emphasized nutrition and healthy eating with both our students and the parents. We took advantage of the kitchen at our school site, and found that hands-on cooking classes were effective in changing unhealthy diet patterns.

∞

The success of the Kennett Migrant Head Start program is largely dependent on the communication and collaboration with the broader community. I sit on the Advisory Board of MCHC's Family Center, and, because of my involvement, I understand that The Family Center and Migrant Head Start share a similar mission on kindergarten readiness. I'm a familiar face among the mushroom employers, who allow parents time off from work for teacher conferences and parent education classes. I regularly attend Bridging the Community meetings to inform the community of our programs and to help with recruitment of families and employees. Yes, I need to start asking for volunteers, too. We are so fortunate to have Anne Humes, our treasured volunteer from Kendal. Technical College High School-Pennock Bridge Campus is a valuable source for employee recruitment. And, I partner with surrounding daycares, which may supply childcare during the months that Migrant Head Start is not in operation.

Our Kennett agricultural community is different than most migrant communities because our mushrooms are grown and harvested year round. When Kennett Migrant Head Start closes its doors from March to September, many of our families scramble to find another daycare for their children. There are home daycares provided by some of the migrant women, but the children are not receiving the pre-school education that is critical to prepare them for kindergarten. This issue must be addressed as we work towards a continuum of care.

Our greatest challenge is funding the children's transportation to and from our facility. The cost is very expensive, however, offering transportation is what makes or breaks our attendance. We will continue to explore ways to reduce this cost.

To experience the children's and family's progress is very fulfilling. I thoroughly enjoy interacting with the employees, and appreciate and support their involvement in the daycare and pre-school as a way to move ahead in their employment careers. We are working on establishing a partnership with PA Keys to expand professional development programs and an opportunity for our employees to move to their next level of education.

11

"When I approach a child, he inspires in me two sentiments—tenderness for what he is and respect for what he may become."

— Louis Pasteur, French scientist and inventor —

Chester County Head Start Program
Tamara Acuna, supervisor

05/25/2016. I was born in North Carolina. During my growing up years, I lived in several areas around the country because of my father's different job assignments. I was in the southern Chester County area during my early school-age years when I attended Kemblesville Elementary School, and then during my high school years when I went to Unionville High School. I have worked for Head Start in several capacities since 2009 and became the supervisor of Chester County Head Start in 2013. We serve six hundred and fifty children throughout the county. I live in West Grove with my two sons, Josh and Jeremy.

Head Start is a program of the United States Department of Health and Human Services, which is now celebrating its fifty-first year anniversary. Chester County has conducted Head Start programs for forty-five years, and the Chester County Intermediate Unit has hosted Head Start for thirty of those years. We have nine centers throughout the county under the operation of the Chester County Intermediate Unit. In the earlier years, the Kennett Square Head Start's program was housed in several different churches and was operated by the Community Action Program. In 2008, a developer in town, LGB Properties, built a facility that was designed for pre-school success. We are located at 380 W. Cypress St., Kennett Square, Pennsylvania where we are serving seventy-six children and families.

The mission of Chester County Head Start is to provide comprehensive, high-quality early childhood services to ensure that children and families can achieve individual success. We are funded federally, and we receive funds from the State of Pennsylvania as well. Our capacity to serve is determined by the amount of money we receive. We have two hundred and fifty more youth in the Kennett area that would qualify for Head Start if we had more funds.

Fortunately, we are known in the area, so we receive many referrals. After a parent contacts our agency, a family service worker visits the home and assures that qualifications are met. The family must be living at or below the 100% federal poverty guidelines, and the child must be between three to five years old. Please refer to the Glossary (Note*) for a description of the federal poverty guidelines. The child closest to kindergarten age receives preference, and the parents must have the means to provide transportation for their child to the Head Start Center. If the family does not qualify for our program, we try to refer the family to other programs, although there are few options due to cost and criteria for other pre-school programs.

We conduct two sessions a day; morning and afternoon. Each session is three and one-half hours each. We serve breakfast and lunch on site and serve family-style with staff included. We have our own food service on site and have a nutritionist from the county who plans the menus so that they are nutritious, as well as culturally appropriate. We also have cooking activities twice a month and send home recipes, which promote healthy foods and preparation.

In our Kennett Square Head Start center, 80% of our students speak mostly Spanish, with a little English, and three of our five staff members are bi-lingual. We have two classrooms of mixed ages from three to five years old and have two (one bi-lingual) teachers in each classroom. We are implementing the family model, whereby different ages benefit from each other. The teachers do a great job and really take an interest in the children, which provides a sense of "family."

The family service worker is bi-lingual and develops a close relationship with families in their homes. Instead of seventy-six families, the worker has about fifty families to serve because two or more children may be from one family. On her first visit with each family, she conducts a survey and learns about the information, education and resources that the family needs, as well as the risk factors. She makes more home visits to families that are high risk and also makes referrals to the many services in the area.

The center hosts two programs for parents each month. Some of the topics have been homebuyer options, parenting classes, behavioral health, as well as information about medical services.

Being a federally funded program, Head Start has high standards to meet, which are assessed regularly. The positive side of this is that we are challenged to maintain a high performance. On the down side, there are some standards that are out of our control, such as parents' compliance with such things as timely medical and dental exams and lead screenings, and this can affect our rating.

Our teachers have higher pay than pre-school teachers, but lower pay than the school districts; however, they do receive health benefits and pensions from the CCIU. We have observed that the teachers who have just graduated from college enjoy starting at Head Start. Since 2013, the federal guidelines require that all of our employees have at least an associate's degree, with one-half of the staff having a bachelor's degree; however, in Chester County our teachers all have at least a bachelor's degree. We also continue with training classes and updates.

We follow a curriculum, and when our children enter kindergarten, 88% are developmentally at par with their peers. A few years ago, we had the unfortunate limited study that came out of a university that said our Head Start Program did not make a difference in a child's education, by the time the child reached third grade. Head Start has conducted expansive studies and this is not accurate. In fact, the studies have been able to contribute Head Start participation during the pre-school years, as a factor that has reduced the involvement in future crimes by 60% nationally.

$$\infty$$

As you would guess our greatest challenge is financial. It is difficult to fundraise beyond our current government funding, because it appears to the general public that we are adequately funded. If I had a large sum of money, I would like to enroll the 3,000 eligible children from the county in Head Start programs. Finding sites to conduct our childhood services is not the problem, as we have churches and businesses approach us with offers to set-up at their locations. We would need funds for staff and administration. I also would fund transportation, which was ended a while ago. This is a real hardship for families, even though they have learned the art of car-pooling. On the practical level, when one compares the cost of ameliorating education of a child in later years versus the cost of pre-school, it isn't difficult to see where we need to be making our investment.

There are two state-funded Pre-K Counts programs that have started in southern Chester County. This is an effort to accommodate families, who have incomes that are below or equal to the 300% federal poverty guidelines. Please refer to the glossary for a description of the federal poverty guidelines. The program runs for six hours a day, five days a week. The Chester County Head Start is also starting up some efforts in other parts of the county, but will not be starting one in Kennett.

There is a future trend that is in the works; next year Head Start will be moving from our half-day sessions to six-hour days, which would run from 8:30am to 2:30pm. In addition, we are pursuing the option of being licensed as a before and after school daycare center, which will accommodate working parents. Another new endeavor on the horizon is developing a teacher home visiting program. This would involve having teachers visit families with children from birth to three years, to provide materials and education that will provide instruction and earlier support. The first five years of a child's life is probably the most critical in creating a healthy foundation for a life time. We, at Head Start will continue to look at creative ways to utilize our funds and ways to gain more community support in joining our mission.

"If our American way of life fails the child, it fails us all."
— Pearl S. Buck, author and activist —

United Way of Southern Chester County
Interview with Carrie Freeman, CEO

06/04/16. I was born and raised in Elizabethtown, PA and graduated from Smith College with a degree in education. In searching for that first professional job post-college, I interviewed with Charles Patton from the Unionville Middle School and was hired as a teacher there from 1979-1990. When my two sons, Scott and Bradley, were young, I was a stay-at-home mom until I returned to work as executive director of Tick Tock Early Learning Center in Avondale, a nonprofit educational daycare for low-income families. I was there for ten years. I transitioned to CEO of United Way of Southern Chester County in 2003. Kennett Square has been my home since 1979, and I moved to the Stenning Hills neighborhood in the borough in 1981.

The United Way started in the Kennett area in August 1944, as a Community Chest. That year it raised $29,790 from the community to give to 17 War Fund Appeals Agencies and 11 Home Front Agencies. In 1974, the organization morphed into the Kennett Area United Fund. In 1987, it because the United Way of the Kennett Area. Avon Grove's United Way merged with Kennett soon after. Oxford had the Oxford Civic Foundation, which was not a United Way, but helped financially serve the needs in the Oxford area. In 1991, we became the United Way of Southern Chester County, serving the four school district areas of Kennett, Avon Grove, Oxford and Unionville-Chadds Ford, which include about 110,000 residents.

Throughout the years, our fundraising ability has been up and down based on the economy. We receive pledges starting in September and send the amount we can allocate out to local nonprofits by March. When I started in 2003, we allocated $535,000 and we have gone as high as $1,000,000 in 2014. This year, 2016, has been painful for us since we can only allocate $780,000, cutting allocation amounts by 22% due to the reduction of employee donations coming from Delaware companies home to southern Chester County.

∞

In the past, DuPont Company employees have been our greatest donors, with up to $300,000 per campaign season. With their merger with Dow Chemical, and other Delaware companies' downsizing, we lost many leadership donors. Donors, who live in southern Chester County and work out of the area, comprise about 43% of our campaign. They are responding to our slogan, "Live here? Give here. Stays here!" 30% of our campaign comes from donors responding to a direct mail appeal. 20% of the campaign comes from local workplace campaigns at area businesses and schools. Grants and our Chocolate Lovers Festival comprise the rest of the revenue.

Our allocations are focused on three areas:
1. Crisis Intervention
2. Stability and Sustainability—mainly senior programs and health programs
3. Transitioning to Independence through Education—our youth and adult literacy and job training programs.

We also have an Unmet Needs Fund for creating new programs to address unmet needs in our area. We allocated funds to 27 programs at 19 local nonprofits this past year. Four of these agencies will receive $100,000 or more.

In the past year, the Board of Directors of United Way of Southern Chester County (UWSCC) put in place tougher eligibility requirements related to non-discrimination at every level of the applying agencies' organizations. In other words, there can be no discrimination in delivery of services to clients, in staffing, in volunteer participation, or in the selection of board members. This led to two previous agency recipients not applying for funds this year. UWSCC believes non-discrimination is a vital component to any organization, and we mentor area agencies to adopt best practices and a strong non-discriminatory policy.

We have an accountability process for the agencies that we fund. We ask each agency to identify three measureable goals and report statistics back to us at the end of the funding year. If the goals haven't been met, we have a discussion about the reasons and evaluate, which still may leave the agency eligible for the following funding year. We have had many professional board members and area volunteers who give their time to help agencies that are struggling. We will do cash analyses for agencies and work on sustainability plans. Yes, we have defunded agencies; mainly for poor use of funds or having a model of operation that we didn't believe was sustainable. Our goal is to have all our agencies be successful in meeting their missions while being fiscally sound.

∞

I have several great concerns about the future. In southern Chester County, we have wonderful philanthropists who are quite elderly, which leads us to ask, "Are there any others that will follow?" In the area of volunteerism, the trend today with the millennial is short-term volunteer projects; many of our programs are heavily supported by long-term volunteers; in fact 70%. The large corporations moving out of the area or downsizing robs us of a wonderful volunteer base in the future as well as that corporate enticement to collectively donate.

My goals as CEO of United Way of Southern Chester County are:
1. To grow in the future, we must reach more donors. We need to tell our story better and highlight the value of giving to us. United Way is the collective heart of the community and best understands the whole community picture of needs. With this perspective, we can assure that needs are met in a balanced and accountable fashion.
2. To discern unmet community needs and work to develop programs to address them.
3. To provide yearly workshops and ongoing support to develop professional capacity in our local nonprofits.

I am grateful that Family Promise was established this past year to address the homelessness issue we are facing here in southern Chester County. This was an unmet need in our community and United Way worked on a solution for several years. Concerned citizens and area nonprofits led the search for a solution, which was the formation of Family Promise of Southern Chester County. Homeless families with children now have housing in a traveling shelter situated in thirteen different host churches. We helped fund their start-up and develop their organizational policies.

Kennett Square is an incredible community. Everyone is willing to work together for a common cause with every section of the community stepping up to help. I enjoy working here because I have so many committed and concerned residents who deeply care about their fellow community members. In spite of the changing trends and challenges in front of us, I still believe we have the community strength to deal with them.

13

"*Children are our greatest treasure. They are our future.*"

— Nelson Mandela, former president of South Africa —

Chester County Futures
Marie McDonald, executive director

06/16/16. I am a lifelong Chester County resident, born in Berwyn, PA. My father owned a catering business called Jimmy Duffy Catering, which established our roots here. I received my business administration degree from Immaculata University and worked for my father's business throughout my twenties. I married Hugh in 1986 and together we've raised our two daughters, Maria and Stephanie. I entered the nonprofit world in 1991, and decided that it was where I would stay. I was employed at University of Pennsylvania, Peoples Light and Theatre Company, Elite Charitable Foundation, and Breastcancer.org before accepting a position at Chester County Futures as their director of development in 2012. I began my current role as executive director in 2014.

Chester County Futures was founded in 1996 by three Chester County philanthropists working with the Chester County Community Foundation to address disparities in county school districts with the highest levels of poverty. Their vision was to create a nonprofit after school program that would increase the high school graduation rate in these schools and encourage students to pursue a college education.

The mission of Chester County Futures is to provide comprehensive academic support, mentoring, and scholarships for motivated economically disadvantaged youth to succeed in school, higher education and in life.

Chester County Futures is celebrating its twentieth year as a nonprofit organization offering direct program support and services through after-school academic enrichment meetings, mentoring and post-secondary scholarship support. We serve four school districts, listed in the order of enrollment size: Coatesville, Oxford, Kennett and Phoenixville. Our main office is located at: 704 Haywood Drive, Exton, PA 19341.

Our student population in 2014-15 consisted of 210 high school students, 87 middle school students, and 159 post-secondary students. We serve 42% Hispanic, 26% Caucasian, 25% African American, 2% Asian and 5% other. Our programs have 56% females and 44% males.

We maintain a million dollar operating budget. We are a privately funded nonprofit organization with a fundraising effort that yields 40% from foundation funds; 35% from individuals; and 25% from corporations, of which 10% comes from the Educational Improvement Tax Credit Program. To secure these annual funds, I work closely with members of the development team and am actively involved in grant writing, fund raising events and personal solicitations for support.

Kennett Square and Coatesville were the first two school districts we served in 1996. In 2007, when the Walk In kNowledge (WIN) program was implemented in Kennett Square, we added Phoenixville and Oxford. As the WIN program got started, we developed a middle school program. We have since followed those original middle school students and have returned to Kennett High School. Both the administration and teachers of Kennett Consolidated School District believe we can build a stronger desire for higher education by starting earlier and continuing to work with these most vulnerable young people throughout high school. We offer enrichment camps to seventh and eighth grade students, who counselors have identified as fitting our criteria. We involve two school districts on one project to provide a broader student experience.

∞

Chester County Futures identifies a STEM project to be worked on, and incorporates the arts in all we do to transform our curriculum to STEAM. Our corporate partners offer their sites, expertise and mentorship, but the students stay at the helm of implementing the project. One recent example occurred at Longwood Gardens. The project that was proposed was Design Thinking through Bio-mimicry. The students learned about a variety of plants, then designed a playground that would include various plants that provided shade, cushioning, definition to the area etc. They left feeling proud of their design and creation and could easily communicate the purpose of each plant they used in their plans.

Chester County Futures' Kennett Middle School students meet with mentors once a month. Chatham Financial has generously offered its meeting space and covered transportation expenses to their site. Twenty

Chatham employee mentors are matched with our students. The ninety minutes is spent addressing an identified topic that prepares students for the challenges of high school. The topics include: critical thinking; communication; collaboration; creativity; teamwork; career exploration and more. All in all, one of the greatest benefits of this time is that each child has concentrated time with a caring adult, which in turn helps build student self-esteem and self-confidence.

∞

In the spring of the eighth grade, students in our program, re-apply to be participants in Chester County Futures high school program. Our coordinators have meetings with the parents, who need to show a strong commitment and buy-in to the program. Again, the students need to show motivation and accountability. During high school, a coordinator for each grade level holds a ninety minute session once a week, which the student must attend. We select curriculum topics for each grade level. We have strict class attendance rules and, fortunately, we only have a 5% attrition rate annually.

We also have a mentor component, which we set-up for our most vulnerable high school students. The mentor is required to stay in touch weekly either by phone or text and to spend face-to-face time once a month, which can be a shared activity. The commitment is for one year, however many of the mentors stay on, as they build a caring relationship with the student, which also enriches the mentor's life. The primary goal is to keep the college encouragement and dialogue alive.

We have access to the student's report card status, which helps us stay in tune with the progress or issues of the students. If a student is having academic difficulty, we work together with the schools, parents and student to develop a strategy to help, sometimes involving tutoring and advocacy.

Before graduation, our students will visit at a minimum four college campuses; frequently it is six or more. This is to expose them to the variety of choices and to help them find the best match for them. Upon matriculation into college, our students receive a $1,500 scholarship every year with the maximum of $6,000 for the total college period. To receive the scholarship the student must take twelve credit hours and have a "C" average. The students also need to check in with us twice a year via personal interviews. Beyond this, we help students explore other funding options and private scholarships to help make college affordable.

My dream for the future is addressing some challenges our students face as they transition into college. This year, we will deliver our first college bridge programming to out college freshman. We competed for and were awarded the opportunity to work with three consultants from SAP America for six weeks, who lead us in the development of our new program, "Steps for College Success." We have a boot camp, of sorts, that we have conducted at SAP (Systems, Applications, and Processing) America Headquarters in Newtown Square,

PA. Some of the topics that are addressed are: financial literacy; time management; advocacy with professors; and social adjustments. Eight-five percent of our students are the first in their families to attend college, making the transition from high school to college challenging at best. We find that we need to have a more hands-on approach during the first eighteen months of college to guide and support them during this transition. We have recruited our alumni to become mentors of the new college students. We also will have a closed Facebook page, which will use gamification to encourage student participation. The students will receive reward points for following the recommendations on the Facebook page.

As another dream, I am hoping we can find additional community partners to offer other educational options for students whether they are attending trade schools, community colleges, or traditional four year colleges and promote internship opportunities. Ultimately, we want to find the best fit for each individual Chester County Futures student. Our goal is to assure that the choices a student has available are the most viable and effective for them.

Currently, 45% of our students graduate from college, which is four times the national average for the economically disadvantaged. My goal is to move that rate to 60%, which is the average for the middle class economic group. It's then that we will know that we have truly removed the economic barriers to a self-sustaining and fully empowered life for our talented students.

I can't say enough good things about our Chester County Futures' staff and the commitment of our mentors and community partners. Kennett has a true sense of community and offers our students a wide-range of opportunities and talent to tap into. We all share the challenge and joy of working together on making a difference in the life of our students. Ultimately, I want to see our students returning to Chester County and giving their time and talent to a young person from the community they grew up in.

14

"Children are not things to be molded, but are people to be unfolded."

— Jess Lair, author —

The Garage Community and Youth Center
Patti Olenik, past executive director and board member

11/15/15. I moved to the Kennett Square area in 1998 with my husband and my growing family of three sons. In 2001, I met Mike Bontrager and Mike Miller, founders of the current Garage Community and Youth Center. I whole-heartedly resonated with the mission to support the potential of vulnerable youth, so I became actively involved as a volunteer. In 2003, I was hired as the executive director of The Garage and served in that capacity until 2013. With an educational background in social work and business administration/management, I helped the organization grow as a solid nonprofit with a priority for building relationships.

The history of The Garage Community and Youth Center (i.e. The Garage) starts with Mike Bontrager, CEO of Chatham Financial, and Mike Miller, a youth pastor from Willowdale Chapel, joining together to develop the first Garage Community Youth Center. They located an empty garage (previously used as an automotive repair shop) in the heart of town and were able to secure an arrangement for renting the site. Community members volunteered to renovate the garage and made it an appealing site for the youth to gather. The space was large and open, with an area for a pool table, couches for smaller group sessions, a large stage for entertainment and a closed-off area for quiet schoolwork. The Garage opened its doors in January 2001 with Janet Strike as the executive director. The initial hours of operation were 3:00 to 7:00 pm two nights a week. Because of its popularity, The Garage increased its hours to four nights a week the third year and five nights a week from then on.

We now have two Garage Community and Youth Center locations:

- The Kennett Square center is located at 115 S. Union St., Kennett Square, PA 19348 and is celebrating its 15th year anniversary.
- The West Grove center is located at 122 Rosehill Ave, West Grove, PA 19390 and is celebrating its 4th year anniversary.

The population that attends The Garage in Kennett has changed throughout the years. The first attendees were primarily Latino students, but now have expanded into a diverse group of students. The Garage provides a structure and infrastructure that is lacking in low-income families, possibly because of a lack of education and/or limited experience. In West Grove, the majority of students are Latino, just as it was in the beginning with Kennett.

Our Mission: Our mission is to empower youth to reach their potential.

Our Core Values are:

- Building relationships. Many tutors/mentors remain in a youth's life even after he/she graduates from high school because of the mutual bonds that have developed.
- Focusing on the uniqueness and needs of each child and setting goals. We can change the trajectory of an at-risk student's life with this focus.
- Communication. We help the community "see" the youth in a different light, and we help the youth communicate to the community in a positive manner.
- Volunteerism. We need volunteers for tutoring, mentoring, fund raising, et cetera. We have a high caliber of volunteers, who gain as much or more than they give. We also believe in engaging our youth in community volunteerism. They learn how to "give back" and become a part of the bigger picture.

Funding is always an organizational challenge. We have substantial support from the United Way of Southern Chester County, corporations, foundations and individual funders, but we must always investigate ways to sustain future funding. Aside from our executive director, the directors at the Kennett and West Grove centers, and the academic & workforce program coordinator, our staff is part-time. A common thread among all the staff is the strong belief in the mission. Another challenge that has developed over time is the need to become more corporate. Because of the popularity of The Garage and the successes in empowering youth to reach their potential, we have had to invest in administration to keep track of our finances and data to measure our outcomes.

Opening the West Grove facility was not without obstacles. Members of the community were uneasy about the ramifications of opening a youth center and the disruption that would be created in the neighborhood. We held a town meeting for two purposes, to answer questions by the community and to build relationships with the community. With patience and perseverance we worked through many issues, including zoning and parking restrictions, and focused on allaying the fears of the community. Ultimately, The Garage in West Grove opened its doors to a welcome reception. In fact, one of the concerned neighbors now has youth to help her with her yard work and shovel her steps when there is a snowstorm.

A societal challenge we encounter is the increased availability of heroin and other drugs. Our youth are susceptible, and our greatest protection against drug use is educating our students, building relationships among one another and the community, and nurturing their self-esteem. The issue of drugs is not going away. Cameras installed in The Garage's parking lots and surrounding areas, and an excellent relationship with the Kennett Square police and the West Grove police help to maintain a safe haven from drugs.

We collaborate with guidance counselors, social workers and teachers to support a student's path toward success. In September, students set individual goals, and these goals are reviewed mid-year and year-end. In many instances, our students are dealing with family issues that create higher hurdles, making it even more difficult to attain their goals. Because of The Garage's nonprofit status and strong partnerships with various human service agencies, wrap-around assistance is available to the student's family. Often times a youth cannot succeed until the family issue is addressed.

For The Garage to be sustainable in the future, we must be more creative around funding. Relationship building with our funders is integral to our success, and we must continue to "tell our story" to the community detailing the successes of our students using our newsletters, social media, newspapers and verbal communication. I believe we will always need a community youth center. Beyond technology, we all need personal, caring relationships and interactions.

> **"The potential possibilities of any child
> are the most intriguing and stimulating in all creation"**
>
> — Ray L. Wilbur, 3rd president of Stanford University —

The Garage Community and Youth Center

Kristin Proto, executive director

12/16/2015. I joined The Garage in 2011 and served as the first director of the West Grove Garage for two years. In 2013, when Patti Olenik retired, I was promoted to executive director. I hold a Bachelor's Degree of Arts in Political Science and History from University of Pittsburgh, and a secondary education certification in Social Studies from St. Joseph's University. Through my work with AmeriCorps, Greater Pittsburgh Literacy Council, and Path Stone Corporation, I have over 11 years of experience in the nonprofit sector, working with immigrants, refugees, and at-risk youth, while developing educational and work-readiness programs. I currently live in West Grove with my husband, Anthony and our daughter, Lydia.

Mission: Our mission is to empower students to pursue their potential academically, relationally, and spiritually.

Guiding Principles: The Garage executes its mission through five guiding principles, which govern everything that we do.

- Community Relationships: We connect students to each other and to the wider community, believing our world is healthiest when diverse people know, respect, and serve each other.
- Community Leadership: We empower the skills, insights, and creativity of the students themselves to serve The Garage family and the wider community.
- Core Spirituality: We guide students to establish a set of core convictions from which they can build meaningful lives.
- Academic Potential: We assist students in successfully graduating high school and preparing for higher education or gainful employment.
- Irresistible Fun: We embrace the spirit of youth and channel it into life-giving activities that keep kids coming back for more.

Vision: The Garage will be a source of life and hope, recognized for how we nurture students, how we deploy them for service, and how they contribute to vibrant, welcoming communities. Our students will credit The Garage for helping them find purpose, direction, and joy as full members of the communities in which they live.

Goals: The Garage's goals are organizational, and are in addition to the specific programmatic goals that we strive to achieve. We are currently working under a strategic plan that emphasizes the following four goals:

1. Position The Garage as a widely recognized and valued force for good in our communities.
2. Develop and engage in program planning, implementation, and evaluation processes that will energize youth programs, cultivate youth leaders, and enhance The Garage's position in the community.
3. Increase communication with and engagement of parents.
4. Invest in The Garage's leadership, systems, facilities, and infrastructure to strengthen the organization's sustainability.

The Garage currently employs a staff of twelve, four are full-time and eight are part-time. Our current full-time employees consist of the executive director, the Kennett Square center director, the West Grove center director, and the academic and workforce program coordinator. We also have a part-time development director and a part-time marketing and event coordinator. The Kennett center also employs a part-time volunteer and mentor coordinator, a girls' program coordinator, and a boys' program coordinator. The West Grove center also employs a part-time volunteer & mentor coordinator, an academic coordinator, and a boys' program coordinator. Our 2016 budget is $615,420. In 2015, our revenue was $606,211.

What We Do

Students come to The Garage during the critical after-school hours when many would otherwise be unsupervised. Instead of filling those hours watching TV or hanging out alone, students find a sense of belonging and purpose by coming to The Garage. After grabbing a snack and catching up with staff and volunteers students are encouraged to take advantage of our core program offerings.

Academic: The academic program offers one-on-one support, general homework help, assistance with college and job applications and a fully-equipped Mac computer lab for middle and high school students, all of which improve academic motivation and school performance. Volunteer tutors are matched with students to provide individualized homework help in specific subject areas, including English language assistance. The Garage employs an incentive system to instill motivation and to teach students persistence towards attaining a goal. Strong relationships with area schools permit parents to have their children's report cards sent directly to The Garage to maintain academic progress.

Mentoring: The Garage invests heavily in the lives of individual youth in our mentoring program. Our diverse group of volunteers draws from a variety of age groups and professions, representing companies like DuPont, Chatham Financial, Exelon, and local law enforcement; and all demonstrate the meaning of professional success for our students. Mentors help students with academic goal setting to find internships and jobs, and often, to change negative behavior patterns and to make better choices. Volunteer adult mentors meet weekly with students to provide encouragement, support and resources.

Community Service: Through our service program, students learn relational skills like civility, respect, interdependence, honesty and responsibility. These service projects come in a variety of forms – short and long-term, both volunteer and court-mandated – and yet, each community service endeavor reinforces our efforts to encourage students to reach their potential both as individuals and as members of their community. To promote the value of engagement with the broader community, students and staff participate in a variety of service projects throughout the community like calling bingo at the senior center, repairing homes with Good Neighbors or sorting clothing at The Bridge or the Kennett Clothing Closet.

Enrichment Programs (Boys' and Girls' Programs): Our enrichment programs fuse tutoring, mentoring, and service in order to holistically support our students. Girls' programs designed for girls, by girls, empower middle and high school girls to make positive life decisions by exploring topics including healthy relationships, self-esteem and gender expectations as well as by participating in career workshops, mock interviews and leadership conferences. Boys' programming brings together middle school boys to discuss critical topics, build a positive community through activities, and provide a venue to bring mentors and students into relationships.

Career Compass: The Garage Career Compass is a program for youth between the ages of 14-19, which combines a summer-long (8 weeks) service placement with a challenging life and leadership skills development curriculum. Youth are placed individually or in pairs at Host Sites, where they participate in part-time, meaningful direct-service activities. These activities must be specific and identifiable with measurable outcomes, address a community need, and provide a direct benefit to both the community and to the host sites. Throughout the summer, youth take part in extensive life and leadership skill building seminars, in which local, expert practitioners and staff present workshops. In addition, they participate in team and community building activities and engage in service reflection activities, all designed to provide valuable skills and support their healthy and positive development. Although Career Compass is a short-term program, our goal is to equip youth with transferable life, work-readiness, and leadership skills along with the knowledge to actively support their community. Employers in the greater Kennett Square area make this program possible by volunteering to serve as host sites, providing structured job opportunities and a supervisor to mentor youth during the summer, and/or subsidizing the cost of wages for the Career Compass participants.

As a community center, The Garage strives to collaborate with everyone in the community. Our success is based on the support that we get from the community. Our strongest programmatic partnerships include the Kennett Consolidated School District and the Avon Grove School District, as well as the CCIU Technical College High School and 21st Century Learning Program, Chester County Art Association, the YMCAs of Kennett Square and Jennersville, the Borough of Kennett Square and the Borough of West Grove, Delaware County Community College, the Kennett Library, the Avon Grove Library, and Point Look Out Farm.

The United Way of Southern Chester County, approximately 50 corporations, 30 foundations, 20+ churches and other nonprofits, and over 400 individuals provide financial support annually. We also have hundreds of businesses and individuals from the community who donate in-kind to our programs and our annual auction fundraiser, as well as attend and contribute through our events.

There are a variety of ways that The Garage measures success. Academically, we measure success by tracking and analyzing our students' grades, attendance, and graduation rates. Socially and behaviorally, we ask our students to complete pre and post school year surveys which include questions about how The Garage influences students to avoid risky behavior or promotes positive behaviors in their lives. Program attendance and participation affirm that students are engaged in our services. Parent, volunteer, and community surveys give The Garage an outsider's view of our programs.

One of our biggest challenges is funding. The Garage is entirely privately funded, and we spend a great deal of time writing grants, soliciting individual donors and business sponsorships, and coordinating fundraising events. None of our income is guaranteed, and it can create a challenge when budgeting for what is ultimately unknown.

The Garage students face immense challenges: peer pressure, bullying, difficult home environments, language barriers, domestic violence, learning differences, doubt, mistrust, poverty, addiction, or incarceration of a parent. The nature of working with a youth population, let alone a disadvantaged youth population, can be draining and emotionally difficult. Our students are members of our family, and it can be heartbreaking to see them face struggles of which they have no control. It is our great commission to humbly walk alongside our students in whatever hardships they endure and to love them fiercely, regardless of those factors.

The Garage relies heavily on in-kind donations to keep our operating and programming costs at a minimum. Here are some of our current needs:

- Pens, markers, colored pencils, and paper supplies for school
- Graphing calculators
- Craft materials such as beads, thread, yarn, glue, colored paper, etc.
- Non-perishable snacks and beverages for our café incentive program
- White paper for printers
- Printer ink
- Paper towels and toilet paper
- 13-gallon trash bags and 39-gallon trash bags
- All-purpose cleaner and Windex

Volunteers: I would be remiss if I did not mention the army of volunteers who truly make The Garage function. Words cannot describe the immense gratitude that we have for them. They are an essential piece of The Garage family, and without their selfless gift of time and resources, The Garage would not function. Volunteers support students directly (tutoring, mentoring, etc.) and indirectly (fundraising, cleaning, making repairs, information technology, etc.).

The Story of Tony Gomez: During the summer of 2009, nearly 7 years ago, an 11-year-old boy was riding his bike in Kennett Square with a friend. The sun was blazing hot, and his friend suggested that they go down to "The Garage" to hang out in the A/C. There he met a group of caring adults and a community of students who would quite literally become his family.

Tony was born in southern Mexico. When he was 3 years old, his father was murdered, shot in the heart at close range, and their home was burned down to the ground. Everything they owned was destroyed; he has never even seen a photo of his father. Fearing for their lives, Tony and his mother fled to the U.S., specifically to Kennett Square. His mom remarried and their family grew to six children, however, things did not get easier for Tony. They moved many times, jumping from apartment to apartment, never truly settling in. In 7th grade, his step-father was caught selling drugs and went to jail. With six to support, his mom started selling drugs also. Within a few months, the police searched their house in the early morning with the drug dogs. All six kids were home. She was taken away by the police, and eventually deported back to Mexico. Tony and his siblings moved in with an aunt and his cousins, 9 children with one adult in a 2-bedroom apartment, which was only a temporary solution.

Throughout all of this turmoil, Tony continued to find support at The Garage. He came through our doors nearly every day, seeking stability and consistency when his life was in tremendous upheaval. He was paired with a mentor in the 7th grade, a mentor who has continued to work with him for the last 5 years. He has kept his grades up and will graduate this June, the first in his family to complete high school. He plays football for Kennett High School and runs track in the winter and spring. He is in four clubs: Students against Destructive Decisions; the Humanitarian Club, where he helps organize donations for the Kennett Food Cupboard; Earth Club; and every Monday, he spends his lunch hour reading to Daniel, one of the special needs kids at school, as part of the Special Friends Club. He volunteers to help younger students with their homework at Study Buddies, and he recently became the Junior Council Person on the Kennett Square Borough Council. He has always been fascinated with aeronautics and will join the military upon graduation this June.

Last summer, The Garage had the privilege of sponsoring Tony to attend the National Academy of Future Scientists and Technologists in Boston, MA. This is a conference for of the country's finest high school students who aspire to have careers in science, technology, engineering and mathematics (STEM) fields and have at least a 3.5 GPA. And in the midst of this achievement and celebration, Tony's family was preparing to move again, this time to Delaware. As a rising senior in high school, Tony was reluctant to leave Kennett Square and the life that he had pieced together here. Once again, he was faced with homelessness and abandonment. But once again, The Garage community had the privilege of intervening. Two former Garage staff members and volunteers, Dave and Maggie (along with their infant son, Roman) opened their home. On February 1st of this year, they became Tony's guardians – legally his family.

Unfortunately, Tony's story is not all that unique. Yes, the specific details may change, but there are many "Tonys" in our community who have similar hardships – migration, learning a new language, homelessness and unstable housing, abandonment, death of a parent, incarceration of a parent, lack of resources, and quite honestly – lack of a loving and safe life. They are caught in a cycle of poverty, and, without a place like The Garage, they have no one. But fortunately, The Garage is here. The Garage works with students like Tony every day, every year, for the last 15 years. We support the "Tonys" of our community, not only so that they can survive, but so that they can thrive and become leaders for their peers, their siblings, and their community.

Tony spoke at a Garage fundraiser this past year, and I will end with his words to you now. "I would like to encourage you to continue supporting The Garage. Invest in The Garage because this has had a big impact on my life and the person I am now. If we can help others reach so many kids like me, it would be amazing. Thank you for giving your support to The Garage. I'm not the only one who is working to break a cycle."

"Tell me and I forget. Teach me and I remember. Involve me and I learn."

— Benjamin Franklin; diplomat, author, inventor —

The Garage Community and Youth Center
Comments from "The Garage" Youth, four female Kennett High School students

12/6/2016. *An interview was conducted with four girls, who are regular attendees at The Garage Youth and Community Center (The Garage). Following are the interview questions and responses focusing on the girls' background, their community outreach involvement, their dreams for the future, and their current perceptions of the Kennett community and their ideas for improvement.*

Tell us how long you have lived in Kennett; your family background, and why you come to The Garage.

KHS Freshman 1:

> I moved to Kennett Square from Oxford in the 7th grade. I am a middle child in a family of six children. My older brother is at Williamson College and my younger sister comes here to The Garage. The Garage has become a great support system for me. It keeps me out of trouble, and I am able to get homework help. Since I moved here, I have been a "regular," and I plan to continue coming to The Garage most every night after school.

KHS Freshman 2:

I have lived in Kennett Square all my life. I have a younger brother who is 4 years old. I just started coming to The Garage this September because my friend encouraged me to attend. I really like it here because they treat us like "family." I am sad because I will be moving to Florida next year, and I will miss this kind of community.

KHS Sophomore:

I have lived in Kennett for 5 years. Our family of five moved from Delaware to be closer to our extended family and to live in a bigger house. I have been coming to The Garage since I've been in the 6th grade. I really enjoy it here because people care, and I am able to get help if I need it. The staff at The Garage are available any time you need someone to talk to, and I also can ask to be assigned a mentor, if I wish.

KHS Freshman 3:

I have lived in Kennett for 4 years. I am originally from the Dominican Republic and my dad came first and traveled back and forth before our family moved here. My dad is a gym personal trainer and a professional body builder. I still spend my summers in the Dominican Republic. I like the way The Garage has a close connection with the school system. I heard about The Garage when the director, Mikey, spoke to the middle school about The Garage and all the programs offered. The school also knows that they can recommend The Garage to students that need support, so they work together well.

How does The Garage get youth involved in community volunteerism and engagement and what is the benefit?

KHS Freshman1:

I volunteered with Good Neighbors Youth Camp this past summer for a whole week. (Note: Please refer to the Good Neighbors chapter.) It was an amazing experience. I have never done home repair before, but now I have some skills that I can apply in the future. I learned how to put siding on a house and how to repair a roof. We were helping people and really made a difference; I felt like we were changing people's lives.

KHS Sophomore:

Last summer, I was a paid group leader for "Wipeout" at Willowdale Chapel, which was a two-week program playing and connecting with 5th graders. Part of the program was an overnight 'zip lining' field trip for the camp leaders in which all participants learned teamwork. This experience took me way beyond my normal experiences, and I learned so much. The Garage's Career Compass Program started this year. The goal is to go out in the community and experience different jobs to help us see what our future careers could be. I worked at the Kennett Area Senior Center, and this experience taught me how to communicate with a generation different than myself and will help me when I pursue the field of psychology.

KHS Freshman 3:

I take part in the Garage's outreach programs. I have accumulated seven community volunteer hours by working with The Garage volunteers to paint the Kennett Food Cupboard's new office. I had never painted before, so I learned the "rules of painting" and we actually did a pretty good job. I also liked the great bonding experience by working together on a project with other youth and community members. Another Garage outreach program that we all get involved with is volunteering to read to the children at the Tick Tock Learning Center. The Garage has a 15-person van that is used to transport us and we make that visit to Tick Tock several times a year.

What are your dreams for the future?

KHS Freshman 1:

I first want to graduate from high school and then I would like to go to college to become a registered nurse or a social worker.

KHS Freshman 2:

I would like to attend college on a lacrosse scholarship and major in health sciences. After that, I would like to go to medical school to become an OB/GYN surgeon.

KHS Sophomore:

I would like to pursue the field of psychology and become a counselor.

KHS Freshman 3:

My goal is to be a graphic designer or animator. I am currently in Arts Honor Society and taking basic art classes in school. I have a talent in this field and I would like to develop it.

What do you think of Kennett, and do you have ideas for change?

KHS Freshman 2:

I will be moving to Orlando, FL in June to live with my father full-time instead of just for summers. I feel there is no other place like Kennett. The town is not really busy, but not too quiet. I will miss this town and The Garage friends so much.

KHS Sophomore:

I have lived here all my life, so I don't know any other town, but I do like it. I attended Study Buddies on East Linden Street, along with my two friends. We have helped with the East Linden Street Block Parties in August and this has been great. I just think it would be nice to make this bigger and inviting to the broader community. Now I have the idea of expanding the block to include Kennett Square's State Street. We could keep the shops open and ask permission from Borough Council to close the streets; that would be so fun and nice for the town.

KHS Freshman 3:

I think it is great when youth get involved with the bigger community. Last summer I painted and decorated about 40 backpacks for the East Linden Street Block Party which were handed out to the Study Buddies participants. I would like to expand my art into the town.

17

"We worry about what a child will become tomorrow, yet we forget that he is someone today."

— Stacia Tauscher, dancer and artist —

Kennett Area YMCA

Doug Nakashima, executive director

04/27/2016. I have been with the YMCA my entire life, even working as a day school counselor in my high school years. I started at the Kennett Area YMCA in 2012. My wife, Kate and I live in the borough and have two grown sons, Brett and Jeff.

YMCA Mission: To put Christian principles into practice through programs that build healthy spirit, mind, and body for all.

YMCA Vision: To be a catalyst for improving the quality of life and well-being for all in our community through youth development, healthy living and social responsibility.

The history of the Kennett Area YMCA is a story of community leaders gathering and raising the funds for a six million dollar YMCA in 1998. Mabel Thompson and Marshall Newton III were two key figures who led the vision, and Marshall served as board president when it opened. Michael Walker, Tom Musser, and Aaron Martin led the fundraising efforts and were instrumental in seeing the vision become a reality. Today, we serve 12,000 members. In 2013, we went through a major building project. Our Kennett Area YMCA has a branch advisory board consisting of twenty-four members. The board helps with business and strategic planning. We have 322 employees; 25 are full-time employees. We are fortunate to have over 300 volunteers.

Our greatest strength as a YMCA is that we work closely with the community. This includes collaborations with the local nonprofits and Kennett and Unionville-Chadds Ford School Districts. Kennett Police Chief Zunino and Chief McCarthy credit the YMCA with reducing the number of youth offenders in our community. I have the following examples of how we are helping the kids in the area:

- Saturday Night Lights provides children in grades 4-12 a safe and fun place to be on Saturday nights.
- We collaborate with the Kennett Middle School After-the-Bell program. Students participate in activities in the fall and spring. Volunteers from After-the-Bell and our staff provide the activities.
- We have a strong collaboration with the Kennett High School and Unionville High School swim teams. Both teams use our pool for practice and for their swim meets.
- We collaborate with La Comunidad Hispana (LCH). We have supported their health fair, Viva tu Vida, and this year we will be helping with the LCH 5K Walk/Run.
- We collaborate with The Garage Community and Youth Center by offering indoor and outdoor swimming as well as activities at The Garage and at the YMCA.
- We have seven events this year that we will be participating in as a member of ACTIVATE Kennett Square.
- We support the Kennett Run as their registration and runner packet pick-up central.
- YMCA Water Safety Program – 220 2nd graders from Greenwood and Bancroft Elementary Schools learned about water safety over three days in 2015. We are expanding the program to include New Garden Elementary and a Unionville-Chadds Ford elementary school in 2016. Volunteers assist YMCA staff in providing this important program.

These are just a few examples of our collaborations and activities that the YMCA provides and supports in our community. And, we are always open to a discussion with other nonprofits or youth programs. We offer financial assistance on a sliding scale fee for our programs and membership. For example, we collaborate with Family Promise, the southern Chester County program for homeless families, and provide a free full membership until the family is established in a home and has a stable income. And we take pride in that last year we provided $623,000 in scholarships to the community. Our major fundraiser is our Annual Campaign, which is how we provide financial support for all.

We have hosted Healthy Kids Day, a national YMCA initiative for twenty-five years. We are trying to bring awareness to the obesity issues and the need for activity/exercise. The Centers for Disease Control's prediction now stands that this will be the first generation of children that will not live as long as their parents. We have a wide range of programs, and we are constantly working to bring awareness to families. We also have a fresh fruit and vegetable truck that visits two times a month outside our facility to encourage purchase of healthy foods.

∞

I believe the Kennett Area YMCA is strong and will sustain itself, as long as it continues to receive the support of the community. My greatest concern about the future is how the youth are "feeling," both emotionally and physically. I would say many students are not happy individuals. I have participated in focus groups and have met with recovering heroin addicts. These interactions have helped me gain insights into what many of our youth are experiencing and feeling. Pressures from life, from so many angles, are weighing on our children. We will need to pull together as a community to build a supportive culture that addresses and alleviates these pressures. It is different than our working on helping our youth gain an excellent education; it is the mental and physical health of students that I'm concerned with. The Kennett Area YMCA offers a full-year complimentary membership to all seventh grade students, regardless of income. This is the age that youth are most vulnerable to negative behaviors and peer pressure. The hope is that they will have a place to exercise, renew their spirits and develop some balance in their lives.

The Kennett area community has done a good job of providing programs for the at-risk students. I still like to look at the math and say that we have 10,000 students between Unionville and Kennett Square. We probably are affecting 2,000 of these kids with our programs. We need to assure that all children are provided the resources they need to be happy and fulfilled. I have been interested and invested in the "Search Institute's 40 Developmental Assets for Adolescents." We need to assure that we meet all forty of these assets. To assure that these assets are met, we need the collaboration of schools, churches, nonprofits, government, and businesses; in other words, the entire community.

When you ask how we have adjusted to the growing population of Latinos in the borough, I would say we are always trying to improve our services, programs, and activities. One example of how we are trying to improve our service is hiring a bi-lingual staff member who is available at the member services desk. We have an outreach coordinator who is bi-lingual, and have had this position for fifteen years.

My reflection on Kennett Square is that it is a small friendly town that provides a nice place to raise a family. Our challenge is one of continued growth, which will impose infrastructural demands. Transportation is a huge issue. We are primarily a rural area in southern Chester County, so there are no possibilities of cost effective mass transportation at this time. We are always looking at ways to fulfill our mission and to live out our vision of being a catalyst for improving the quality of life for all. I take a strong personal interest in this and will continue to stay invested in helping make a difference.

"Free the child's potential,
and you will transform him into the world."

— Maria Montessori, Italian physician and educator —

Montessori Education and the Happiness Project

Nancy Pia, community organizer

06/07/2016. I have the fondest memories of growing up in this cozy little town of Kennett Square. It's a community filled with diversity, culture, and the friendliest people; some of those people I started first grade with at St. Patrick's School and still call my closest friends. After attending Bishop Shanahan High School in West Chester, I left for college and chased the adventure of living in a big city. It was very different from what I was used to, but it didn't take me long to became quite comfortable with an urban lifestyle. In 1974, I graduated from Loyola College with a Master's Degree in Elementary Education and accepted a teaching position in one of the most challenging schools in Baltimore. For five years I loved the ambience of the city and had no intention of returning to a small town atmosphere. Nothing could ever lure me back, or so I thought. Everything changed when my sister got married. My brother's best friend, Mike, happen to be at that wedding, and he pulled off what I'd convinced myself was never going to happen; he brought me back to Kennett Square. It only took a few dates to decide we were meant to be together, and the rest is history. Mike and I now have four children, four grandchildren and are soon to have another. And there's no other place we'd rather call home. My children have all followed in my footsteps by moving away for college and job opportunities, but have returned to their hometown roots to raise their own children. I couldn't be happier.

I've seen Kennett Square grow and change so much over the years, but the one thing that never changes is the wonderfully supportive group of people who live here. I always say, if you can think of an initiative that will benefit the town, you will never be at a loss for volunteers to lend a hand and support you. I have proof of that.

The Kennett YMCA is an extraordinary asset to our community. Like so many other local organizations, it offers a variety of programs for children and adults and lots of volunteer opportunities for anyone who wants to get involved. While serving on the board of directors in 2003, I brought the idea of creating a Montessori preschool to the Executive Director, Denise Day. It was a long shot. There are 2600 YMCAs in the country, and it is the largest childcare provider in the world. Denise explained something like this had never been done before and would be quite risky for a variety of reasons. For starters, it was an unknown philosophy at the Y. It would be costly, and it would take an incredible amount of work to get it into place. My children were educated in the Montessori schools, and I was a firm believer in the Montessori method that respects the unique individuality of each child. I was willing to take on the risks, and Denise supported my enthusiasm. Initially, the board of directors did not share my excitement and were skeptical of the change, but they were willing to listen. To make a long story short, with a team of committed Montessori advocates who believed in the axiom, "if you build it they will come," and the financial support from the Michael & Nancy Pia Foundation, the directors gave their approval and voted in favor of this new venture.

∞

We opened the doors for enrollment at 5:00 am on April 6, 2004 to a line of parents who had been standing under umbrellas in a pounding sleet for close to an hour. Our two classrooms were filled on the spot, and we had a waiting list by 11:00 am. The Kennett Montessori School continues to do well as we've doubled in size from the beginning, and I'm so pleased that our young children are receiving this outstanding developmental foundation. It is an effort on the part of so many. We've educated over 600 children from all socio-economic backgrounds, and our students have received $50,000 in tuition assistance from the Y as well as additional contributions from other outside sources. This is just one of the many successful collaborations that exist in our amazing little town.

Through our foundation, my husband Mike and I also helped launch the Michael and Nancy Pia Imaginarium at the Kennett Y. This is a wonderful space specifically reserved for the creative arts. I'm thrilled to have taught art classes in both the Montessori School as well as the Imaginarium in the past few years.

Most recently, I was asked to lead the YMCA's Togetherhood Initiative. It is their signature program for social responsibility. This program invites a volunteer Y member to lead a service project that benefits the community. It is designed for members to identify ways they can give back through their own ideas, skills, energy, and network of the Y. Since "happiness" has exploded as a serious hot topic worldwide, I wanted Kennett Square to be a part of something so powerful. Happiness is unarguably what we all want for ourselves and, above all, for our children. Togetherhood's Community Happiness Project has spread into the local schools and businesses since its inception two years ago; with professional speakers and a book club, as well as classes in nutrition, yoga, and art. International Day of Happiness on March 20th is a global celebration in which Kennett Square now takes part. Our initiative continues to grow because of the dedicated team of volunteers that work together for a cause that brings meaning and purpose to our lives.

Our townspeople know that great happiness is found in reaching out and helping others. There was such a request for more of the same that the *Alive* Program has now sprouted with even more sustainable programs. It was developed to elevate the well-being of our neighborhoods by offering enriching programs and activities. It gives me the opportunity to respond to additional interests and needs in the neighborhood. So far we've built over 10,000 square feet of community gardens that gives 20% back to the Kennett Food Cupboard, conducted collaborative art projects to enhance the workplace, and provided laughing yoga and meditation workshops. In addition, mindfulness training in the elementary schools is being planned for September.

Kennett Square is a family friendly town filled with lots of history, charm, and community-minded people. Along with that, our holiday parades, annual festivals, world famous gardens, walking trails, park, fine restaurants, a symphony, and free concerts are just a few of the reasons why people are always happy to return. I'm sure glad I did!

"Never doubt that a small group of thoughtful, committed citizens can change the world. Indeed, it is the only thing that ever has."

— Margaret Mead, cultural anthropologist —

Camp Dreamcatcher

Patty Hillkirk, founder and director

04/14/2016. *My personal journey started with my undergraduate and graduate education at Penn State University (PSU) in the College of Health and Human Development. After graduate school, I completed three years of training through the Pennsylvania Gestalt Center. A life-altering event occurred in 1986 when my friend, Biff, told me he was HIV infected. I wanted to do something to help with the epidemic locally and became an HIV/AIDS instructor through the Red Cross. I also volunteered as a therapist with what was then called Chester County AIDS Support Services and facilitated weekly groups for adults living with HIV/AIDS. In 1991, I started a private practice and worked mostly with trauma survivors. In 1995, I watched a program on "60 Minutes" about a camp for HIV/AIDS impacted youth, which really touched my heart. I had lost friends to AIDS related complications and had many friends facing the disease. I had a vision of creating a therapeutic camp for children coping with HIV/AIDS. My dear friend and colleague, Charlotte Bartlett, also saw the program and called me to tell me I should think about starting a camp for HIV/AIDS impacted youth in the Philadelphia region. I started to share my dream with a small group of people and also decided to volunteer as a camp counselor at Camp Bright Feathers, a recreational camp for HIV/AIDS impacted youth. I was a counselor in a cabin of seven-year-old girls, and I met a seven-year-old HIV infected child, who was deaf as a result of the disease. We communicated by her reading my lips. My relationship with her, and the conversations I had with other children coping with the devastating reality of HIV/AIDS, inspired me to create a therapeutic camp community that would offer a safe place for children to share their problems and concerns. In January 1996, I met with Burroughs Mack, the executive director at Family Service of Chester County, who agreed to have Camp Dreamcatcher come under the umbrella of their nonprofit 501(c)(3) status. After obtaining our own nonprofit status in 1999, we created a separate organization.*

Camp Dreamcatcher just celebrated its 20th anniversary. As founder and director, I relate to the philosophy of Ubuntu, which speaks particularly about the fact that one can't exist as a human being in isolation. Archbishop Desmond Tutu defines it as: "We think of ourselves far too frequently as just individuals, separated from one another, whereas we are connected and what each one of us does affects the whole world. When one does well, it spreads out; it is for the whole of humanity. I am what I am because of who we all are." Far too many of the children and families served by Camp Dreamcatcher still face the stigma and isolation association with HIV/AIDS.

HIV/AIDS affects all of us. Many think that the Kennett area is free of this disease, but this is not true. We have children infected and affected just like any other community. There are 50,000 new HIV infections every year in the United States, and that number has remained steady for almost two decades. This number does not include the 13% of people that don't know they are infected with HIV. Unfortunately, the number of children in need of our programs continues to increase.

We offer a "disclosure" camp, which means that all who attend our programs must be aware of their own HIV/AIDS infection, have dealt with the HIV/AIDS infection of a family member, or have suffered the loss of a family member due to an AIDS related complication. We offer a safe place for kids to be open about HIV/AIDS and to step out of secrecy and into a space of unconditional acceptance and love. In the beginning, we recruited children from ages five to thirteen years old to attend a one-week camp. I reached out to the HIV case managers in the counties of Chester, Lancaster, Montgomery, Berks and Bucks for applicants. We had our first camp in August 1996 with 53 children and 28 camp counselors. The set-up at the camp was very primitive, but we were creative and, more importantly, we were providing a variety of creative modalities for children to express themselves.

∞

Over the years, we expanded our programs to meet the changing needs of the children. In 1999, we were encouraged by Hershey medical physician, Dr. John Dossett to provide puberty education at the camp. We created two programs for the campers between the ages of 11 and 13, "Celebrate Girls" for the girls and

"Keepin' It Real" for the boys. With this, we soon realized that we needed to extend our camp ages to include 14 and 15 year olds and focused on developing our teen camp program.

Today, the teen program specifically deals with issues that are known to impair self-esteem, which could lead to an increase in HIV transmission. These issues include abuse, addiction, depression, bullying, eating disorders, relationship & community violence, HIV/AIDS stigma & secrecy, and more. The camper program expanded further to include Counselor in Training and Leaders in Training programs for 16 & 17-year-olds and a Junior Counselor program for 17 & 18 year-olds.

We've learned through the evaluations and psychological questionnaires completed by the children that 70% of them have experienced some form of abuse, 50% have lost a family member, and 25% have been diagnosed with a mental health condition. Our programs have expanded to offer a variety of creative therapeutic modalities to encourage the safe expression of feelings. During the one-week camp session, we offer 60 to 70 therapeutic programs (art, music, psychotherapy, movement, mindfulness meditation, acupuncture, massage, and yoga), 40 to 50 educational programs (HIV/AIDS, depression, addiction, bullying, HIV disclosure & medication adherence) and 140 to 150 recreational programs (swimming, basketball, horseback riding, fishing, canoeing, arts/crafts, lacrosse, archery, etc.).

∞

The one-week camp is certainly our core work, yet we have evolved our mission to provide services throughout the year. We now conduct teen leadership workshops, which provide a variety of therapeutic and educational programming. Over 10 years ago, we held our first teen leadership retreat and challenged the teens to share their stories of how HIV/AIDS had impacted their lives. The exercise was so successful that our Teen Speaker's Bureau was formed. Participants in this group accompany Camp Dreamcatcher volunteers and staff in providing HIV/AIDS education and outreach to schools and community groups. In 2013, we created a mentoring program for 16 to 25 year-olds, which at this time has thirteen mentors assigned to thirteen mentees. We have transformed over the years to become an organization that provides consistent support to HIV/AIDS impacted youth throughout their life-spans, which can mean attending college, getting a job, starting a family, coping with the loss of a family member to AIDS, or dealing with their own declining health or impending death due to the disease.

Our therapeutic model and the number of long-term committed volunteers definitely make Camp Dreamcatcher unique, and I believe this will be the key to our sustainability. 70% of the children and volunteers have been attending our programs for 10 to 20 years and keep coming back because of the bonds they have formed over the years. We have a core group of volunteers who return each year determined to provide a fun, safe and therapeutic place for children coping with HIV/AIDS and other issues.

Since 2000, we have held most of our weeklong camps at Camp Saginaw in Oxford. Each summer, 130 to 140 youth attend the camp session, and, over our 20-year history, we have served 5,000 unduplicated kids. It is an amazing how we have grown. Camp registration is on a first come, first serve basis and there is always a waiting list for the camp session. We now serve children from Pennsylvania, Delaware, New Jersey, New York and Maryland. 70% of those served are from Philadelphia and the surrounding counties. All of our programs are free, and 97% of the attendees are low-income. Family foundations, fundraising events, corporations, groups, the United Way of Southern Chester County and individuals all generously support our programs.

∞

Our budget is $330,000, and I am the only full-time employee. Part time employees include two program directors, a health center director, and a therapeutic director. We also are fortunate to have many interns. In 2011, a student who was from the same college at Penn State that I attended was our summer intern. In 2013, she nominated me for the PSU College of Health and Human Development Alumni Recognition Award, which I was honored to win. She accompanied me to the ceremony at PSU. As they say, all roads lead to home. Over the years, we've also had interns from University of Delaware, University of Chicago, West Chester University, University of Maryland, Penn State, Immaculata University and University of Pennsylvania.

A small group of seven committed volunteers serve on our board of directors. In 2015, we completed a strategic planning session that included a review of Camp Dreamcatcher's programs ("Sharing the Dream"); an analysis of our fiscal sustainability ("Strengthening the Dream'); and a sustainability plan ("Sustaining the Dream") that sought to establish a cash reserve fund that would assist the management of cash flow in between grant cycles and build the financial sustainability of the organization. We also conducted surveys and interviews with the stakeholders of the organization, which included parents/guardians, volunteers, children and donors.

The community has been very generous with donations and volunteerism. The Kennett Lions Club and the Longwood Rotary Club provide help before, during and after the camp week. Another generous community donation is the Paul Harris Human Potential Leadership Scholarship for college-bound teens who attend Camp Dreamcatcher. Doug Harris, who owns a business in town, has set up this fund to honor the memory of his uncle, Paul Harris. A male camper and female camper who demonstrate positive leadership abilities and service for the community and for Camp Dreamcatcher are each awarded a $1,000 scholarship.

There is so much to say and if you don't mind, I would like to include part of the message I gave at our 20th year celebration as a summary. Thank you for including us in this book, <u>The Story of Kennett: Shaping Our Future One Child at a Time.</u>

∞

I recently heard about the Salutogenesis theory of well-being and health, which identifies the three factors, and if all are present, contributes to a person's propensity to move towards health and a sense of coherence. This theory made perfect sense to me and describes what we have been able to achieve over the years.

The first is comprehensibility, which means that my life has structure, order and predictability. If you've ever spent time with us during the camp week, you know that our days are very structured and provide a sense of safety and predictability for children who may be living in unpredictable households.

The second is manageability, which means that you have access to resources and tools to cope and manage, including a trusted person who believes in you and truly recognizes who you are and who you can become. The children tell us in their evaluations that they find it easier to talk about things at camp because of the level of trust, the lack of judgment, and the understanding and support they receive from the volunteers. I can speak to this factor personally because Camp Dreamcatcher would have just stayed a dream within my own heart if not for the people who believed in me. One of my favorite quotes is this one from Margaret Mead: *"Never doubt that a small group of thoughtful, committed citizens can change the world. Indeed, it is the only thing that ever has".* Our small group has grown into over 240 counselors, medical personnel, professionals and community members who come together with the common goal of providing a safe, loving and supportive place for children coping with HIV/AIDS. Their dedication to the children we serve warms my heart.

The third is meaningfulness, which means that my situation has meaning and my struggles are an opportunity to develop and learn. If there is no sense of meaning, there is no reason to comprehend or face challenges. As one camper stated in her evaluation last summer, "I had somebody I could talk to and learned that I'm always going to be perfect just the way I am."

Twenty years ago, we united with the common dream of providing a safe and supportive camp session for HIV/AIDS impacted youth. Our program was created to serve young people facing the issue of HIV/AIDS, and we have transformed over the years to become a place where these young people learn and grow and become leaders. We've realized that HIV/AIDS doesn't define who they are, but is one part of who they are.

My hope is that we offer each child, teen, young adult and volunteer a safe space to explore their own dreams, to discover who they are, and to take what they have learned into their own communities. To dream and follow one's unique path in life is a human right and defines the Camp Dreamcatcher spirit.

20

"For the whole law is fulfilled in one word, even in this; Thou shalt love thy neighbour as thyself."
— Galatians 5:14, <u>King James Bible</u> —

Good Neighbors Home Repair
Jay Malthaner, founder

07/14/2016. I was born in Summit, New Jersey and grew up in New Providence, New Jersey. I grew up at a time of great opportunity and lacked for nothing. My father liked to use his head and hands and had an electrical contracting business; he taught me many handyman skills growing up. I graduated from Monmouth College, New Jersey with a degree in Business Administration. In my first job, post-college, I was a case manager with Children and Youth Services in Elizabeth, New Jersey. My uncle, who was involved in social work, introduced me to this type of work. After two years of good work and too much bureaucracy, I left and helped my father with his business. In the mid-70s, I started working in the film department of the DuPont Company in Wilmington, DE, later taking on many functions over a thirty-one year career. In 1990, I was inspired by a presentation that Good Works Home Ministry made at my church, Kennett Presbyterian Church. I knew in my heart that I was being "called" to start a similar effort in southern Chester County, which became Good Neighbors Home Repair. I recruited a few volunteers and, with a start-up generous donation of $5,000 from a community member as well as donated home repair materials, we began repairing many of the homes on East Linden Street, Kennett Square. Our small team slowly moved on to include homes throughout southern Chester County. We worked under the umbrella of the Koinonia House nonprofit status until we formed our own 501(c)(3) nonprofit organization in 2008. I retired in 2011 when Rob Ellis became the executive director *and Bill Stecher became the operations director. The current executive director of Good Neighbors is Harold Naylor. I live in Avondale with my wife, Vicky Malthaner.*

Location: 224 E. Street Rd., Kennett Square, PA 19348

Our Mission: To make homes warmer, safer, drier and healthier for qualified homeowners as an expression of our faith in Jesus Christ.

Our tag line: "Repairing Homes – Restoring Hope"

Our Vision: To eliminate substandard housing in southern Chester County, PA

Our Core Values: Compassion, Integrity, Excellence, Safety and Impact

Our Financial Model: Discounted materials and the work of many volunteers allow us to leverage our home repair dollars. For every dollar we spend, we accomplish about $3 worth of repairs.

We have approximately 250 volunteers who, in 2015, donated over 7,330 work hours allowing us to complete over 151 projects. (Note: Most of these are for different homes, but some homes require more work and can have two or three projects. We regard the number of projects as a better metric than the number of homes.)

Our Staff: Our executive director, office administrator, development director, operations director, application coordinator and six project managers all work on a part-time basis. Starting in 2016, our senior project manager is our first full-time employee. All other work is done by volunteers.

The word is out about our ministry, so we receive referrals from many sources. Our newsletter has been helpful in getting the word out, as well as our brochures, which are printed in English and Spanish. The person that is referred must live in southern Chester County, fit our low-income guidelines, own their home, and owe no back-taxes. About 60-70% of our referrals result in approval for repairs.

Throughout the years, many of our referrals have been widows who are left with an older home and do not have the resources to invest in repairs. It is heart-warming to help them, as they are immensely grateful. We are finding that many of the Latinos in our area do not own a home, but purchase mobile homes that often are in need of repairs. These residents qualify for our services, but repairs are expensive since there are few standard parts for mobile homes. Recently, we have been fortunate to find a contractor who specializes in mobile home repair and donates a portion of the cost. We are now able to cost effectively serve these homeowners. And, there are homeowners who have fallen on hard times and have not been able to maintain their homes. Our long list of referrals helps us move towards our vision of eliminating substandard housing.

We are blessed with volunteers and funders. Our financial model certainly gives the donor a "bang for the buck." We believe we will be sustainable in the future for this reason. While *Good Neighbors* is a faith-based ministry, we place no belief or religious restrictions on our donors, our volunteers, or the homeowners we serve. We know who we are and want to continue to respond to the voice of the Lord saying, "Whom shall I send? And who will go for us?" And I respond, "Here am I. Send me!"

"Coming together is a beginning. Keeping together is progress. Working together is success."

— Henry Ford, American industrialist —

Good Neighbors Youth Work Camp
Bob Johnson, founder

07/14/2016. *I was born in Louisville, Kentucky. My father worked for the DuPont Company so we moved to Wilmington, DE where I graduated from Brandywine High School. I received my Bachelor's Degree in Chemistry from Brown University and my PhD in Chemistry from Northwestern University. I had a forty-year career with the DuPont Company. I currently live in Hamorton Woods, Kennett Square, with my wife, Janet Johnson.*

In the late 1980s, Janet and I coordinated weeklong home repair trips to Appalachia for the youth at the Presbyterian Church of Kennett Square. Projects were set up by another organization, and we stepped into the jobs that were assigned. The work was meaningful, and the youth gained quite a lot from the experience. Then, in 1997, our church youth group ended up going to a camp in Butler, PA. It was here that I met with a local organization that had written a notebook about how to develop one's own local youth work camp. Being familiar with Good Neighbors' ministry, I knew we had a perfect venue for getting our youth involved in our community. I brought the notebook home, showed it to Jay, and we started the first Good Neighbors Youth Camp the next year, 1998. The camp has been held every year with the exception of 2000, when we went to help out with the devastating floods caused by Hurricane Floyd, and 2008, when Good Neighbors was in the midst of being incorporated as a 501(c)(3) nonprofit.

For the past sixteen years, Good Neighbors has had between forty to sixty high school students from the southern Chester County area working together for one week in repairing homes. The youth are housed at Avondale Presbyterian Church, where they convene on Sunday afternoon and stay together until the following Friday evening. Monday through Friday, the group arrives at the work sites by 8:00 am and returns for dinner at 5:30 pm. The Kennett and Jennersville YMCAs provide access to showers at the end of each workday. My wife, Janet Johnson, used to be in charge of the meals for the week for most of the camps but now serves as assistant to Veronica Young, who is in charge of providing meals for the attendees of the Youth Camp at the Avondale Presbyterian Church. Church volunteers provide help with the meals, biblical devotional time, group discussions and overall support. The group even adopts a spiritual theme, which is kept in mind throughout the week and discussed in the evening. In recent years, these evening programs have been led by the Chaplain of Good Neighbors, Rev. Joshua Knott. We have scheduled the third week of July as our annual camp, which usually ends up being one of the hottest weeks of the summer. To take the edge off the discomfort, unannounced community members stop by with bottles of cold water and other goodies. We are now known in the community, and I believe we are an inspiration to many.

What is unique about our camp is that most of the youth have started out with very few home repair skills. This is a great learning opportunity, and the mentors are wonderful in taking the time to teach the steps and then guiding the youth as they take on progressive responsibilities. It is a win-win situation, three-ways around. The homeowner certainly receives the benefit of home repair and good-hearted workers; the youth acquire skills and receive the experience of helping and caring about the needs of others; and Good Neighbors expands their impact by accomplishing their home repair mission.

Many youth have spoken about their work experience as one of the most impactful of their high school years. There are so many boundaries to cross and new frontiers to discover. It is a short week that carries fresh insights and newly developed skills that will last a lifetime. And, one of the greatest testimonials and most rewarding experiences is when one of these youth returns after college to volunteer with Good Neighbors or help out with the Youth Work Camp.

"We humans can choose how we look at the world. I choose potential over problem and essence over existence."

— Terry Anderson and Sandra Maslow, philosophers —

Boy Scouts of America
Clarke Green, Scout Master

A Boy Scout leader's reflections: "Taking the Path of Potential"

In the early 2000s, a group of us looked at our Boy Scout Troop and wondered why it did not look like our community. Kennett Square is a wonderful diverse community; yet somehow that diversity never reached our scouting program.

In seeking answers and direction, we approached people that were familiar with different sectors of our community. We learned about cultural barriers…but they did not look all that formidable. We discussed financial and logistical barriers, and tried to craft solutions. Nothing really seemed to be all that promising. Some people in the Scouting community said that there were types of families that just weren't interested in the program.

After some false starts and dead ends, we came upon the realization that there was only one thing in the way of our goal; our program. We made some pretty big assumptions about how families should approach our program, and these assumptions created barriers. All we had to do was remove the barriers – and not just for a few select families – for everyone. More importantly, we needed to treat our community as a whole, not as a number of sub-groups. Our outreach became very simple; any boy in Kennett Square can be a scout. We also resolved that no boy would ever have to make his decision to be a scout based on finances.

We approached the question of finances by telling each family what the cost was, and asking them to be responsible for whatever they could afford. Some pay nothing, some pay something, and some pay the whole amount. We left the determination of how much a family could pay to the family itself. There was some concern that we would be taken advantage of, but these concerns were unwarranted. Families immediately understood that we trusted them, and responded by being honest. In the end, far more families that we had projected have paid some, if not all, of the cost.

Finally, we made the program family friendly. Traditionally, when a boy becomes a Scout, his family goes to the store and gets him a uniform and a book. The stores in our area with Boy Scout merchandise are few and far between. All we had to do was arrange for the books and uniforms on hand when the boys signed up. Also traditionally, Scout meetings are held during the evening, and we depend on families to get their boys to and from the meetings. To meet the needs of the boys in our community, we changed our meeting to after school, and we worked out transportation solutions for some of the boy's return home. As a result, we have a program that looks like a cross-section of our community, and have a lot more boys participating.

The principles applied to this situation may be helpful to other community efforts that are stalled or ineffective. The most crucial realization was the understanding that the problem was not with the boys we wanted to serve, but with our fixed program approach.

Another big jump in thinking came when we started looking at our community as a whole instead of thinking of it as a collection of groups. Instead of targeting one or two groups, we opened the program to everyone. After all, can't every young boy benefit from being a Scout?

In essence, we moved from attacking a problem to realizing potential. The problem as we saw it, was families being unresponsive. The potential was released when we sought the answer to the question: "How should our program change to serve all the families in our community?" The difference was powerful and liberating.

This experience has taught me that focusing on a problem does not necessarily advance a solution. Working from potential is helping regenerate our Boy Scouting effort in Kennett Square, Pennsylvania.

**"The early years of a child's life are very important for
his or her health and development. We can work together as partners
to help children grow up to reach their full potential."**
— Centers for Disease Control and Prevention —

Chester County Health Department
Public Health Nurses Pat Yoder, Nicole Hoffman & Charlotte Kelly

06/09/2016. **Pat Yoder RN/BSN, MSN**: *I was born in Texas, where my father was stationed for the military. I attended Eastern Mennonite College, Harrisonburg, VA where I received my BSN in 1979, and in 1985 I received my MSN from the University of Virginia. Before starting with the Chester County Health Department, my nursing experience was in the fields of orthopedics, drug and alcohol treatment and public health at the Prince Georges County, Maryland Public Health Department. My husband and I moved to the area in 1986, and I started at the Chester County Health Department in 1987 as a public health home visiting nurse. Currently I am serving as the Maternal and Child Health Supervisor. I live in Narvon, PA with my husband, Nelson. We have three grown children and three grandchildren.*

Nicole Hoffman RN/BSN: *I was born in Media, PA. I graduated from Neumann College in Aston, PA in 1998 with a BSN. I first worked at A.I. Dupont as a nurse's aide and as a new graduate for a year. In 2001, I was hired by the Chester County Health Department as a public health home visiting nurse. I currently make home visits in the Kennett area. I live in Aston, PA with my husband, Shawn and our two daughters and son.*

Charlotte Kelly RN/BSN: *I was born in Hartford Connecticut. In 1988, I received my BSN from Seton Hall University in South Orange, New Jersey. I have an extensive background in labor and delivery having worked at the Wilmington Birth Center for several years. Also, I have had experience in pediatrics. I came to the Chester County Health Department in 2013 and serve as a public health home visiting nurse in the Kennett area. I live in West Chester, PA with my husband, Kevin. We have six children; three daughters and three sons. We have three children still at home and three have graduated from college.*

The Chester County Health Department (CCHD) has consistently maintained a public health emphasis on health promotion since the start of the organization forty-eight years ago. It is one of ten local public health departments in Pennsylvania. In contrast to acute health care services, CCHD services focus on promoting the health of families, groups, and communities. The public health principle of "community as client" is embraced. In conducting a countywide needs assessment in 2013, the findings noted that maternal-child health indices are a key indicator of a community's well-being.

The following is an interview with the three nurses that captures the CCHD maternal-child health nurse home visiting program in the Kennett area.

Pat Yoder: The mission for our Maternal-Child Health (MCH) Nurse Home Visiting Program is to help promote the long-term health and well-being of moms and children through relationships that are developed through home-based visits. We have a range of nurse home visiting services, including a more intensive "Nurse-Family Partnership" program for first-time mothers and shorter term services funded by the federal Title V program for pregnant and postpartum moms who already have a child. All of our home visiting services are voluntary, free of cost to the client, and based on the consistency of having the same nurse for visits in order to build relationships.

We are primarily funded by federal, state and local funds. We also are required to have matching grants as a demonstration of local community support. We continue to receive funds from local foundations including the United Way of Chester County, and the Chester County Departments of Drug and Alcohol Services and Children, Youth and Families.

There are three public health nurses who make home visits to pregnant moms and children in the Kennett and Unionville school districts. Currently, about seventy families are being served in the area. Also, there are three additional public health nurses covering the rest of southern Chester County with the same service.

Our home visiting process starts with a referral. We take a referral from any agency or community member, even a self-referral. We are fortunate to be an independent service and do not require a physician's order or insurance coverage. We have risk criteria that need to be met in order to be eligible for our home visiting services, and we focus on the areas of prenatal, postpartum and child health. Once the referral is received, the nurse makes a phone call informing the client of our program and, with the service being voluntary; the client may accept or refuse. In most cases, the person making the referral has explained the advantages of the program at no charge, and the client accepts when the nurse makes the initial contact. Fortunately, our reputation precedes us, and most of our clients are respectful in keeping the times we schedule for home visiting.

After going through several iterations of models for our home visiting services, we now are pleased to offer a continuum of care. We start with first-time moms, and they receive more intensive services. Other referrals are evaluated for need, and the clients are visited accordingly; again with the intent of building a working relationship. The home visiting schedule is worked out between the nurse and the client, and the key word is flexibility.

Our public health nurses have been trained and equipped to provide an educational curriculum in the home, called "Partners in Parenting Education (PIPE)". This education focuses on social and emotional health and helps build a strong base for parent-child engagement. This home-based education certainly helps promote kindergarten readiness. Bonding is such an important element in the early stages of life, followed by concrete activities whereby the parent and child interact in a personal, loving manner. There has been research on the effects of toxic stress and the importance of early assessment in a child's life. Fortunately, there are protective factors that can be put in place to help mitigate the future effects of chronic stress.

Nicole Hoffman: My caseload consists of twenty-five families made up of first-time moms, some of whom are Spanish-speaking. I have an interpreter who accompanies me on my home visits. I visit clients who have a wide range of issues including limited resources, medical concerns and social barriers. The Nurse-Family Partnership (NFP) program starts in the prenatal period, and I provide the client with knowledge about what to expect during pregnancy, prevention of preterm labor, tests that are required, monitoring of blood pressure and proper weight gain, breastfeeding, and labor and delivery. I think that one of the strengths of our program is that we offer affirmations and positive energy to this new experience of parenting, which is something that all new parents can benefit from receiving. Once the child is born, I am in the home at least bi-weekly; coaching, helping the mother adjust to breastfeeding, and answering questions about her newborn baby. This is followed by teaching her about the care of a growing infant and the child's developmental milestones. This time is so important for building the foundation of health and well-being for both the child and the parent-child relationship. Research has shown that this time period in a relationship with a home visiting nurse has a lasting effect on healthy future outcomes for both the child and family. Our goal is to remain with the client until the child turns 2; however, we sometimes are unable to continue due to work or school schedules, or the client may move out of the service area.

Given that we visit with the client frequently during the prenatal phase, we are able to help monitor the client's health during pregnancy. For instance, we may see clients who have gestational diabetes; for them we discuss their nutrition, check their food diary, and monitor insulin injections. As previously mentioned, we take blood pressures during the prenatal period. There are visits when the client's blood pressure is elevated. I am able to connect with the prenatal provider and inform them of the client's blood pressure reading and other symptoms that may be of concern. There are instances when the client is brought in to the hospital due to preeclampsia and ends up delivering the baby. Clients may also be unaware of preterm labor symptoms. The frequency of our program's visits can help in prevention of preterm labor, facilitate healthy pregnancy outcomes and provide support for clients who may have difficulty communicating concerns or questions to the physician.

Charlotte Kelly: My caseload of thirty to thirty-five families consists of first-time moms and other pregnant and postpartum women. Ninety percent of my cases are Spanish speaking, so an interpreter accompanies me on these visits. My goal is to provide whatever education and support is needed during the pregnancy and postpartum period. I follow an assessment and educational protocol, but have the flexibility to adjust my visits to address the needs at hand. In addition to physical health concerns, I find that often clients are dealing with complex social and environmental situations. With our program's more extensive assessment tools and the trusted relationships I build, it may be that the clients are more willing to speak about their issues. These issues can include domestic violence, postpartum depression, over-crowded living conditions and a lack of resources.

I am receiving some referrals for women who have recently relocated from countries outside the United States culture. Beyond their pregnancy, they have little idea about how to navigate the health care system in addition to the social system. The cultural beliefs and practices around some of these social issues vary in different countries, so I find some women don't reach out for help. I am grateful for the many agency partners I have in the Kennett area community. I make referrals and frequently have joint conferences to work out a coordinated plan when working with a difficult situation.

As a visiting public health nurse, I have been able to make a difference in helping clients access services. This help includes referring them to a counselor, helping them to call the pediatrician, or even telling them that their baby needs to go to the emergency room. For example, there were several occasions when I came to a regularly scheduled home visit and came upon an infant in distress. Each time the mom had been afraid to call the doctor again, as she had already been to the doctor the day or week before. These moms don't understand that an illness can change and worsen, sometimes even in an hour's time. They knew in their hearts something was wrong, but didn't know how to advocate for their child or ask for help. In two of these different situations, the babies ended up being admitted into the ICU after I called 911 with the family.

Pat, Nicole and Charlotte: Our work presents us with many challenges. We are providing services to the most vulnerable population during a time when there are many risks, not only to the mother, but also to the unborn and newborn child. We are serving a variety of cultures, each having their own belief system. We must learn about the cultures in order to be effective, and we don't speak the native language of many of our clients. We also are visiting clients who are living busy lives. Many of them work in the mushroom industry, and their work hours are never certain. We could set up an appointment at the end of our work day, and the client's work hours have been extended. We do our best to schedule our visits on the client's day off, but we are managing large caseloads, which makes it a juggling challenge.

In looking at trends, mental health needs are becoming more visible. Just today, our department, in partnership with the Chester County Hospital Prenatal Clinic, conducted a Maternal-Child Health symposium for prenatal and postpartum care providers. We heard repeatedly about the need for support for depressed moms. One of our roles as a health department is to build collaborations; coming together as a system to address mental health will be paramount in the future.

All of us are passionate about our work. We are in the business of changing lives; however, we, too, are personally growing every day because of our clients' lives. We can't be in this role without becoming compassionate and inspired by how our clients rise above so many obstacles every day. In other words, we become equal partners, growing together and working towards building a better life and community.

24

"A person's a person, no matter how small."
— Dr. Seuss, *Horton Hears a Who!* —

YoungMoms
Linda Mercner, executive director

12/29/2015. I stepped into the director role at YoungMoms 2 years ago, excited to help teen moms achieve goals and to use my skills and experience to bring structure to the organization. I received my Bachelor's Degree in Accounting from the University of Delaware and worked as a CPA with KPMG in Philadelphia before leaving to raise my family. Over the years, I served in numerous volunteer roles, most recently in a local chapter of Community Bible Study where I trained and supported many small group leaders.

As YoungMoms grew, we established policies and procedures, and implemented more efficient methods of tracking participant, donor and volunteer activity. All the while, we continued to provide individualized and comprehensive support to teen moms in our community. Many of the young moms we work with face significant socioeconomic and relational challenges. I am amazed daily at the resilience, commitment, and hard work of the women who participate in our program, and consider it a privilege to help them overcome obstacles and reach goals.

YoungMoms started as a program of The Garage Community and Youth Center in 2010. At the time, there were two pregnant students who needed services beyond those offered by The Garage. A master social worker intern, Lisa McMain, together with Molly Henry, an employee of The Garage, began providing support, connection and encouragement to these teen moms – and from there, YoungMoms was born! What makes YoungMoms uniquely effective is our holistic approach and the long-term investment we make in the lives of the moms we serve. Most participants remain in the program for 2-4 years during which time we help them see their potential, achieve goals, and create a more stable future for themselves and their families. We have operated under the fiscal sponsorship of The Garage, and are excited to launch as our own 501(c)(3) nonprofit organization on January 1, 2016!

The mission of the organization is to empower teen moms to reach their potential as women and mothers. We do that through a combination of case management services, goal setting, connecting to resources, one-to-one mentoring, life-skills training and community building activities. We work with each young mom to develop academic, employment, relational, and parenting goals and to create a plan to achieve them. Our objective is for these young women to see their potential, achieve their goals, create a more stable future for themselves and their families, and become productive members of the community. The program is provided free-of-charge, and is open to young women between the ages of 15 and 21. Last year, we served 39 young moms from southern Chester County. Currently we have 35 participants enrolled.

With only two paid employees, myself and a part-time social worker, we are heavily dependent on volunteers to accomplish our mission. We currently have about 80 volunteers who serve in a multitude of ways, including providing transportation, meals, and childcare for our monthly large group gatherings. Others provide administrative, special event, and fundraising support. Thirteen are serving right now as one-to-one mentors. Our current budget is $140,000.

Our board is composed of members who have the following community skills/roles: public health nurse, director of nursing at Lincoln University, human resources manager at Genesis; executive director of The Garage Community and Youth Center; communications professional, and a registered nurse who was a past YoungMoms participant!

Our program has three main facets:
1. Case management, which involves an assessment and setting of academic, employment, relational and parenting goals. The participant is encouraged and connected to resources in the community.
2. Mentoring, whereby a participant is paired with a trained, adult mentor who walks alongside providing support and encouragement.
3. Community building and life skills instruction, which is provided at a monthly club session and through special programs and activities.

We also just kicked off a YoungDads program in November, which includes bi-monthly large group gatherings and one-to-one mentoring. This new initiative aims to strengthen the entire family unit by empowering the partners/spouses of YoungMoms participants to reach their potential as men and fathers.

Collaboration with other organizations in the community is essential for us to provide the support our young moms need. We have strong working relationships with: La Comunidad Hispana, Chester County Health Department Public Health Nurses, KACS, The HOOD, The Peacemakers Center, Safe Families, Family Promise, MCHC/Healthy Start, Holcomb Behavioral Health, Wings for Success, Delaware County Community College, Community Volunteers in Medicine, Legal AID, Home of the Sparrow, and others.

Yes, we have challenges too. We are always revisiting the make-up and expansion of staffing. We have recently seen an increase in Spanish-only speaking young moms and recognize the need to hire additional bi-lingual staff members. Funding is another challenge. Currently we receive support from private foundations, the United Way of Southern Chester County, individuals, churches and corporations. Programmatically, we are challenged in knowing when to graduate our participants. We recently developed a peer advisory group for young moms who have achieved most of their goals and are ready to provide feedback & ideas on programming and serve as peer mentors.

If I had $100,000 dollars, I would expand staffing to reach out in a broader way to the Oxford and Coatesville communities. I would love to explore having a residential facility for young moms facing homelessness. This would provide safety and stability to the young mom and her child(ren) while she completes school and training programs, and saves money to afford a place of her own.

∞

We measure outcomes by taking a quarterly snapshot of participant employment and education. We also regularly evaluate progress toward participant short and long-term goals. But the personal stories of transformed lives are what really communicate the impact of our work. One young mom, who faced multiple personal and relational challenges, recently returned to high school and is on track to graduate this spring. She is committed to raising her 2 small children, finding a job after high school, and enrolling in additional training or degree programs. YoungMoms played a critical role in building this young mom's confidence and self-esteem, removing barriers for her return to school, and providing the support necessary to allow her to finish her education.

YoungMoms is a community where teen moms find the support they need to face the challenges of navigating adolescence and parenting simultaneously. We are proud to work alongside our young moms as they achieve goals and create a brighter future for themselves and their families.

"The essence of our effort to see that every child has a chance must be to assure each an equal opportunity, not to become equal, but to become different—to realize whatever unique potential of body, mind and spirit he or she possesses."

— John Fischer, distinguished professor of Philosophy (University of California) —

Kennett Square Family Center

Maritza Rivera Cochran, supervisor

05/24/2016. *I was born and raised in Puerto Rico. My parents have seven children, and I am the fifth child. Our family was poor. My mother was a wonderful athlete, so I think I inherited her talent. I was involved in multiple sports in high school, but I was best at track & field. I received an athletic scholarship to attend American University in Bayamon, PR, and I also attended the University Central of Bayamon in Puerto Rico and majored in business administration. I moved to New York City in 1993 with my parents and my boyfriend. I was pregnant when I arrived and shortly thereafter I had my daughter, Tiffany. To survive, I enrolled in public benefits while I attended Bronx Community College. It was a difficult time but, after three years, I earned an Associate's Degree in Applied Science in Marketing Management while improving my English and raising my daughter along the way. My father then wanted to relocate to Pennsylvania to be closer to some of his extended family that lived in the Kennett area. He started a mechanics business in Toughkenamon, PA called "Rivera's Auto Repair," and he has been in business for 18 years. My first job experience was working at Mendenhall Inn setting up conferences and banquets. One day, I went to La Comunidad Hispana looking for a new job opportunity, and Margarita Quiñones encouraged me to apply for a position as a family health advocate serving Kennett Square in the Healthy Start program at the Maternal and Child Health Consortium (MCHC). In 2002, I started at Healthy Start making home visits and focusing on Spanish-speaking women needing prenatal, postpartum and child health support. Four years later, in 2006, I was promoted to the parent educator at MCHC's newly launched Kennett Square Family Center. I enjoyed the position very much, and I also received excellent training. Then almost ten years later, in the fall of 2015, I was promoted to be the program director of MCHC's Kennett Square Family Center. Currently, I live in West Grove with my partner, Bradley Spangler and my two wonderful daughters, Tiffany and Kimberly.*

The Kennett Square Family Center is an initiative of the Maternal and Child Health Consortium designed to address the unmet needs of Spanish-speaking families in southern Chester County. The center is located at 637 Millers Hill Road, Kennett Square, PA 19348. We serve families in southern Chester County by helping parents fulfill their roles as their children's first teachers and, by doing this, closing the kindergarten readiness gap. Our bilingual, bicultural parent educators use the nationally recognized, evidence-based Parents as Teachers (PAT) Born to Learn Curriculum™ during bi-weekly home visits. The parent educators equip the parents with activities and demonstrate proven methods in which they can engage and help their children develop, learn and grow. The parent educators also provide information, support, resources, and encouragement to the families to ensure the children have a proper foundation for a lifetime of learning.

∞

We are a staff of seven. I supervise five parent educators and a program assistant. The parent educators are assigned to one of three different programs we operate out of the Kennett location. The Parents As Teachers (PAT) curriculum is wonderful. We use PAT during our bi-weekly home visits exposing the parents and children to math, art, literacy and a host of experiences to support the children's age-appropriate growth and development. To qualify to use the PAT curriculum, the parent educators must complete and pass two training courses: a five-day session focused on prenatal to two years old, and then a three-day session to study three years olds to five year olds entering kindergarten.

The PAT curriculum limits the parent educator's caseload to a maximum of twenty-four families. Intense, home visiting programs provide a powerful resource for the vulnerable, low-income Latino families we serve. Though there are no restrictions on participation, all of our families qualify for public benefits. We work closely with many southern Chester County nonprofits and accept referrals from all of them. We are even qualified to work with families with a child in the prenatal stage. Though the child is the target of our support, we serve the whole family and provide social service referrals as needed. In some instances, we have worked with different children back-to-back in the same families to prepare them for early learning success. Currently, we have a waiting list of about twenty-five families.

We make referrals to so many agencies. There are more needs than any single organization can satisfy. For instance, we refer our clients to the public health nurses when there is a medical or behavioral health issue; to La Comunidad Hispana for any health and social services issue; to Community Volunteers in Medicine (CVIM) for dental care; and to Misión Santa Mariá for clothing and counseling. Whatever support is available in the community, we make it our business to learn about these resources and then to make the referrals for our clients.

Our parent educators screen all children for developmental delays and then link them to early intervention services, if necessary. I remember once when I was visiting a family as a parent educator, I quickly picked up on a developmental delay with one child. The parent was not aware that the child's behavior should have even been a concern, until I addressed it. As it turned out, the child was diagnosed with autism, and he was able to enroll in a special school that allowed him to thrive.

In addition to the direct one-on-one support our parents receive, we host monthly group connections that provide the parents with additional health, social and community education. These events have covered many topics including nutrition, healthy relationships, medical care and immigration. For many years, The Kennett Square Family Center has been a host site for the annual flu clinic offered by the Chester County Health Department.

We end every year with the Kindergarten Transition Summer Program (KTSP). All of the children who will turn five years old before the start of the next school year are automatically enrolled in our half-day "kindergarten boot camp." Volunteers are essential to the success of the KTSP; many of these volunteers are West Chester University students. In addition, to help the children prepare for the experience of leaving home for the first time to attend school, we use a yellow school bus to pick up and drop off the children.

∞

My current challenge is growing into the role of program director. This has been and continues to be a wonderful challenge as I learn more about supervision. My role as director requires me to deliver presentations to outside organizations. I would like to feel more at ease with public speaking; however, I understand I'm not the only one uncomfortable. After eight months in this new role, I believe that my strong sense of responsibility and work ethic has helped me grow, and I appreciate my business degree every day when I am faced with financial management responsibilities including budgeting and fundraising.

For every nonprofit, the constant challenge is finding funding. We know that the funding is available, and that the work we do has impact. For example, I recently spoke at two local Rotary Clubs on behalf of the Kennett Square Family Center seeking support for bus transportation for the Kindergarten Transition Program. I am so happy about this. We will have full participation of all the five year olds who will be entering school in the fall of 2016.

Our screening tools help us measure our students' readiness for kindergarten. We conduct screenings six months before a child enters our summer transition program. Guided by the screening results, our parent educators work in the home with the parent and child on all areas that need improvement. We re-screen the children both in May and at the conclusion of the summer transition program. The results of the final screening confirm that eighty percent of our students score at the high end of the grading range, and the remaining twenty percent receive satisfactory readiness scores. In other words, all our students are ready to enter into kindergarten with the exception of the children who are diagnosed with special needs.

All parents who have children enrolled in the Kennett Square Family Center program are requested to complete a survey. Our performance has consistently received high scores. But what we notice is the parents' increased confidence as they become more and more active in their children's education.

If I were given a windfall of funds, I would spend it on many program additions. First, I would double or triple the size of our program because the need is so great. I would hire mental health therapists to work alongside the parent educators and the families to help alleviate the stress associated with living and working in a foreign country. I also realize the importance of women-led support groups where women are able to discuss their situation in a comfortable and safe setting and realize that they are not alone. I would employ a trained counselor specifically to lead support groups dedicated to women, which have been shown to empower the participants and build their self-esteem. Of course, I would like to have a wonderful public transportation system. Many parents have no transportation to get to the services that they need. And finally, I would offer more flexible hours for the ESL classes. So many of the parents we work with say that "learning English" is a top goal, but their long working hours and fixed schedule for ESL classes do not coincide.

I love working with our families. They have such an appreciation for our assistance, an eagerness to learn, and a humility that makes our time together very satisfying. In the Latino culture, family comes first, so our method of working with the families as a unit is the right approach. Our goal for our students to be kindergarten-ready is being reached, allowing them to begin their school years with confidence.

"There are two gifts we should give our children: One is roots. The other is wings."

— Author Unknown —

La Comunidad Hispana
Alisa Jones, president and CEO

05/17/2016. I was born in San Diego, California and raised by my mother and step-father. We were a family of twelve. My mother never graduated from high school but, later in life at the age of 45, went back for her GED and attended community college. She worked as a migrant farm worker in the Southwest and Midwest. My step-father is from Mexico and came to the US with nothing. He started a family-run sewing business, and he and my mom owned that business for over 25 years. We kids were the best workforce ever! My parents instilled a work ethic into my siblings and me by example. We saw them working 14 hours a day 7 days a week. Upon graduating from high school, I began working outside of the family business in the medical field. As the first in my family to go to college, it was important that I balanced work and school. I worked full-time during the day, and in the evenings I attended community college. Over the course of 8 years, I received my Bachelor's Degree in Social Science from California State University and a Master's in Public Health from San Diego State University. My career in health care and human services in California included serving as a medical assistant, a health educator and several years as a consultant to community health centers in the areas of program implementation, quality improvement and evaluation. I worked for the University of California, San Diego, in the Division of Community Pediatrics for almost 10 years in the areas of immunizations, HIV/AIDS and US/Mexico border health. In 2005, I moved to Delaware and worked for the state health department as Chronic Disease Bureau Chief and later as Family Health and Systems Management Section Chief. In this capacity I served as Delaware's Maternal and Child Health director and implemented programs to reduce infant mortality and teen pregnancy. In 2013, I relocated to Pennsylvania and came to La Comunidad Hispana in the role of chief operating officer. In 2015, I was appointed chief executive officer. It has been a true privilege to work with amazing leaders and fabulous staff over the course of my career. At LCH, the team brings the mission to life every day, and it's a privilege to be part of such a vibrant organization. I live with my husband Errol, and my fifteen-year-old son, Luke in Landenberg, PA.

La Comunidad Hispana (LCH) has a rich forty-three-year history. LCH is an agency that was born out of a social justice movement and serves as a great example of a caring community coming together to meet the pressing need. LCH was critically important to the southern Chester County Latinos in the early 1970s, and it continues to be a primary source of support today. Recently, our agency developed the tag line for LCH— Life Changes Here—and we take this to heart. We are inspired by the level of change that can happen in a short period of time. Residents who walk through our doors can be assured that they will receive the support that they need. It may be one or two things that we can help with to meet a critical need, or it may be support for an ongoing period of time until a sustainable change is made. At LCH, we help to improve lives, thus benefitting the broader community as well.

∞

LCH started as a social service agency at 223 E. Birch Street, Kennett Square. About ten years later, a health clinic, Project Salud was added, in addition to other services such as education classes and job placement. In the early 2000s, the agency moved to three different locations due to being displaced by a flood. The next level of expansion occurred, when two generous major donors, Mrs. Betty Moran and Mrs. Alice Moorhead, spearheaded a capital campaign to build a new state-of-the art, LEED (Leadership in Energy and Environmental Design) certified center. This new location is located just outside of the Kennett borough at 731 W. Cypress Street, Kennett Square. The capital campaign was very successful. In the campaign appeal, it was easy to point out the harmoniousness of the open space movement and the horse farm owners, with the competent and willing Latino labor work force; all helping to maintain a healthy economy. We received major donor contributions and matching contributions, which led to our paying off our mortgage soon after our move to our existing location in 2009.

The mission for LCH is to help low-income residents of southern Chester County to stay healthy, build strong families and live productive lives by providing high-quality, culturally welcoming services. This mission drives everything we do at LCH. For example, at every monthly staff meeting we make time for "mission moments". These are stories from the past month that illustrate how our mission comes to life to positively impact a person or family. It's amazing to hear staff describe how LCH saved a life, improved a life or comforted a person in need. Our values of being an organization that is welcoming, integrated, dedicated and dynamic guide us, as we interact internally and externally. They help us focus on customer service and improve the member experience.

∞

Since I have moved into my current role, I have stewarded the transition of LCH from program silos to a fully integrated organization with a service model called Person-Centered Care. Our service model is a holistic continuum of care. The LCH team spent over 18 months and hundreds of hours re-designing work flow and processes and investing in internal staff development and change management. The leadership team and I have spent many hours at the front desk, interacting with LCH members, as well, to learn about their experience of services and soliciting suggestions. At the same time, we could see that our previous building structure did not convey the "welcome" and "integration" to which we were aspiring. So, we have literally torn down walls and opened up space to bring the experience of entering a site that has a menu of services, all available when needed. We offer health, social services, legal counseling, work force development, pre-GED education; civics and ESL classes. We connect all these services in the background via a new data system we call LCH Centricity. This has helped us share information across services and ensure the member has an integrated experience. We are grateful to our donors for supporting this campaign for the facility and data system. The name of the campaign is Fortyforward, and our donor's support has truly helped LCH launch forward!

We have a board of directors that guides LCH with a laser focus on our mission. It's a joy and privilege to have them guiding me and our organization. More than half of our board is composed of LCH members, or people who use our services. All members of our board function in a coordinated manner to help LCH. Each board member is a valuable contributor to the ongoing guidance of the agency. The board has a strong onboarding and orientation process so that each member knows their role and responsibilities. During our meetings we discuss important topics in English and Spanish to ensure all members understand and have the opportunity to fully engage. Although the federal funding we received required us to have a majority of users on our board, it has been such a blessing.

LCH's vision is that, with access to high quality and culturally welcoming services to those in need, all residents of southern Chester County will be able to more fully benefit from and contribute to the social vibrancy and economic prosperity of the region. My goals are to continue to strengthen our ability to meet the changing needs of the community. We have done that by opening a new site in Oxford to better serve that area of our county that experiences geographic and access barriers to care. Our LCH Oxford Community Health Center is located at 303 North Third Street, Oxford, PA 19363. We are grateful to our friends and partners in Oxford who have been very welcoming to LCH as a new service provider in the region. We aim to be fully integrated into the community and work hand in hand with other nonprofit service agencies to coordinate and not duplicate.

The next venture on the horizon is a dental clinic. Based on community survey data, there are 18,000 residents in our county who need dental care and have not received it in the past year. LCH did a survey of 100 LCH members and we learned that it was not a lack of caring or concern about dental health; it was about affordability and access.

Our fiscal year 2016 budget is $3.7 million. About $1.4 million is from federal funding as LCH is a federally qualified health center. Over 35% of our overall budget is received from individual donors. We are so grateful for their generous support! Foundations and other grants along with a small amount of revenue from patient fees and health insurance reimbursement help us cover our costs of providing services. We are pleased to receive support from United Way of Southern Chester County and the southern Chester County Health and Welfare Foundation. In 2015, we saw over 4,000 unduplicated LCH members through 20,000 visits.

∞

Our challenges are the ever-changing needs of our community. We also know that the residents requiring services will grow. We want to continue to broaden our brand to serve all low-income groups. There are many community residents who could use our services but do not know we are here or think we only serve Latinos. We want to reach deeper into the community so that those in need know we are here for them. As with most nonprofits, continued funding and philanthropic support is a challenge. We are always looking for new friends of LCH and to share the impact of our mission.

I believe in collaborations and partnerships. We live in a wonderful community with so many great services. My hope is that we continue to find new and innovative ways to coordinate and collaborate to minimize duplication and maximize positive impact for the vulnerable in our community.

LCH provides services for the entire family, so we serve the "kids" at LCH that you are talking about in this book. I am inspired by the youth in our community. So many have crossed boundaries and are moving into a realm of life they couldn't even imagine in their country of origin. As a child of an immigrant family without many financial resources, I know there are unique challenges, but, more importantly, unique strengths that can help our community's youth become successful. The strengths are that many immigrant families have such strong hopes and dreams for their kids to do better and have more security than the parents might have had as children. They are willing to sacrifice and go without often times, so that the children can have all they need to be successful. The challenges are that youth who are the first in their families to have college as an option often don't have a "road map" or role models to help guide them and the family. Decisions about higher education are family decisions because they have significant financial impact and can be seen as weakening the social ties. Youth need to see examples of success with finding a path for them and one that is supported by their family.

For those not attending college, we need to help support and inform them of great options for employment in Chester County that do not involve college. There are many paths to success in our wonderful community; we simply need to help youth and their families identify the right path for them.

"One of the greatest feelings in the world is knowing that we as individuals can make a difference. Ending hunger in America is a goal that is literally within our grasp."

— Jeff Bridges, actor and activist —

Kennett Area Community Services
Melanie Weiler, executive director

05/02/2016. I started as executive director of Kennett Area Community Services in 2013. I had a previous work history with the YMCA, where I was part of a small start-up, which now is the Rocky Run YMCA, part of the Philadelphia Freedom Valley YMCAs. This gave me my first experience of reaching out into the community to develop a program that met the needs of the broader community. I came to the Kennett Area YMCA in 2003 as member services director and worked with the financial assistance program. I loved working at the YMCA, but felt ready to move into a more direct line of human services, where I could develop resources to meet some of the community's needs. Before I started at KACS, I had the experience of meeting a homeless man in Walmart, and for the first time I saw for myself that there was homelessness in southern Chester County. I live in West Grove with my husband, son and daughter.

Our Mission: Serving people in their time of need

Our Vision: We are an organization committed to serving families and individuals in the fight against hunger and homelessness in the Kennett area and surrounding communities. We are responsible stewards of the community, helping members of the greater Kennett community to lift themselves out of the cycle of poverty in a dignified manner.

Our History: Our history goes back to 1954. Kennett Area Community Services (KACS) began by distributing Christmas baskets of food to a few families in need in our area. This grassroots effort was begun by Norm Connell and Bill Buffington with community support. KACS was incorporated as a nonprofit organization in 1993, followed by the Kennett Food Cupboard opening in 1996. In addition to food, KACS has aided residents in crisis with emergency financial assistance for rental and utility payments, heating oil, medical and transportation assistance, as well as other emergency needs. KACS has two programs, Emergency Assistance and Kennett Food Cupboard, and sometimes they overlap. Over the last eight years, our Emergency Assistance program went from serving a handful of households to serving 300 families this year; families receiving funds and counseling for homeless prevention, rapid rehousing and other emergency programs. The Food Cupboard program serves 410 families each month. KACS has become a significant access point for families in need in southern Chester County.

The staff consists of an executive director; two emergency assistance case managers; one nutrition services manager and one administrative assistant. All the rest of the work is covered by sixty-five plus volunteers. Our annual budget is 1.3 million and our administrative costs, including fundraising costs, are 8%.

Kennett Square is a community that believes in and is committed to taking care of its own. It is heart-warming to work with all the individuals, groups, clubs, farmers and agencies, who enthusiastically bring their food donations to our center. Last year, we received over $800,000 worth of donated food.

∞

When I first came to KACS, there were no nutritional guidelines for food donations and distribution. This has been a real cause for me. All of us deserve food that promotes good health. And, we were on the same page as the Chester County Food Bank, who decided to move in that same direction. We started making up lists for donors of requested items, which included foods low in both sugar and sodium. As we progressed, we started receiving many more fruits and vegetables from farmers and others. We also reduced the number of dessert items that a client could receive. During the past two years, clients were able to participate in planting and harvesting from community raised-bed gardens. Our latest development is that of contracting with a nutritionist, who has developed an eight-month nutrition education program for our clients, who visit us once a month. The educational approach will include food models for portion sizes, recipes in English and

Spanish, videos, and we will even raffle off cooking utensils and cookware to reinforce the lessons. We understand that obesity is a major national issue; our hope is to be one of the change agents.

Since I have been in my position, our board went through its first strategic planning process. This was very helpful in moving us into our next phase of evolution. We could see that beyond providing emergency food and financial assistance, we also needed to address the underlying issue of poverty. The number of families we served since 2009 went from 135 to 520 families. We were not able to sustain this process. We knew that we were serving a population, who for the most part wants to be self-sufficient, but due to family and community circumstances needed a broader support.

∞

Our first change was to blend the existing Emergency Assistance and Food Cupboard programs. When an individual begins the relationship with KACS, it is typically through the Food Cupboard program. With the blending of intake, assessment and relationship building, the staff has an opportunity to catch household crises in the early stages to prevent both homelessness and to bring an end to a cycle of food insecurity.

We now are on a path of providing professional and community education about poverty. Several board members and I attended a national conference focused on the constructs of Bridges Out of Poverty. This comprehensive approach to poverty reduction was a real eye-opener for us, and we hope to bring that same awareness to our Kennett area community. It is so easy to stereo-type and to blindly accept myths about the poor. Many times we think if we could just help those in poverty with a budget, this would solve their problems.

Financial management is only one of the ten resources needed by those who wish to leave poverty. We learned that the definition of poverty will be the "extent to which an individual does without resources." The resources are: financial, emotional, mental, spiritual, physical, support systems, relationship/role models, knowledge of hidden rules, and coping strategies. I will be starting the community training at the end of May, and the hope is that we will start impacting the mind-set that also holds a low-income economic group in its place. The idea of "pull yourself up by your boot straps" does not work when someone is coming from generations of poverty; new managing tools and support are needed.

At KACS, we will pilot a program for participants called "Getting Ahead in a Just Getting-By World," which will be offered in Spanish and English. There will be twelve students in each class for sixteen weeks/2 hours a session. The participant will receive a $25 gift card for attending each session and may only miss two classes in total. We will now be doing assessment and measurement of success with this tangible program, which has an element of goal setting. Nationally, 80% of the enrolled students graduate from the program.

We envision the next step for these graduates as one of becoming candidates for our KACS Board. We would like to have two graduates on the KACS Board in the next couple of years. We also look forward and see that these graduates will move into playing other roles in the community and join the team which is creating "bridges out of poverty."

The Kennett area school district is doing a tremendous job with educating the Spanish-speaking students and helping them become integrated and adjusted to the American life. We will be working with their parents, of whom many are doing without the ten resources mentioned above. At this time, 50% of KACS's clients are Spanish speaking.

In August 2015, KACS acquired and began renovations on the adjacent facility at 138 West Cedar Street. This new facility will provide a number of opportunities for under-resourced individuals and families to connect with valuable services while improving their situation:

- Bathing and laundry for KACS clients seeking housing
- Expanded raised bed gardens
- Office space for partner agencies to deliver services on-site to current KACS client base
- Expanded case management offices to deliver family-friendly private intake, consultations, and stability services
- Training and meeting space for KACS and partner agency programs
- Increased food storage at current KACS facility

This facility will provide a client-centered space to build healthy connections and begin to rebuild the client's resources and skills. Partner agencies are currently being secured, with the end goal of becoming a partner in the individual's pursuit of stability and success.

As we start our effort with Bridges Out of Poverty, I see that it is paramount that we seek to build a strong collaboration between service agencies, churches, employers and others that have a direct impact on poverty. The model asks for the development of a Bridges Steering Committee, a group that focuses on creating a continuum of care, minimizing duplication and advocating to reduce poverty. In our training, we learned that there are communities which have a centralized database that any individual or medical service agency is eligible to access when addressing a client in front of them. Access to a centralized database would inform the client where to go instead of running from agency to agency, and would prevent duplication and abuse of the system. Kennett Square still has some roadblocks toward true collaboration; however, my dream is that we will overcome the obstacles and experience ourselves as one community with the common goal of empowering our clients towards independence.

This work continues to be very rewarding and challenging at the same time. I believe we need to treat each person with dignity and walk with them through the journey out of poverty. We laugh sometimes when we say, "Are we trying to work ourselves out of job?" In all honesty, I would say that a reduction of clients is our new sign of success; which is a total paradigm shift from years past.

"Success means having the courage, the determination and the will to become the person you believe you were meant to be."

— George Sheehan, physician & author —

Youth Story – Through the Adult's Eyes

Lenda Carrillo, Kennett area resident

12/01/2016. *I was born in Uriangato, Guanajuato, Mexico in 1979 as the third child of a nine-member family. I completed middle school in Mexico and moved to the Kennett area in 1995 at sixteen years old. My father had been traveling back and forth between Kennett Square, PA and Uriangato, Mexico since 1976. With amnesty, my father received his green card and my parents decided to bring our entire family to Kennett in 1995. I begged to stay with my grandparents in Mexico, but my mother was insistent that we all stay together.*

As a teenager, it was a very challenging time for me to not only move, but to join a new culture and learn a totally different language. Why did we have to leave my friends and my familiar home in Mexico was my ongoing question and tantrum? I recall my first day at Kennett high school. I almost felt like my feet were floating, because I didn't know the ground I was walking on. The school was a giant monster and I felt so small with so many students rushing down the halls. When I went to the cafeteria, the new smell of pizza filled the room, and to this day, I really don't like that smell, because it brings back memories of this difficult time.

But, as any change, I started to find my way. Mrs. Jane Cornell was my ESL teacher and she was really the reason that I started to calm down. She would say comforting things like, "Don't worry, it is all going to work out." I recall her smile and that kept me coming back to class. I was mainstreamed into computer, math and science classes and I started in tenth grade, because I was sixteen years old. I worked hard and actually ended up doing well and graduating from Kennett High School in 1998. A group of five other Mexican girl classmates were another salvation, as we encouraged and supported each other and built on each other's understanding of a subject helping us all get through.

One nice memory of my high school years is when Kathleen Snyder brought in a movie to school called "La Broma." The actors were Latino youth and it was produced in the Spanish language to teach us about conflict resolution. I felt like my culture was being recognized by the school and this made me proud to be from my culture.

∞

Migrant Education was a wonderful support to me. Eileen Steinbacher stands out as a mentor, who strongly encouraged me to pursue my dream of college. I always wanted to become a teacher and she helped me see that it was possible with grants and scholarships. After I graduated in 1998, my mother wanted me to wait one year to attend college, so I could go with a group of friends, who would be graduating one year after me. My parents were always protecting us, as they did not know about college campuses and feared for our safety. I ended up working for Migrant Education at New Garden Elementary as a Student Support Specialist for one year after high school graduation.

After my Migrant Education experience, I decided that teaching wasn't for me and that I would do better if I went into something different. I attended Penn State Main Campus for one year, then attended Brandywine Penn State Campus, living at home to save money for the remainder of my college years, and graduated with a Bachelors in Business Administration in 2005.

I was so fortunate to receive scholarships and financial support for my college education. And, I also worked part-time as a receptionist at Phillips Mushroom Farm on Saturdays and Sundays to pay for my books, transportation and other college expenses. I continue to tell the community that there is college financial help available for minorities, women, and children of agricultural workers. The American Mushroom Institute gave me a scholarship for four years, and currently is giving me a scholarship for my Master's program at Immaculata College. I am a go-getter and continue to pursue these opportunities; they all didn't just come to me, but they are available to many if you are a good student and search them out.

Children of migrants would be on their own, without Kennett area's strong community mentoring and support. My parents have only attended school through the second grade. They both work in the mushroom industry, with my mother packing mushrooms, and my father involved in the watering of the compost. They are grateful for their consistent work and paychecks, and only through experience with their children have they learned the value of pursuing a higher education, as preparation for professional work. I am proud of them, and as part of their successes, they have fully paid off their home.

After college, I was hired by the Kennett Area YMCA as the Community Outreach Director. I worked there for ten years and it was a rewarding job. I was able to help Latino families see how the YMCA could meet their child care needs, memberships as well as provide scholarships for summer camps. When I started at the YMCA, there were few Latinos in the place. I promoted the membership scholarship program and now you see many more Latino families attending the YMCA regularly.

∞

My husband, Jose Luis Lopez is also from Mexico. I met him through my sister when I was in college. We dated for three years before we got married. Even though he has not attended college, he has continued to progress in his work and has the dream of owning his own landscaping business someday. He started out working on the mushroom farm and now is doing patio design and installation. Fortunately, he is very supportive of my higher education, as I pursue my master's degree. My sister Esmeralda also encourages me to continue with my higher education as well (she is my best friend).

Jose and I have two sons; Sebastian, who is 8 years old and Mateo, who is 3 years old. Sebastian attended the YMCA babysitting when I went back to work and attended their Montessori School. At 5-years old, he went to Upland Country Day School on a partial scholarship and he will be there until middle school, when he will attend the Kennett middle school. He is very smart and after attending kindergarten for two weeks, he was advanced to first grade, as he was reading already. Our son, Mateo attended Tommy Tinkers daycare and this past year he has started at Hockessin Montessori School.

The children have adapted very well to this culture because of course they were born United States citizens and I have only been naturalized since 2007. We speak Spanish at home only, so they retain this language, and both are learning English very quickly. Mateo sometimes only wants to speak English, and I continue to assure that he hears the Spanish language to give him this gift for later in life when he will be happy to be bi-lingual.

When I was pregnant with my first child, I was working at the YMCA and knew Joan Holliday, a public health nurse, who was providing prenatal preventive health services. I asked her if she would help me during my pregnancy, and she said that the Chester County Health Department public health nurses provided prenatal education and support for first time mothers and I fit the criteria for a referral. I think now that every first-time mom should have a public health nurse as there was so much to learn, and I think I had a healthier pregnancy and birth because of these services. There were things I couldn't ask my mother or husband, but was able to talk to "my nurse." I also received visits after delivery for six months to assure my son was progressing and receiving the medical support he needed. The Family Center also provided in-home services for me, when Sebastian was young, and they helped me learn ways I could educate my child and assure that he was ready for kindergarten; remember he skipped kindergarten because he did so well.

∞

In August of 2015, I started at Kennett Area Community Services. In fact, every significant event has happened to me in August; moving to the United States, graduating from college, becoming a citizen, starting my master's degree, buying our home and now this new employment.

I left the Kennett Area YMCA because I noticed that Latino families that I was serving at the YMCA needed help with issues beyond receiving discounted YMCA membership and camp scholarships. The issues went deeper than money and I wanted to be a part of helping change lives. We have started a "Getting Ahead" program at KACS, and I facilitate the Spanish group. Our goal is to help families move out of poverty towards a sustainable lifestyle. This is very rewarding work and I am learning so much about teaching our participants "how to fish" so to speak. We help people learn how to make financial choices and identify their priorities and values, as well as help they access education and jobs that will raise their income.

If I were going to suggest any thing that we need to work on in our Kennett area community, I would identify the need for more affordable child care. We have made progress with some of the services that are now provided by Path stone, Tick Tock Early Learning Center and the Kennett Area YMCA, but we need so much more. Even with both parents working, high child care costs can mean that the rent or electric bill isn't paid. I am hoping we can develop more options for affordable childcare.

Kennett Square is now my home and I love it. I am so proud to be a resident here. It feels like a safe place to raise a family and the community is amazingly supportive. I have my extended family living in the area and we all have adopted this area as "home." Yes, we will be living here for a long time and every other year, we get to travel to Mexico to see the relatives that still live there.

29

"Seek the wisdom of the ages
but look at the world through the eyes of a child."

— Ron Wild, author —

Tick Tock Early Learning Center

Jackie Neidigh, executive director

05/12/2016. *I was raised in New Jersey and attended Merion Mercy High School. I then matriculated at Bloomsburg University where I received a Bachelor of Arts in Social Work and a Master's Degree in Education from Farleigh Dickenson. My first professional position was as a residential specialist at the New England Center for Children in Massachusetts. I then took a position with the Philadelphia school district as a social worker and a behavioral health specialist. In 2013, I began at Tick Tock Early Learning Center as a Pre-K Teacher. For the past two years, I have been the executive director.*

Our Mission: Tick Tock Early Learning Center prepares children from working families for school and life in a loving environment at affordable rates.

Our Vision: Tick Tock Early Learning Center envisions a world where every child has hope, is loved and valued, and is given the opportunities to develop the skills and confidence to achieve success.

Our Philosophy: To accomplish our mission, we are committed to keeping our program affordable. Our rates are determined on a sliding scale based on family size and income. We accept state sponsored subsidies and offer private fee subsidies so that quality child care is within the reach of hard-working, low-income families. Sometimes the lack of reliable childcare is the only impediment preventing a parent from obtaining, keeping, or excelling at a job. We remove that obstacle. We are committed to providing a curriculum and a summer camp program in a safe and supportive environment that is stimulating, hands-on, and linked to the Pennsylvania Early Learning Standards. We nurture young learners while emphasizing school-readiness and English language acquisition.

∞

Fifty-two years ago, four Quaker women got together to discuss child care options and soon opened Tick Tock Early Learning Center. The leadership included Sally Lighty, Connie Nichols, Jean Tennent and Jane Vincente. They voiced a concern that some of the area's disadvantaged students were struggling in school and recognized the need for an educational outreach before children reached kindergarten. They established a Head Start program before there was Head Start. With little fanfare and a large number of dedicated volunteers, including primarily teachers and drivers, this committee of four moved forward. They worked with the Kennett school district and reached out to many local funders and to the Commonwealth of Pennsylvania for guidance and funds. They rented the Tic Toc Bar for a short time as their initial facility and, soon after, purchased the building. It now stands as Tick Tock Early Learning Center, 1694 Baltimore Pike, Avondale, Pennsylvania with colorful ceramic flowers covering the front of the building.

We have the capacity to enroll ninety-eight children and are usually full. We always keep a few positions open for emergencies, and we always have a waiting list. Our hours are from 7am to 6pm Monday through Friday. We serve breakfast, lunch and a healthy snack, but do not provide dinner because we hold to the philosophy that children need to eat with their families. Tick Tock is scheduled to close only for major holidays. We subscribe to the philosophy that families need to have time together, and these breaks provide that opportunity.

We have twenty-four employees: four administrative, two cooks, one housekeeper and seventeen teachers consisting of leads and assistants. To start at our center our teachers are required to have a high school diploma and two years of verified child-care experience. This entry level employee is partnered with a teacher who has a higher educational level or has received a CDA/Child Development Associate Certification. Two teachers have a bachelor's degree and one has an associate's degree. All of our staff receives twenty-four hours of training annually, which fosters professional growth and development. We value higher education for the center's employees, and strongly encourage and assist the staff in locating funding to further their education. When their goals are reached, we celebrate!

We are members of the Pennsylvania Keystone STARS Quality Child Care Assurance Initiative and have earned the highest rating, a STAR 4, for several years. This program is an incentive for us to do our best by requiring the center to meet the highest standards. As a result, we provide the best child care and pre-school education in the safest and healthiest environment. We have strict protocols for everything. It is also helpful for recruitment. Consequently, we provide the same level of quality service as is provided by a for-profit daycare/pre-school.

All of our staff has had training in CPR and in responding to seizures. If a parent wants us to administer medicine, we require an action plan from a pediatrician which must be signed by the parent. We are focused on allergies. We work closely with the Chester County Health Department if we have any infectious diseases and follow all of their protocols. The Department of Human Services inspects us and issues our child care license. Our on-site kitchen is inspected by the Chester County Food Services on an annual basis.

∞

Our budget is close to one million dollars. The government awards us thirty percent of our funds, and the remaining funds are obtained from United Way of Southern Chester County donations, grants, fundraisers, sliding-scale fees for service, and individual contributions. Currently we are formulating a strategic plan, refreshing our mission and vision statements, and developing our new logo. We also have just started a Building Expansion Campaign. We need to enlarge our facility which will increase enrollment and also allow for reduced operating costs through bulk purchases. Our overall capacity of part time and full-time students will increase. Property limitations will probably prevent any further expansion at this site.

Our uniqueness is our reputation for caring. We are small enough to maintain a family atmosphere. Working together as a team has always been a significant part of our culture. Teamwork is an aspect of the center that I, personally, continue to emphasize. It is very important that each employee feels valued and that his/her personal concerns are addressed. Demonstrating care and concern in a professional atmosphere helps make the center special. We are one of the few child care centers in the area that has a bi-lingual staff. This helps tremendously in communicating with the parents and for providing a familiar environment for the children. While immersion in the English language is important, we strongly value the Latino culture and language.

As part of my individual continuing educational improvement, I am studying Spanish with the goal of becoming fluent. I am also taking a course load to receive my director's credential. Although the current interpreter is helpful, I look forward to the day when I can clearly and directly communicate with my students, their families and my staff. In the meantime, we are fortunate to have a wonderful social service bi-lingual employee, who has a great rapport with the parents. She has proven to be invaluable in a wide variety of areas such as making referrals, completing documents, and helping parents sort through an issue.

∞

Challenges that will always exist are funding and community awareness. As we observed the difficulties that Pennsylvania, on the state level, was having in formulating a budget, we began to recognize our level of dependency on governmental funding. We diligently pursued new grant opportunities and sought out additional support from our longtime supporters. The response was very gratifying. We are extremely fortunate to have so many stakeholders in our venture that believe in what we do and who support us in so many ways.

It is difficult and sometimes heartbreaking to tell families that they will have to be placed on a waiting list. The need is so great. If I had a windfall, I would open another identical center. So many vulnerable children are hindered if they can't receive pre-kindergarten preparation. We can see the difference in the children who are registered in our program. Our daycare service benefits both the families and the children. It allows hard working families to retain their dignity and their family cohesiveness.

Many of our families return to enroll their younger children in our program. And graduates of Tick Tock, and/or the family members, have returned as teens and adults to volunteer or apply for employment at the center. This is gratifying; an indication that we are doing a good job and making a difference. We are a part of the fabric of the community, and this brings to everyone a warmth and satisfaction that keeps on giving.

Please come and visit us. Everyone is welcome.

**"The more that you read, the more things you will know.
The more that you learn, the more places you will go."**

— Dr. Seuss, children's book writer, poet, and cartoonist —

CCIU Family Literacy Program

Patricia Quynn, program coordinator

06/01/2016. I have lived in Kennett Square my entire life. I graduated from Kennett High School and received a Bachelor's Degree in Elementary and Early Childhood Education from Millersville University. I grew up on our family's mushroom farm. I can remember my dad working long hours, 7 days a week. My mom packed the mushrooms, so my three brothers and I went with her as soon as we got old enough to spend the day in the mushroom house. I can remember stamping the lids and papering baskets (two things that are no longer done in a mushroom house) and carrying the baskets of mushrooms to the packing room. It was a family business, and I have fond memories of my time and work in the mushroom house. We kids were the best workforce ever and working in the mushroom house taught us the importance of work. In the summer, my dad and brothers spent hours in the hay fields cutting, raking and baling hay which would be used in the mushroom compost. My dad made sure to take a week off each summer and would take us all to the beach. It was his way of showing us his appreciation for all we did for the family business. When the students in our classes talk about the mushroom business, I know firsthand what it is like to work in a mushroom house.

I worked for the Even Start Program from 1993 until 2011, when we transitioned to the Family Literacy Program. I live in Kennett Square with my husband Norman. We have four children: Norman, Sarah, Andrew and Kelly.

When federal funding ended for the Even Start Literacy Program, the Family Literacy Program started in 2011. It provides services through a combination of center-based and home-based components. Primary services include: adult education, early childhood education, parenting education, and parent and child Interactive Literacy Activities (ILA). A family unit qualifies for family literacy services if there is a child from birth to eight years old and a parent is eligible for Adult Basic Education. These services are offered in the Avon Grove and Oxford Area School Districts. There is no fee for the service.

The foundation behind this comprehensive approach is one that builds the whole family system.

- Parents become literate in the English language and receive formal education towards a high school diploma. This improves their opportunity for higher-level employment.
- Children have exposure to educational opportunities from birth until kindergarten. This helps the child become kindergarten-ready. At this time, 80% of our students are kindergarten-ready.
- Parent-child relationships are built through not only parenting classes, but through regular parent-child interactive literacy activities with books, which sets the stage for future parent educational support with their child.

With this outstanding family literacy model, there are many challenges. The Family Literacy Program is funded through the Pennsylvania Department of Education (the Adult Basic Literacy Education division), and they require us to offer three hours, per week, face-to-face parent-child interactive literacy activities (ILA) at our centers. Parents are also required to attend two hours of parenting classes and five hours of adult education a week. Some of our participants find it difficult to attend all of these educational sessions because they have other work and family obligations.

To encourage good attendance at our weekly parent education classes and parent and child interactive literacy activities, we prepare healthy kid-friendly lunches during the educational sessions. Once we started to do that, we found we had the best attendance. We build further incentives to attend by giving donated books to our families because many of the parents lack good books at home. We teach and model reading behaviors during ILA sessions with parents and children. We work with parents to help them learn how to "read" picture books if they cannot read the words. For many of our parents, this was a new concept; many think if they cannot read the words, they cannot read the book.

The rewards of this work is hearing about some of the children that I taught in pre-school now going on to college and doing well. One of our adult students approached me the last day of class this program year and told me how proud she was of her children. One received a science award and the other a reading award. She wanted to thank her teacher for the skills she developed in the pre-GED class that helped her to gain the skills she needed as a parent to help her children.

The Family Literacy Program is founded on the premise that with literacy, there are increased opportunities, and, with more opportunities, a family can rise to a new cultural and economic status and life. The Family Literacy Program's approach of providing services for the whole family is certainly a key to opening opportunities for families.

31

"Children are our most valuable resource."
— Herbert Hoover, 31st president of the United States —

Kennett Consolidated School District
Dr. Larry Bosley, superintendent from 1980 to 1999

01/06/2016. I was in my mid-30s when I took the job as superintendent of Kennett schools. I acquired previous administrative experience in larger school systems, and I believe I was hired because the school board wanted a younger pair of eyes to look at taking the school system to the next level. Board members, who had graduated from outstanding colleges and had unusually successful careers, mentored me throughout my tenure, for which I felt privileged. They were leaders in the community and had a firm grasp on academic standards. They were all more mature than I, most were twenty years my senior. This board, as well as Dr. Forrest Schaeffer, former KCSD superintendent, were a tremendous help to me. My relationship with these mentors and my love of Kennett Square brought on the successes we achieved during my service. I retired for the same reason I was hired; I loved what I was doing, but thought it was time for a person with a fresh outlook to take the lead. When I left office, the budget was $50 million. Today, I believe that the budget has doubled, which makes it an entirely different ball game.

The school district faced critical issues when I started. As a whole, our students were behind academically, and there was no vision for moving forward. In contrast, the academically talented students and their parents were pressuring the district to offer advanced placement courses. I had to determine solutions for both.

The board dictated that I create a "world class faculty." When I asked if they were willing to pay for a top-notch staff, they replied, "Yes, reasonably." I recruited both nationally and internationally, and successfully hired several quality, diverse faculty members. As a team, we developed an up-to-date curriculum that met competitive national academic standards

In the mid-1980s, the federal government directed schools to include all Hispanic students, and we were not allowed to ask if the students were documented or undocumented. The 1980's decade was a difficult time for the school district. The faculty juggled a diverse student population; at one end of the spectrum were the immigrant students dealing with a language barrier and a foreign culture, and at the other end were the financially secure students who came from families that often bought their children expensive cars. My goal was to ensure that each child was educated, and that each child reached his/her potential regardless of economic status.

∞

To help attain my goal, I sought professional support to train my staff. We had total English language immersion at the kindergarten level, and then English as a Second Language (ESL) classrooms for the upper grade levels. The intent was to orient the student in the ESL classes, and then have the student attend regular classes. We were promoting the ESL classes as a way to integrate the student into the American culture. Studies have shown that the success rate for learning a language is much higher when the student is immersed in the language. Often a teacher asked, "How do I grade the Spanish-speaking students?" I responded, "Kennett teaches to the kid. That is our gospel!" I studied the grading distribution every marking period and kept a close eye on the outcomes. I had a wonderful staff, and I felt their commitment to helping each student to be successful. When I started in 1979, I employed one bi-lingual staff member; when I left my position in 1999, we had at least two ESL teachers for each school in the district.

To address the "kindergarten readiness" of our young students, we instituted the two-year kindergarten program. Kindergarten was still a half-day; however, if the student was not ready to graduate to first grade, he/she would attend another year of kindergarten to continue to work on skills. The two-year kindergarten program was a lead-in to a full day of kindergarten. I worked closely with the area pre-school programs such as Even Start and Head Start that focused on school readiness. As a land developer today, I am happy that I was able to build a school site in town where both of these pre-school programs are now permanently housed, as the programs were always dealing with moving to and from temporary sites.

To achieve success with the Hispanic students, I knew I must involve the parents in their children's education. In the beginning, there was little or no communication between the parents and the teachers. We scheduled several parent nights throughout the school year, one conducted in English and one communicated in Spanish. Hispanic attendance was low in the beginning, but gradually grew over time. These gatherings gave us the opportunity to encourage Spanish-speaking parents to enroll in the ESL classes at the Kennett library, enabling them to become more active members of the school community and of the larger local community.

It was also important for me to develop a healthy relationship with the Kennett black community. Often I was told that I was favoring the Hispanic community because of the efforts related to integrating their culture into the school system. In my role, I was responsible for every student, and I believe my actions consistently showed that I cared about each one of them. I was fortunate to have a strong rapport with our Home School Visitor, who helped me develop a relationship with the black community and a trust that I believe I continue to have today.

∞

There were several community factors that helped me do my job. I was willing to attend the first Bridging the Community meeting, in which we looked at the "white spaces" in our community and quickly agreed that we needed community after-school youth programs/processes if we wanted to stay on the positive/potential-side of things. To address the issue, I signed on to After-The-Bell, an after-school program for middle school students which proved to be an effective partnership between school and community; Mentoring Youth in Kennett, which provided volunteer mentors to support elementary students during the school day; Study Buddies, which provided after-school tutoring to at-risk students in four different local churches; The Garage Community and Youth Center, which provided after-school tutors and programs for high school students, and, of course, all the other clubs and sports! Why not cooperate and collaborate with the community? We all shared the same vision, "Kennett is about each kid – It is our gospel!"

The relationship I had with Kennett's chief of police was invaluable. Because we shared the same vision of helping the kids, we worked together to educate the children about right and wrong. Police Chief McCarthy had his responsibility of enforcing the law, and he allowed me to contact the parents and deal with any legal situation in a way that the student could learn a lesson from the offense. The chief was very visible, both in the community and in the schools. His regular presence in the elementary schools teaching DARE (Drug Abuse Resistance Education) and seeking the parent's buy-in was extremely helpful in keeping our kids on the right track.

Our community was invited to send representatives to a statewide training on Communities That Care (CTC) in 1998. The chief of police and I attended the training in Harrisburg. We accepted the funding and went through the process; however, we realized that our community was already creating a direction for "promoting positive development among youth" through the above efforts. CTC legitimized what we were doing.

Note: Communities that Care (CTC) is a risk-focused and evidence-based approach for promoting positive development among youth. CTC began in Pennsylvania through seed grants from the Pennsylvania Commission on Crime and Delinquency (PCCD). These grants allowed the prevention boards in each community to convene, hire a community mobilizer, perform the risk and resource assessment and develop a community action plan, which often included the opportunity to implement evidence-based programs.

∞

As I look at the trends of the future for Kennett I have some concerns. The lack of available low-cost housing is a key issue in our area. Taking a look at the big picture, however, I feel that additional low-cost housing will greatly stress the schools. Affordable housing already exists in the Stenning Hills development, as well as on East Linden Street and Walnut/South Streets. Statistics indicate that low-income families have 3.4 children compared to .75 children in higher income families. Area townships outside of the Kennett school district must also tackle the need for affordable housing. On the other hand, low-income housing for seniors would be a great addition to the Kennett community because no school children would need to be accommodated. I regularly study things from an Economics 101 viewpoint and believe we must continue to attract businesses, restaurants, and shops to our area, which, in turn, will make Kennett Square a great town to live in and visit.

The merger between DuPont Company and Dow Chemical and the subsequent restructuring will have a major impact on the Kennett area community. DuPont employees live, shop and donate in Kennett, and local businesses have a strong working relationship with DuPont. The absence of DuPont will require quite an adjustment for the community.

My work today as a developer is living out the Bridging the Community vision – *"Kennett Square: every day a better place to grow up in and grow old in."*

32

"Children are one third of our population and all of our future."

— Select Panel for the Promotion of Child Health, 1981 —

Kennett Consolidated School District
Dr. Rudolph Karkosak, superintendent from 1999-2010

02/25/2016. Before my time in Kennett, I earned my educational degrees at West Chester University of Pennsylvania and the University of Delaware. I began teaching social studies in Wilmington before moving into different administrative positions in the Delaware and Maryland school districts.

I think that the Kennett community is a great and unique community. It is very supportive of the district, its children and new ideas. After serving in several educational and administrative roles in Delaware and Maryland, I was happy to spend the last of my 45-year career in Kennett as superintendent. The main reason is that I realized that I was leading a school district within a small community that had a sense of belonging. Maybe it is the Quaker background, or maybe it is that the residents are looking to make a difference; because I experienced people very willing to go the extra-mile to meet their community's needs. Other communities are jealous of the culture that exists in Kennett.

When I started my role as superintendent in 1999, I enjoyed an enlightened board of education composed of community members who possessed integrity, dedication, and a true concern for all students. I vividly remember calling two snow days and then losing two board members in my first two weeks. The two board members resigned to pursue other tasks, but we fortunately found new members made from the same cloth. Even though we scheduled a monthly Monday night business meeting, all board members usually attended additional committee meetings on the other Monday nights. They cared and wanted to stay informed on all community topics. This made for an informed board, ready to take action on the many issues facing the district. I stood strongly on the ground of mutual respect and staying on the positive side of issues. We also understood our assigned roles; the board members set policy, and I put policy into action. Right from the beginning, I expressed the guideline, "You evaluate me, and I evaluate everyone else!" This worked well, because it kept me solely in the implementation role.

During the first few weeks as the new superintendent, I listened to the board, the staff, the students and the community to gather information about the schools and to establish a plan of action. Ironically one issue that seemed to be heard most often was starting a football program. Alas, this was not to be the first matter addressed. The goals that I established were filling administrative vacancies, handling the infrastructure issues in the district, negotiating a teacher's contract, strengthening the curriculum at all levels, tackling the needs of all students, and quite a few more. No one of these goals was given top priority. I attempted to undertake them all with the support of the board and the staff.

∞

I started officially January 1 with a district office staff of three including a business manager, a director of special education, and myself; and had to attempt to take on the issues at hand. My first plan of action was to hire a director of human resources. Good fortune presented Nancy Tischer, an experienced personnel director who was well known in the state and who possessed great skill in finding outstanding candidates. With her assistance, we hired really great teachers and staff throughout my tenure. When we found an exceptional person, no matter the position, we were willing to pay a competitive salary. It also helped that Kennett had a great reputation that brought excellence to our door. I believe that Kennett Consolidated School District (KCSD) is an outstanding school district because of the exceptional staff that we hired.

The second most important position to be filled was a director of curriculum and instruction. Dr. Bureau accepted this role and was in charge of developing a course of study in every subject over the next three years, reviewing textbooks and instructional materials for all subjects, and advancing technology throughout the district. We established a realistic plan spread out over a number of years that included input from the teachers and staff at every level. The goal was to develop a comprehensive K though 12 curriculum that addressed the needs of each student. Having a very diverse student population added to this challenge, but the results were well worth the effort.

One of our major accomplishments was raising the number of credits needed to graduate from 18 to

25.2, the highest in Chester County. Graduates were required to complete four years of English, Math, Science and Social Studies; and students were encouraged to take a foreign language. We increased offerings in Spanish, Latin, French and German at the middle school and high school, persuaded eligible eighth graders to take Algebra 1, and added more Advanced Placement (AP) classes with a higher weight for grading. Despite the addition of numerous electives and interesting courses, we were never able to achieve my personal objective – the total elimination of study halls. Scheduling, space, and staff seemed to dictate the necessity for them.

∞

In the early days, my first priority was developing a positive relationship with our teachers. The most pressing issue was negotiating a new contract with the Kennett Education Association. My plan emphasized that no board member should be on the negotiation team. The goal was to protect them and to put a process in place with my business manager. The previous superintendent had maintained a bare-bones contract, which helped us in our negotiations. We kept complicated language out of our discussions, and as long as we worked together, we saw no need for a lot of legal language. We negotiated for months with little success. We brought in a skilled attorney to assist in the process. As we approached November, we faced the possibly of a strike. Wednesday afternoon before Thanksgiving, we were presented with a letter calling for a strike after the holiday if we did not reach an agreement. On Thanksgiving Day, my wife Carol was preparing dinner while I was on the phone with the attorney and staff developing a strategy to avoid the strike. We decided that if a strike happened, schools would close until we reached a settlement. All parties involved in the negotiations were willing to meet and did so the following Monday afternoon. After hours of talk, all parties shook hands and agreed to terms. My philosophy was that a successful negotiation was when no one leaves totally happy or upset; that was called compromise. The good news was that a teacher's strike was avoided, and we were the first school district in Chester County that had teachers contribute toward their health benefits.

Today, all of the Chester County school districts have this stated in their contracts. Three years, and then six years later, we had two amicable "Early Bird" contracts in a row, which I think is a record in Chester County. We had set the stage for working together by focusing on what was best for the kids, teachers and community.

My third focus was confronting the over-crowding at the elementary schools and the infrastructure of the district. The plan stretched over ten years in order to address all the needs and be able to finance each project in turn. During that time, the enrollment continued to grow. When I arrived in 1999, we had 3,375 students. When I left in 2010, the enrollment increased to 4,300; the equivalent size of a large school.

The plan's first step was to build a middle school. Kennett High School needed renovations, so the time was ripe to move the middle school to a new location and restructure the entire building during renovations for use as only a high school. We developed a great middle school building campaign with staff, teachers and community members involved in the discussions. We still take pride in the beautiful facility that we have in the Landenberg area. Even though I am not an architect, I know how school buildings work from my years of administrative experience. When I was presented with a traditional school model from the architect, I asked to change the specifications so that each of the three grades had its own separate section, thus providing increased protection for each age group while improving student interaction between the classes. All three grades share the gym, cafeteria, and other supporting classrooms in the center of the school. To this day, the concepts are working well. We built a true middle school.

We initiated the plan for renovating the high school while the middle school was under construction. After an extensive tour of the high school, the architects proposed building a new high school and destroying the existing one. The immediate answer was absolutely not. Kennett High School was built in 1932 and had served as the historical center of the town and community for decades. There was no way we would destroy it. After numerous plans and multiple decisions, we decided to demolish the old middle school in the back of the building and build a two-story science and math wing. That first step would be followed by an elaborate schedule to renovate the original building, a renovation that was to be accomplished while the students were attending classes in the building. Construction noise, dust and confusion were everyday occurrences during the renovation that could never have been completed without the cooperation of the principals, the staff, and especially the students. We finished the project two months ahead of schedule and under budget. To the community's delight, we maintained the façade of this historic building while creating a state-of-the-art school inside.

∞

We finally created a football program in 2003 and started a varsity program two years later. Our first game was played on Unionville's high school field, and the first comments we heard from the Kennett community were, "When are we going to get our own field?" Our campus site was limited, so our challenge was to build an athletic complex suitable for all sports offered at the high school. Although the complex was successfully completed, we developed Legacy Fields years later to meet the growth of the sports program.

By 2007, because of the increase of students in the elementary grades, we needed to build another elementary school. We also had to address the concern about the image of Mary D. Lang having a large Hispanic population. Several parents had moved their children to the new Avondale Charter School because they thought they would receive a better education. After much deliberation and interactions with my board, a teacher committee, business manager and community members, we felt the best decision was to transform Mary D. Lang into a kindergarten center and to build Bancroft Elementary School as the third elementary school in the district. I was relieved to have the approvals and building plans in place for Bancroft Elementary by the time I retired. Yes, that was a tiring process! The good news was that it was a perfect time for bidding, as construction work was down and jobs were competitive. We actually saved money on the Bancroft Elementary project. Once again, I was able to influence the architectural model of the school, and I continue to be pleased that it works so well for our students and faculty.

∞

The "No Child Left Behind" legislation created quite a challenge for our schools, primarily Mary D. Lang Elementary School. Over 40% of the Mary D. Lang enrollment was Latino, with English as their second language. Because of poor test results, Mary D. Lang was placed on the "Warning List". I appealed to the state, but was unsuccessful in having Mary D. Lang removed from the list. The PSEA, PASA, ACLU and many other organizations filed amicus briefs to point out that the test was only offered in English, with no accommodations. Many of the students at Mary D. Lang were just learning the English language. The test was unfair! After many efforts, the case was scheduled to be heard in the Commonwealth Court. Soon after, we were informed by the state that Mary D. Lang was taken off the "Warning List".

Another priority was getting our fiscal house in order. We had to raise taxes almost every year because of the infrastructural improvements and capital expansion. We strove to have clean audits, which occurred throughout my tenure. Unfortunately, the state auditors always found one issue to note. I almost felt like the object of the auditors was to find at least one flaw. The community accepted the financial demands of increased taxes and provided the support we needed to create a school system that has the high school on the "Best Public High Schools" list since 2010.

In the 1990s, the trend of increased Spanish-speaking student enrollment started and continued to grow while I was superintendent. We needed programs in place to deal with their special needs, so very soon after I arrived, we hired more ESL teachers. The U.S. Department of Education visited us in 2000 and determined that we did not provide sufficient services for our Spanish-speakers. We accepted this as a challenge, resulting in us being more creative and resourceful. We first reinforced strict residency requirements by calling for a verification of address. Then, we examined how we could better educate a first language Spanish-speaking student through ESL classes and immersion. We had a strong relationship with Migrant Education, so we continued to draw on their expertise and support. We increased our school nursing staff by hiring one nurse for each of the six schools. All of the nurses went beyond the call of duty and promoted preventive health care, as well as health care. We shared the philosophy that a healthy child can be a better student.

It was at this time that we applied for funding for the Walk In kNowledge (WIN) program at the Kennett High School. With the help of Loretta Perna and Connie Logan, ESL students were given help after school to reach their goals of completing high school and setting goals for college. We discovered early on that Spanish-speaking students could do well in advanced math classes conducted in English. This built their confidence and willingness to pursue other classes. With one of the WIN graduating classes, I was given a report. Of the 28 graduates, 27 students were going to college with scholarships! The remaining graduate joined a convent. The Spanish-speaking students also did well with other languages. In fact, one of my favorite stories was hearing the news that Juan and Jose had won the German awards at the German exam competition in Philadelphia! I also heard from one of the school counselors that the Hispanic population had a nickname for me, "Jefe de la colina," which means "Boss on the hill." I know they felt my support, and I enjoyed this nickname!

∞

One of the difficulties that we faced was how to help a student secure financial college support throughout his/her college years. Low-income students found it especially challenging to remain in college when they had little to no resources from home. Although they were bright students, they were unable to receive loans or aid. This is an issue that continues today. We instituted the Kennett Education Foundation to provide scholarships to students who displayed good skills and a dedication to continue their education. We have awarded thousands of dollars over the past sixteen years, and will continue to do so.

My motto for my staff and myself was, "Have high expectations and provide loving student support." Students were well aware of the school rules and the punishment for breaking the rules. For instance, any fight at school resulted in the participants receiving a police citation and an automatic ten-day suspension from school. The previous administration and the police department had already been implementing many of the rules and disciplining the rule-breakers, and we continued along the same path. All the schools in the district employed strong administrators that enforced the rules. We found that the majority of incidents occurred at the start of the school year when students were tempted to test the limits of discipline. Our goal was to provide an orderly, safe and friendly environment where the students were able to focus on learning and relationships. I tried to visit each school weekly and enjoyed youngsters opening the doors with a ready smile and a polite greeting.

I was always amazed how the community rallied around the schools and also felt close to us. One memory that stays with me is the morning I was called to the high school to join a grieving family, whose son was tragically killed in a car accident. The family had asked to meet with some of his teachers, counselors and administration to share their grief and to work through funeral arrangements.

Looking back, I know I gave the job my all and am proud of the development and accomplishments during my tenure as superintendent. There was a genuine team spirit among the board and myself, and the faculty and staff always put forth their best efforts. The Kennett area community deserves the best, and Kennett schools can certainly be categorized as outstanding today. Now, I am personally reaping the rewards as my four grandsons attend the Kennett schools.

"There can be no keener revelation of a society's soul than the way in which it treats its children."

— Nelson Mandela, former president of South Africa —

Kennett Consolidated School District

Dr. Barry Tomasetti, superintendent from 2010 to present

04/12/2016. It is interesting how I ended up coming to Kennett Square to serve as superintendent of schools. I had been superintendent of the Mifflinburg Area School District in Central Pennsylvania for ten years, and I wasn't really looking to move. I was contacted by the Central Susquehanna Intermediate Unit telling me about the Kennett superintendent position. When I checked out the level of school lunch recipients at 42% and the lower test scores, I decided I wasn't interested. At the advice of the Central Susquehanna Intermediate Unit's Executive Director, Bob Witton, I decided to go ahead with an interview with the Kennett school board. He was a friend of the hired search consultant for Kennett Consolidated School District (KCSD), Bill Leary, who said that the Kennett board was made up of excellent members. It was at that time, I started asking around about impressions of Kennett school district, and they were all positive. Rita Jones, superintendent of the Great Valley School District said, "It is a community that wraps its arms around the kids." I was really impressed by this comment followed by my interview with the Kennett school board. This board was impressive! They had their thumb on the pulse of the school system, on the education process and the district's pressing issues. On my way back to Mifflinburg after the interview, my wife, Linda, called me and asked me what I thought, and I told her, "I will go back for a second interview, if I am called." Well, the story is now told; after the second interview, I was offered for the job, and here I am seven years later and echoing my son, Barry Junior's comment after graduating from Kennett High School, "It was a great decision!"

At the time of my move, my three sons were in 9th, 8th and 5th grades. Now that two of them have graduated from KHS and enrolled in college both planning on majoring in mechanical engineering, I can say they were prepared very well academically. Again, they had the fun of playing sports with a diverse group of guys; culture and race were never a consideration when it came to working towards a common goal on their sport teams and academic goals.

My experience of working with the administration, faculty, students and community has been unique. I think it is unique because we are succeeding even in the face of odds. Our mission states that we will support the academic achievement of ALL students. In other words, it is our responsibility that the kids succeed. And this is the prevailing attitude that exists within the district. We, the faculty staff and administration and board of school directors, may say, "This is difficult, but it is not impossible. We will walk the extra mile towards achievement and solutions." Our teaching staff here at Kennett is uncommonly dedicated and effective in their work with our kids.

∞

Last year, I had the experience of substituting in a tenth grade Social Studies class and realized very quickly that, with the Hispanic students, there is an academic language and a colloquial or idiomatic language deficit. When I said I was substituting so that I could "rub elbows with the students," one of the ESL students said, "Are you going to rub our elbows?" Obviously, we were not on the same language page. We need to learn how to better reach our students who spend most of their lives communicating in Spanish. I had previously contracted with the University of Pennsylvania to perform an audit focusing on our method of teaching the students. One of the findings of this study was that our teachers felt that they never received staff development in this very area. We followed the results of the audit with a think tank with the administrators.

At that meeting, we made the decision to take the Sheltered Instruction Observation Protocol training and phase it into our teaching method. This model offers an empirically-validated approach to teaching that helps students, especially English language learners, to become college and career ready. We started the training with five teachers and principals in every building, with the intention that the newly informed staff will train the other teachers. Our immediate aim is to focus on how to stress content and academic vocabulary with our students. While our staff is adept at teaching higher level cognitive skills to our students, we need to emphasize the understanding of the vocabulary that goes along with this objective. Our goal is to have this teaching method implemented throughout the district, which helps the learning effectiveness for all students. On the other side, we have recently added a new AP course, environmental science, for advanced students. We continue to articulate to all stake holders that it is not only about a paycheck, it is our moral obligation to provide what is needed to help each student reach his/her potential. Our staff demonstrates this notion each and every day. Following is the text of two plaques I have hanging on my wall as well as every principal's office in the district, that remind all of us what we are about.

"What do we want each student to learn?
How will we know when each student has learned it?
How will we respond when a student experiences difficulty in learning?
How will we enrich and extend learning for students who are proficient?" –Richard DuFour

"Nothing splendid has ever been achieved except by those who dared believe that something inside
of them was superior to circumstances." –Bruce Barton

One new initiative that we have started is a parent engagement task force. I strongly believe, and research demonstrates, that parents are instrumental in supporting their child's academic success and we need to work on this in the Kennett district. On the task force, we have representatives from Together for Education, Study Buddies, Holcomb Behavioral Health, YMCA, Spanish Health Ministry, MCH/Family Center, La Comunidad Hispana, and Migrant Education. These community advocates can be agents in developing efforts to bring parents to the table. There are three facets of this parent engagement initiative:

1. The first involves inspiring parents through Witness Talks from Latino students, who have graduated and are either in or have graduated from college and share with the parents the value of higher education and the doors it has opened for them. At a recent session, I was surprised at the emotional experience that this became for both the presenters and parents.

2. The second facet is one of providing parents with objective parenting behaviors that they can practice with their children that will allow their children to understand the importance of school success.

3. The third is one that we soon hope to get off the ground called ASPIRA Parents for Educational Excellence (APEX.) We will provide training for key parent leaders to become resources for their neighborhoods and representatives for communication with the schools.

I was pleased recently, when the YMCA director heard and acted on my comment about Latinos not being on any sport teams in school except soccer. He plans to offer a summer camp that will expose Latino youth to baseball, basketball and football with the thought that without familiarity there is no way any will join the mainstream school sport teams.

We are well aware in the Kennett school district that the number of Hispanic students is increasing. With

Mary D. Lang having 50 % kindergarten students, we can see the future. This adds more cost to the educational services if we are going to do our best job with this population. As I mentioned earlier, we need more supportive after-school tutoring, more investment in the effective model of teaching, and time and effort in working with the parents. 85% of our school district income comes from local taxes and the other 15 % from state taxes. This means that the upper and middle classes are carrying a large part of the load for educating our kids.

I also get questions from persons moving into the area about the quality of education with the growing percentage of Latino students. I continue to speak to our commitment to the academic achievement of every student, regardless of race, color or creed. Our teachers work extremely hard to plan and deliver differentiated lessons with a focus on moving all students forward. What surprises the interviewee is that most of our students speak English with only 13% requiring ESL support.

∞

Testing will always be a contentious issue. Personally, I am in support of standards which help all students reach a basic set of skills. After thirty-three years in education, with twenty-six of those years in administration, I see how standardized testing helps all students if we are committed to helping students reach certain benchmarks. Besides, for most of our students, these tests "are the floor and not the ceiling;" we expect much more from our kids. During its time, "No Child Left Behind" was needed, and it did help raise the standard of education. Although I am in agreement with the PA common core standards, I must say that achievement of the standards has been challenging. The testing requires more language skills, which becomes a challenge for our Hispanic students, resulting in lower test scores this past year. (I believe our Sheltered Instruction Observation Protocol training will address this through time.) At the same time, I don't believe that testing should be a graduation requirement, especially with Hispanic students who are first generation immigrants. So, this discussion continues.

Yes, I agree that the Kennett community has been about "the kids!" Our teachers are a cut above the rest. They are the first to help a student during their planning periods, or stay after school to help a student. It seems to be part of the culture to be committed to the kids and putting in that extra time and effort. The president of the Teacher's Association is a model in this respect, and that sets a tone for the effort. Last but not least, all the gaps that the community after-school programs are filling, as well as the school readiness programs, are certainly the network that brings this all together. These are exemplary practices; these are about a caring Kennett area community.

The Kennett community, that obviously includes our school system, provides every student with the hope that they can succeed in life. Our goal is to provide the type of learning opportunities to make this hope for success a reality.

"We know what we are but know not what we may be."

— William Shakespeare, English poet & playwright —

<hr />

Kennett Area Latino Youth
Christian Cordova

08/23/2016. *I am a child of an immigrant family. My father came to the United States in 1983 and has worked as a farmer —first, on a family farm in the rural Mexican town where my mother grew up, and, now, in the mushroom houses of Kennett Square, Pennsylvania. He worked tirelessly to earn money to support our family then in Mexico for an eventual family move to the United States.*

My father brought my mother and two older sisters, Janet and Beatriz, in March 15th of 1995 and I was born in September of 1995, so I am a first generation United States citizen. We lived in Avondale and Landenberg. I attended New Garden Elementary and the Kennett Middle and High Schools. Currently, I am a junior at Harvard University pursuing a degree in Government and Sociology. I think of myself as a child of immigrant parents who motivate me to excel academically.

My father had no schooling and my mother had the equivalent of a sixth grade education. My father came to this country to seek opportunities, to build a better future for his children, and to contribute the best he could to the country that gave him the opportunity to build a better life for himself and his family. I like to say that my dad, as an agricultural worker uses his hands to cultivate the land, and I, as the next generation, am cultivating my mind, a great privilege I have at the expense of his backbreaking labor.

Kennett Square was a good fit for me to thrive as a student. When I attended school in Kennett, there was enough diversity in the schools that I learned from the contrasts and differences and was affirmed for the similarities. My parents, teachers and friends also supported my growth as an individual and student. In fact, my mother was a school custodian, so I had her support with car rides after school and she knew some of my teachers and was readily available to help me with anything even small things like giving me lunch money. I participated in after-school programs, such as After-the-Bell in the middle school. In high school, I took part in Unidad (the Latino Leadership Club), the Humanitarian Club, track & field, the Academic Team, the school newspaper, and WIN. I appreciated these community programs that helped to enrich my personal and academic development.

∞

One memory I have of my educational experience that really kick-started my love of learning and challenged me to earn the best grades possible occurred in Ms. Uster's academically talented science class in the 8th grade. It was the first time I had taken an accelerated class; I remember some of my friends had been placed in the accelerated track starting in the 3rd grade. I recall learning about the different styles of learning, and was able to determine how I best understand and retain knowledge and process my thinking. This was so helpful and gave me the confidence and a framework for other classes. I ended up taking eleven AP courses in high school and doing well.

I'm often asked the question, "How did you get into Harvard?" To be truthful, I am not sure how it all came about. I know it came down to a good work ethic and a lot of luck. I had a high grade point average and tested well, and I also knew Ivy League schools were looking for students with exceptional backgrounds in their enrollment mix. But seriously, all I can say is that it has been good fortune to be a student here. The classes are outstanding and I am learning how to develop my mind to analyze issues and think through solutions to manage and hopefully solve pressing issues.

There also are some great minds that are associated with this school. For example, on my first day of school I met Miranda DeGrasse Tyson, daughter of Neil DeGrasse Tyson, American astrophysicist, cosmologist, author and science communicator. It seems surreal, but Miranda and I are actually good friends and share a meal from time to time.

Harvard has allowed me to travel and see the world. Last summer I studied abroad in Venice, Italy, taking an Italian language course and a Shakespeare's Venice course. This summer I had two internships— one was in Buenos Aires, Argentina. I worked in the government for the Ministry of Urban Development doing research and analysis. My focus was on how to analyze the socio-economic impact of large scale urban projects. This has helped me to see the importance of urban planning and looking at the macro and micro impacts of how the socio-economic structure is set-up and the critical effects transportation has on the residents.

This second internship has taken me to the mayor's office in Atlanta, Georgia where I am working in the office of immigrant affairs, an initiative of the mayor that tries to build a diverse, talented, and inclusive community for Atlantians. I wear multiple hats on the job. Some days I am in community centers doing outreach for a project called Connect Homes, which helps low-income families with students in Atlanta's public schools understand the "know-how" of technology to better help their child. We provide tablets and technological support to parents and children to assure that they are on an equal playing field with other well-off families.

In light of immigration, I would say communities are pots of soil, the residents are seeds and the "Atlanta Pot" has soil that needs to be fertilized. My hometown, Kennett Square, has rich soil with strong social capital and community building. I also think the Kennett community is in the process of learning how to understand the complex issues and reality related to being an undocumented individual. For example in Atlanta, Georgia, the notorious HB-87 passed in the state legislature in 2005 essentially legalizes racial profiling, incentivizes the arrest and deportation of undocumented individuals, and prohibits them from receiving public services such as necessary medical care.

On the other hand, Kennett Square, thankfully, has no such legislation. Even when a person is stopped by the police for a minor infraction, documentation of residency is not checked as it is in the counties surrounding Atlanta. The same minor infraction could lead to deportation in or around Atlanta.

$$\infty$$

During my time in college, I have been studying the concept of migrant integration. There is such a delicate balance between respecting and honoring the diversity of each culture, while still becoming an integral part of the majority culture. To some, assimilation means, "Be exactly like us!" I personally don't believe we have to erase our cultural background to be part of the larger community or to be accepted. America thrives as a country and as individuals when we accept others into a community

What improvements could the school system make? One change that Kennett High School should work on is hiring counselors and teachers who reflect the diversity of the student body, or at a minimum, who really understand the issues of the changing demographics of the student body. There are no counselors of Latino origin and very few teachers. There are sociological studies that speak to the importance of having a teacher or counselor that "looks like you" in how they make learning accessible and in creating an inclusive learning environment for students. We are fortunate to have Loretta Perna, who is a role model for the Latino students; however, she stands among very few mentors. When Ms. Perna leaves, there will be a real void.

What makes me successful? Part of my success is because of my resilience. In my junior year of high school, our apartment caught fire and we lost everything, though thankfully no one – in my family or in the other seven apartments – was seriously injured. This was challenging both emotionally and economically, as my parents had minimal economic resources. I had SAT exams right after the fire, and I tried to stay focused on my exams and the eventual college application process. I feel sometimes that it takes a certain level of selfishness to stay committed to one's goals. My family always needs me, yet I also need to stay focused on meeting my educational goals, which is difficult to manage sometimes.

As for the future, I don't know exactly what is next. I am the kind of person, who starts on a track, but keeps my eyes and ears open for opportunities. When something is presented to me, I test myself to see if it is "right" for me. If it is, I go with it. At this time, sociology is a strong interest of mine, as well as urban planning. Who knows where this will take me?

35

"Children must be taught how to think, not what to think."
— Margaret Mead, cultural anthropologist —

Educator
Jeff Lee Byrem, consultant

03/31/2016. Based upon my experiences as an educator, there is much I can share about how education is being conducted and about the factors that contribute to student achievement. As I share with you what these are, you may be able to better identify the programs and practices within the Kennett school system and after-school tutoring and mentoring programs that you don't want to lose, and you also may be able to identify practices you might want to establish.

My experience includes a number of years as a middle school and high school biology teacher, a dozen years as an assessment and curriculum specialist and supervisor, and a two-year stint as a high school principal, for which I was hired for the sole purpose of restructuring the school under the auspices of the Elementary and Secondary Education Act, otherwise known as "No Child Left Behind (NCLB)." During a six-year hiatus from teaching, I served as a human resources and training manager at Strawbridge and Clothier and as employment manager at the University of Delaware; opportunities that provided me with an understanding of management science to which few educational administrators are ever exposed. After my retirement from my position at University of Delaware, I worked first for the Delaware County Intermediate Unit and then as a consultant on behalf of the Pennsylvania Department of Education (PDE). In these roles, I was responsible for managing the school improvement plan development and review process for all failing schools (under NCLB) in the Commonwealth of PA. My final position in education was serving as a PDE academic recovery liaison assigned to assist twelve Philadelphia charter schools that were designated by PDE as needing improvement.

The sum of my experiences—my nonscientific sample of one—has led me to believe that what makes for a successful school district is not rocket science. For three decades, American education has spawned a host of experts who claim to have found the silver bullet. Their approaches are usually based upon research; they are seldom implemented with fidelity in schools and districts with the result that the core paradigms of education have not changed very much.

A superintendent is the leader responsible for change, the essential change agent in the district. The average time served in this position in 1999 was 2.3 years, but the tenure has increased nationally to 3.6 years (2010). While this increase is notable, 3.6 years is still a short period of time in which to bring about change that is lasting. Your current superintendent, Dr. Barry Tomasetti, seems to have made a strong investment in the community and apparently plans to stay around, as have his predecessors. Not only is longevity extremely important for causing significant and lasting change within educational systems, school board members also need to maintain student achievement as one of their primary line items.

The Kennett Square community appears to have many committed leaders. I think questions need to be asked such as,

"Are successful programs dependent on a leader's personality and commitment?"
"What happens when a charismatic leader leaves?"
"Has change been sufficiently institutionalized and supported so that your effective organizational practices are sustainable?"

One of my most respected mentors once told me that in America today, "change agents stay for such short periods of time that when they leave, the changes they brought about last about as long as the exhaust from their departing car." This is something to think about.

∞

I like to apply Newton's second law of thermodynamics when thinking about organizations. His second law states that the disorder (i.e. entropy) of the universe is always increasing, which is why all physical and biological systems move toward less ordered states unless energy is used in opposition. A living thing is a complex system that requires the constant input of energy. When sufficient energy is no longer available, an organism dies. The same concept is analogous to what happens in organizations. Right now, things may be going along so well in the KCSD that it is possible success is taken for granted. However, I can guarantee that there is a huge amount of energy in the form of human and financial intervention and support that is responsible for the good things we see, and I can also guarantee that if the input of energy declines, the current success will decline.

An energy loss occurs when a leader leaves an organization, especially a leader upon whom the system has been relying to contribute a significant amount of personal energy to maintaining and enhancing school district systems and to inspiring district staff to perform at their current high levels of effort and professionalism. If the changes the leader has wrought have not been institutionalized, if a systemic culture has not been created that can continue to support success in the absence of the leader, there will be a decline in what we now see as a desirable status quo. Without the input of the focused energy of a powerful and wise leader, or without the collective and focused energy of a systemic culture, a successful system can quickly move toward a less ordered, less effective state.

One suggestion I have is to identify the positive qualities, philosophies, and practices possessed by a leader like Dr. Tomasetti. When the time comes to hire his successor, and hopefully that will not be any time soon, the interview process should attempt to determine whether or not candidates possess the key characteristics you have identified that will be required to continue the good work that has been going on for some time.

∞

In looking at the teaching process, I offer these thoughts. The usual measures of student achievement are highly suspect due to the nature of standardized testing. It is important from a public relations standpoint to identify measures of student achievement that are aligned with KCSD's curriculum objectives, and to ensure that the results of these measures are communicated in a way that can be readily understood by all members of the KCSD community, and by that, I mean parents, students, teachers, and taxpayers in general.

Curriculum objectives, what students should know and be able to do, are sometimes referred to as standards or are derived from standards that are generated at the state level. The first time the term "standard" was used in an educational context was 1913, but standards-based education did not become part of the national conversation about educational reform until after A Nation at Risk was published in 1983. It was the final report of President Reagan's National Commission on Excellence in Education, and one of its recommendations included a challenge to adopt "more rigorous and measurable standards" for learning. This challenge resulted in Pennsylvania's mid-1990s' release of "content" standards, upon which teachers are required, by statute, to base their instruction. The underlying premise of standards-based education is that standards should be challenging and that all students should master them.

Since the early years of the previous century, and unlike the premise of standards-based education, the purpose of schools, especially secondary schools, was to sort students. This remains a pervasive attitude among educators, and among Americans, which allows a teacher to place almost all of the responsibility for learning on students. Such a teacher presents information to students in as engaging a way as possible, and some kids will get it and some won't. Class rank is a vestige of this concept that still plays a powerful role in the college admission process.

Another vestige of this earlier concept is the large proportion of secondary teachers across America that does not base their lessons on standards or objectives; rather, they design lessons that present what they find interesting or think is important about a topic. When done, they then scan a list of objectives and pick those that seem aligned with the lesson already designed. This is like an archer who shoots an arrow at a barn and then paints a bull's eye around it.

The problem with this approach that standards-based education attempts to address is that disadvantaged kids often come to school without the cultural understanding of how American education works, which is an understanding that is implicit in advantaged families. As a result, in a culture where the role of a school is to sort kids, ultimately resulting in class rankings that impact college admission, disadvantaged students start way behind their advantaged classmates. In such schools, it does not matter whether or not all kids master the required standards, which means the teacher is not held accountable for implementing what the research tells us about effective instructional practices or about motivation, both of which are essential to the success of all students, especially those who are disadvantaged.

∞

In unsuccessful schools, where disadvantaged students are not achieving at desired levels, you will often hear teachers referring sympathetically to the fact that those kids can't learn because of the "baggage" they bring with them to school. Fortunately, there are schools across America filled to the brim with disadvantaged students who contradict that point of view because those students are meeting and exceeding achievement expectations despite the baggage they bring with them to school. The difference is that in those schools teachers are expecting every student, regardless of their baggage, to meet exacting standards. In order to do that, those teachers must and do employ research-based instructional strategies, apply what is known about motivation, and subliminally convey to their students that they expect those students to learn.

In school systems where educators' expectations of disadvantaged students are low, the drop-out rate is high, but on the street, many of those same students, thought to be unable to learn, have demonstrated the capacity to manage complex marketing systems related to drug trafficking that are probably beyond my capacity to understand. I think the results we see in successful systems reflect the premise that every student is capable of learning at high levels, and that these students are presented with educational experiences that lead to mastery, not only of content but of critical and creative thinking as well.

One of the instructional approaches that is highly successful with all students is the constructivist approach to learning. "Education is not the filling of a pail, but the lighting of a fire" is a quote that might belong to Plutarch but is attributed to William Butler Yeats, perhaps Ireland's most famous poet. No matter, because the phrase describes the constructivist approach to learning. It begins with the premise that every student is capable of learning and then offers the educational experiences that build thinking skills and mastery. One constructivist characteristic is to engage the student in "playing first" in a way that will allow him or her to construct meaning instead of the student just passively receiving information. I would encourage you to look for constructivist teaching strategies within KCSD so that these known-to-be-successful practices can be validated and replicated.

It is my impression that the Kennett Consolidated School District continues to recruit high quality teachers. Doing so requires compensation packages that are competitive with surrounding districts, which justifies the importance of insuring adequate funding for the district. However, higher teacher compensation does not necessarily result in higher student achievement as measured by standardized tests. The only way that I can figure out how to explain the metrics related to KCSD's overall student achievement is that Kennett's high quality teachers must be able to convey to their students that they believe their students can learn, must be applying what the research says are effective instructional practices, and are consciously or unconsciously applying what research has determined increases a student's intrinsic motivation to learn.

∞

My direct exposure to over fifteen hundred PA school, district and IU leaders over a period of four years—again, my nonscientific sample of one—has revealed what I believe is a remarkable lack of understanding regarding even the basics of human motivation, which I would think should be one of the cornerstones of an educator's foundational understanding. Plain and simple, most educators cannot explain, psychologically, why students do what they do, and I think the primary reason is that there is virtually no concerted effort on the part of schools of education to provide this information to their students! But as I've already said, KCSD's students could not be achieving as well as they are unless their teachers and tutors are personally connecting with them, providing them with some sense of control in their learning experiences, and structuring lessons so that students can ultimately feel competent. There is significant merit in identifying and validating specific classroom examples of these "three C's"—connection, competence, and control—so that those examples can be replicated and expanded.

Kennett seems to have the strong quality of believing in youth and in holding high expectations for educational success. Your examples from The Garage Community and Youth Center, Study Buddies, Young Moms and others back up the research that indicates there is a direct and apparently causative relationship between teacher expectations and student performance. I hypothesize that the achievement of KCSD students, especially those who are disadvantaged and achieve above the level that would be predicted based upon national data, is a probable result of the high expectations of teachers, tutors, and mentors.

∞

Kennett is meeting the challenge of teaching the growing number of Latinos entering the school system. In such a situation, many issues can arise unless teachers build culturally responsive learning communities. Have you identified KCSD and community practices that indicate educators understand the impact of social dominance on minority students, including the effects of stereotyping? The threat of stereotyping individuals, especially as related to standardized testing that unfortunately remains a major measure of student achievement, and social dominance have a very significant impact upon minority student achievement. The success of Latino students tells me that there must be culturally responsive practices within KCSD schools, and I highly recommend that these practices be recognized, validated and replicated.

Gary Howard in <u>We Can't Teach What We Don't Know</u> suggests seven teaching strategies that are important when there is cultural diversity in schools. Teachers and principals should:

- Affirm students in their cultural connections
- Be personally inviting
- Create physically welcoming classroom spaces
- Reinforce students for their academic development
- Accommodate instruction to the cultural and learning style difference of the students
- Manage classrooms with firm, consistent and loving control
- Create opportunities for both individual and cooperative work

You may want to see the degree to which these seven strategies are being implemented in KCSD schools. I suspect they are being implemented to a very significant degree.

In communities with effective schools, there is often a synergy between business leaders and the school district. Business leaders need to be invested in the community because their support can be important in obtaining funding, not only for the schools but for peripheral, nonprofit, after-school tutoring or mentoring programs that help those students who need additional support. And don't forget that business leaders are the ultimate beneficiaries of graduates. When schools produce competent students who can be employed directly, or who can successfully complete post-secondary education and return to town, businesses can hire a loyal workforce upon which they can rely. In addition, the recruiting of employees to a community by a business is enhanced when an HR manager can brag about the quality of the community's schools.

I think one of the things that grabbed my attention as I was preparing for our interview—and it might impress candidates thinking about working in Kennett—was the fact that Kennett High's most recent Pennsylvania School Performance Profile (SPP) score was one point higher than Unionville High School's SPP. This is a primary reason why I believe folks in the KCSD, including volunteer tutors and mentors, must be doing lots of things they should be doing and doing them well.

I have compiled an unpublished manuscript that can be made available to anyone who is interested, which addresses many of the things we touched upon in our interview. Although I am enjoying my retirement after 42+ years in education, I am always open to having a dialogue with any community member about our schools.

"Good teachers know how to bring out the best in students"

— Charles Kuralt, American journalist and author —

Kennett Consolidated School District
Mike Kelly, Kennett High School math teacher

08/18/2016. *I was born in Pottsville, PA, the county seat of Schuykill County. Growing up I remember a very active community and stories about Yuengling's, the Pottsville Maroons and author, John O'Hara. I attended St. Patrick's School and Nativity BVM High School. Education was always a strong interest of mine and thanks to the support of my community and scholarships, I attended Kutztown University and graduated with a degree in mathematics education in 1970; the only member of my family to earn a college degree. When I graduated from Kutztown University, I signed on with Yuengling's Ice Cream, which was the business where I worked summers during college. That summer I received five invitations to interview for math teacher positions. I was very impressed with Kennett and quickly accepted a position at Kennett High School (KHS). I also met one of the KHS teachers who came from Pottsville, and he told me that he felt Kennett Square resonated with many of the qualities of our mutual hometown. So, the rest is history. I have been at KHS for forty-six years. I live in Landenberg, PA with my wife, Pat. I have one son and two daughters.*

In response to your question, "What does Kennett High School do well?," I would say it is the strong educational programs and excellent teachers from kindergarten through twelfth grade. Kennett High School was recently rated thirty-second in Pennsylvania out of 1, 501 schools; this is truly remarkable. The schools also have strong support from the broader community. The numerous cultural and historical venues—

Longwood Gardens, Winterthur, Brandywine River Museum, and the Brandywine Battlefield—provide unique community enrichment. All of this challenges our school system to be our very best.

∞

Excellence inside our high school starts with meeting the students at the door. We assess the abilities of the student and start our teaching from that focus. I believe all of our teachers do this, as this approach is integral to our school district culture. We tune into each child and work to insure a solid foundation for learning.

At the same time, to be an effective teacher requires having the ability to raise the bar at a high level for all students and to challenge the student to raise the bar for him/herself. It is important to create a classroom climate where each student believes without a doubt that we want them to succeed and that we will provide the support to achieve their goals. Currently, I am the KHS mathematics department chairperson and mathematics support specialist. The later position allows me to be available during the school day to assist students one-on-one with their current math courses. We are very fortunate to have teachers and community members taking on after-school tutoring roles, as well, with the WIN program, The Garage Community and Youth Center and others.

"No Child Left Behind" enacted in 2001 presented a challenge to classroom teachers and students. Students learn differently and proficiency based on one test is not the measure of how a student is learning. "Every Student Succeeds Act" passed in December 2015 holds the hope that the individual states and local school districts will return to having local control and that there will be a broader range for assessment of a student's performance. The message should be that a test result is not a message of failure, but a means to help a student learn and progress.

As for SATs scores, I believe a student's grade point average (GPA) is a better indicator of a student's capacity to be successful in college and in life. A strong GPA speaks to a responsible work ethic and is a record of learning over a span of time. Of course, colleges are still using SATs, so I highly recommend that every college-bound student take an SAT prep course to learn about how one is being tested and evaluated.

I also serve as the senior class advisor. Yes, each class has its own personality, some focusing on sports, another on volunteering. They tend to pick up the spirit of the broader community and are influenced by what they are experiencing in the community, as well as in the school.

In response to your question, "How do we help teachers continuously improve their teaching?" I would say that there are several ways. Pennsylvania teachers are required to complete 180 credit hours over five years to maintain their teaching licenses. Teachers have the opportunity to belong to various professional organizations at both the state and federal level and thus have the opportunity to be exposed to the cutting edge of our profession. Fortunately, our school system has followed best practices for professional development long before it was required. As an example, we have had an induction program (assigning a new teacher to a seasoned teacher for one-on-one mentoring) in place long before it became a state mandated program.

I am not ready for retirement as I still am highly engaged and committed to the work I am doing. It is rewarding to have former students come back and let me know about their successes and accomplishments. We have a good number of teachers who have been with the district for a long time. I would say that the pride we feel for being involved in a profession with a school system focused on excellence keeps us here.

"Each day of our lives we make deposits in the memory banks of our children."

— Charles R. Swindoll, Evangelical Christian pastor —

Kennett Education Foundation

Bob George, co-founder

02/11/2016. *In 1955, my family moved to the Kennett area because of my father's job with DuPont. I attended Kennett Middle School, had Mrs. Rupert as a teacher in the 5th grade, and had a crush on Jessica Savitch (one of the first TV women news casters) in the 7th grade. My father's job moved us to Geneva, Switzerland, where I attended 2nd and 3rd Form before returning to Kennett for my last three years of high school year. I received a degree in industrial engineering from Penn State University with a Navy scholarship and served four years driving ships, including four deployments to Viet Nam. I returned to the area and secured a position at the DuPont Company, where I worked for forty-two years. I was given assignments in Virginia; the Nemours building in Wilmington, Delaware; Geneva, Switzerland; mid-town Manhattan; and Chestnut Run. I retired two years ago. I married my college sweetheart and had 5 children, who also attended Kennett schools for some of their education. My background of living in many different communities has enabled me to compare and contrast educational systems, and has led me to take a leadership role with The Kennett Education Foundation.*

The Mission: The Kennett Education Foundation (KEF) is a community-based, nonprofit foundation, committed to supporting and enriching the educational experience in the Kennett community by providing educational grants to educators and students and scholarships to graduating seniors.

The Goal: The goal of the Kennett Education Foundation is to support and invest in the academic success of our children to create a first class academic school system, which in turn strengthens our community.

In 1989, the Kennett Education Foundation had its seed planting when the Kennett High School Class of 1964 celebrated its 25th anniversary. The class decided to recognize those teachers who had the most impact on their lives. They acknowledged Nate Kendig for being their favorite teacher and Ken Webb, the assistant principle, as having the greatest effect on their lives. The Webb Award is still being funded by the Class of 1964, and is awarded to the outstanding citizen of the graduating class.

In 2000, Dr. Rudy Karkosak became superintendent of the Kennett schools. Previously, when Dr. Karkosak was the principal of Wilmington High School in Delaware, he was offered a large donation for the school by Harry Levin, owner of the Happy Harry's drugstore chain, to recognize both his memorable high school experience and Clarence Fulmer, the principal of the high school during the 1950s and 1960s. Dr. Karkosak, unfortunately, was unable to accept the generous donation as he had no mechanism to take the money. By the time he had formed an educational nonprofit, Harry Levin had died, and his family decided to redirect his money to other initiatives.

Dr. Karkosak, in his role as superintendent of the Kennett schools, sought to prevent the scenario from reoccurring. Dr. Karkosak asked me, because of my experience with the Class of 1964 award, and Skip Reynolds, an influential member of the school board, to join him in attending a presentation in Harrisburg conducted by the head of the Altoona Education Foundation. Simply stated, the business plan was to accept donations from their teachers, and the money would then be returned to the teachers and used to purchase the needed classroom materials and tools that the school wouldn't fund. The teachers were able to write-off the donation as a tax deduction, and the classrooms would be stocked with the needed supplies. After discovering how their organization worked, Skip and I just smiled at one another as our Kennett competitive juices started flowing. We knew we could build a better organization.

∞

In 2001, the Kennett Education Foundation was born. The Kennett Education Foundation, a 501(c)(3) nonprofit, has partnered with the Kennett Consolidated School District to encourage innovative ideas, invest in programs that improve academic progress, promote family involvement and recognize the outstanding achievements of educators.

During my eight years as board president, I held my primary role as one of looking at the "white spaces" within the field of education. In other words, what is missing that needs to be addressed? What and who needs to be recognized to hold up models of excellence? What needs to be supported to enrich the educational experience?

The Kennett Education Foundation is an interface between the school district and the community. We offer an unbiased "voice" and reflect the message that needs to be heard from the broader perspective. The school is the social, emotional and intellectual center of the town. The winter basketball games, the summer track meets, and the musical plays provide a stage to watch our next generation become all they can be. When Dr. Karkosak's replacement was being sought, Dr. Barry Tomasetti was asked to apply for the superintendent position. Dr. Tomasetti witnessed the great attributes of Kennett, but he also saw the poverty and poor test scores. A retiring superintendent from the Main Line provided Dr. Tomasetti with his opinion. Yes, Kennett has a lot of kids who have problems, but the town just wraps its arms around them and ensures that they don't fail.

We have continued the Class of 1964's idea of supporting teachers, not only through recognition of outstanding performance, but also in offering grants to help teachers fill the voids and focus on creative solutions. We have provided over $50,000 to help teachers become trained in the STEM educational process. We supported the Kennett football resurgence by being the fiscal agent for fundraising. We filled a similar fiscal role for Communities That Care, which addresses drug use, when the state funding ended. We offer over $25,000 in scholarship money to students who fulfill donors' legacy criteria. In the past, we provided $10,000 to a teacher who taught film-making, and, more recently, gave $10,000 to a teacher who is providing after-school student engagement and competition.

Our budget is small, between $50,000 and $75,000; therefore, we have no paid employees. We hold approximately $750,000 in the bank for grants, ongoing legacy scholarships, and awards.

∞

The Kennett Education Foundation relies on donations to fund the many programs that we support. These contributions originate from individuals, businesses (including matching gifts programs), foundations and other organizations such as the United Way and the Chester County Community Foundation that align with our mission and the success of our initiatives. Our biggest fundraiser is an annual dinner. Many Kennett teachers attend this event, which gives them the opportunity to appreciate the community as it celebrates their vocation.

As we are approached to receive funds, we assure that the funder has the best fit with our organization. We keep in mind that there are other educational organizations in the community; i.e. after-school programming. In our interaction, we assure that both the educational need and the funder are being satisfied. At this time, we are our own fiscal manager through committee, and this seems to be working for us. Some of our funds are managed by the Chester County Community Foundation. We are always seeking the best return on our funds, and, at this time, we have no managing fees.

∞

Our greatest challenge in the next few years is assuring that we are meeting the needs of our wide spectrum of students. With Mary D. Lang Kindergarten having 50% Hispanics, Kennett is a great place to offer English as a Second Language classes, the after-school WIN program and others. We also address the needs of the academically talented by offering nineteen AP classes, which is more than most schools. We will need to focus on the group in-between. How do we get them excited about education? These students slide through, but how can we help them to become all they can be? These formative years are so important, and everyone has a hot button. Every student is unique, and it is our job to find each and every one's hot button. We also need to teach the social skills and foster interests and talents that will move the students towards productive and meaningful lives.

Kennett Education Foundation continues to evolve because we have a board turnover. We have a parent representative from each school in the district, and as their child moves up to the next school or graduates, new members come on. And some of the members stay around. Each board term is 3 years and you can't serve more than three terms. This keeps the board fresh and brings new ideas. One of our most popular events is the Monster Mash Dash, a 5K scheduled on the Halloween weekend. The kids design the t-shirts for the race and run in their costumes.

There are many ways we measure our success by answering these questions: How well does the town and gown integrate? Do people realize how awesome our school system is? Do we have a vibrant board? What is the quality of our teachers? Are the kids all graduating and going on to further their education? Are the realtors saying, *"Yes, you can live there and send your kids to a school where everyone is like your child, but if you want a real American education, Kennett is your school"*? Do we have the money to do what we need to do? But, most of all we measure our success by the look on the graduates' faces in June as they see the whole world in front of them, and they know that they are prepared to take it on.

"If we are to teach real peace in the world, we shall have to begin with the children"

— Mahatma Gandhi, peace activist —

Kennett Square Police Department
Albert McCarthy, former chief of police

03/24/2016. *It's funny you asked me if I lived here my entire life. The answer is, most of it. My family is originally from Philadelphia. After WWII, my father's company transferred him to Baltimore, MD, and then to Wilmington, DE. We would have settled in the Wilmington area, but neither Dad nor Mom wanted to live in Delaware. Back in those days, to get to Baltimore from Philadelphia, you would drive right through the center of Kennett Square. State and Cypress Streets were the southbound and northbound lanes of U.S. Route 1. There was no Route 1 bypass or I-95. Back in those days, we would often stop in Kennett since it was only 15 to 20 minutes from Wilmington. Both my parents thought it was a great place to raise children. It was the kind of community where your kids left the house in the morning, met friends at the playground, went home for lunch and home for dinner. Every mother watched out for every child.*

Like most communities, society started to change. The playground (recreational center) was torn down to make room for a new school. Economic conditions required both parents to work. Kids were experimenting with drugs. As for me, my parents always stressed education. By 1972, my five older siblings had already graduated from college; two sisters were teachers and three brothers were naval officers. My other two brothers enlisted—one in the Navy and one in the Army. This put five brothers in the service during the height of the

Vietnam War. After one year of college, I tried to enlist but was told by the Navy that I couldn't because no more than five members of the same family could be in active duty at the same time. Rather than return to college, I decided to remain home and work to help with the family expenses. My plan was to return to college later.

I never even considered becoming a police officer. I first went into road construction, and I enjoyed seeing what I accomplished at the end of each day. I also became a volunteer fireman with the Kennett Fire Company. While laid off during the winter of 1971, Fire Chief Ralph Hunter asked me if I would work as a Chester County police radio dispatcher. They were so short-handed there were few days off, and the job paid so little that no one would take it. I tried it and was hooked—something about the challenge of the job. I enjoyed the officers in the field. I worked with Bill Davis and Dick Posey through police radio and the fire companies. They were Kennett Square police officers and Avondale firemen. Both of them persuaded me to apply for an open position with the Kennett Square Police Department. I scored well on the test and, on November 14, 1972, Dick waited for me to come out of an interview with the town council. At 9:20 pm, I told Dick I would be appointed at the next council meeting. Dick went home and changed into uniform for the midnight shift. I went home and told Mom and Dad. I remember Mom commenting, "I have five in the service with Vietnam then you do this. But what could happen in Kennett Square?" At 2:38 am on November 15, 1972, dispatcher Jay Groce called me and said Kennett Square Police missed their roll call, and they can't get anyone to look for them. Believing they probably forgot to turn on the portable radios, I went to the police station where I found Bill and Dick shot. Both officers were pronounced dead when we got them to the hospital. Because both Bill and Dick encouraged me so much, I decided I owed it to them to try policing.

∞

I served as a Kennett Square police officer from January 1973 until 2007. At the time I was first appointed, there was no law requiring any training. For most police officers, it was on-the-job training. After being sworn in, I met with the mayor and town council and they proposed that if I enrolled in a training class, the borough would pay my salary. So I was the first Kennett Square police officer to complete training at the PA State Police Academy, but I was not the last. The town council must have believed the training provided valuable instruction on how to deal problems facing the community, because soon the entire department completed the training. Kennett Square was one of the first fully trained police departments in Chester County.

I became chief of the Kennett Square Police Department in 1988 and retired in 2007. I then founded the Kennett Township Police Department in 2007 and served as its chief until retiring in May 2015. Kennett Square does seem to employ a large number of officers for its size; the most at one time was 15, including 6 part-timers. The borough presently has 12 full-time and 3 part-time officers. The township has 4 full-time and 2 part-time officers. It's a safe place to live now.

The borough is located in the very southeast corner of Pennsylvania, bordering Delaware and Maryland with New Jersey close by. Major highways connect the Kennett area to Philadelphia, Baltimore, Lancaster, Reading, and Wilmington. All of this movement brings traffic, which brings crime. Over the years, many of the individuals arrested were from out of the area. At one time, drugs flowed through town easily since they went unchecked. There were also five bars, not restaurants, on the main street.

Homicide was not something you expected to see in a community the size of Kennett Square. Yet, in the first half of my tenure as chief, we had ten killings. Yes, the police department was good, and they handled every case as professionally as any investigator could. Arrests resulted in convictions, but the conduct of those visiting the community didn't seem to change. Surveys told us the local residents felt safe. Several times the police organized neighborhood watches. When the neighborhood watches fell apart, residents said they weren't concerned as long as drug dealers kill drug dealers. Certain apartment complexes in the area became drive-in drug stores—LSD, heroin, marijuana and others were readily available. The police couldn't do a lot about this because we had the serious crimes to solve. Major drug investigations consumed a lot of time, as did assaults and homicides.

At the same time, a group of residents and businessmen wanted to revitalize the town. I was sent to a seminar on this where I learned people want three things from their community:

1. They want to feel secure
2. They want to have pride in their community
3. They want economic development.

I took this information to the mayor, the council and the businessmen interested in revitalizing the town and translated it into three things:

1. For people to feel safe they need police. The police department needed to be re-evaluated.
2. To have pride in the community there needed to be effective code enforcement – not just a building inspector that issues building permits.
3. You can't get to #3 if you don't have #1 and #2.

Using this information, Marshall Newton and other churches aided in conducting a community-wide survey, which produced the YMCA and Nixon Park. Council developed the parking garage. All of this brought the first Genesis building and later the second Broad Street building.

The police department continued to handle the major crimes but was always looking for ways to better police the area. New York City developed a "Zero Tolerance" policy for any crime and, after studying the

NYC program, the Kennett Square police department adapted the policy to fit Kennett Square. The idea was that individuals were not going to come into our community and pick on our residents or trash the area. The police met with many groups so we could explain how the program would work and when it would start. The Philadelphia Inquirer assigned a reporter to investigate whether or not the police were targeting the Spanish population. She quickly learned the Spanish were actually in favor of the strict policy because these criminals were giving the Spanish a bad name. The police presence was amped up in the community with the goal of building relationships with the residents. Police on foot patrol were told to ask, "What can we do for you?" The police department adopted a new slogan, "Caring for Our Community".

The police department and the Kennett school district collaborated on handling the students' behavior. For any misdemeanor committed on school property, the police were called in but the school administration was able to meet with the parents and discuss the offense. In most cases, depending on the severity of the crime, the discipline was handled by the schools. Within a short amount of time, student assaults and bullying greatly declined.

Later, when students became impressed with gangs and gang action, the school administrators and police educated themselves together and the school adopted policies on using gang signs or wearing gang colors. I credit Dr. Larry Bosley with his stance – a child can't get an education if he/she has to worry about a fight breaking out in front of them.

∞

When I think back over the years of my tenure in the police department, I realize that my greatest achievement is tied in with my interaction and collaboration with the committed groups focused on making the Kennett area better. These groups include Study Buddies for the kids who needed tutoring, CTC, Bridging the Community, After-The-Bell, The Garage, DARE, the church youth groups, La Comunidad Hispana, and the YMCA. While involved in these groups, the youth were kept busy and learned to respect each other regardless of race, color, or creed. Juvenile crime was nearly eliminated.

In response to your question about youth in the next three to five years, we need to pay attention to them. We need to praise the good work that is being done. We need to encourage them to get involved. Tell them always be willing to aid anyone – you will never know when you may be that person that needs someone else's help. Policing a borough is a community operation!

"Children are the living messages we send to a time we will not see."

— Neil Postman, The Disappearance of Childhood (1982) —

Kennett Square Police Department
Corporal William (Bill) Holdsworth, second in command

04/19/2016. **Background of Chief Edward A. Zunino:** *I was raised in Kennett Square, PA and attended St. Patrick's School and Kennett High School. I joined the Kennett Square Auxiliary Police Force in April of 1974 and attended the Police Academy the following year. I started working part-time for the Kennett Square Police Department in August of 1975 and went full-time January 1976. I was Second in Command under Chief Albert McCarthy and, for a period of time, also conducted criminal Investigations. When Chief McCarthy retired in 2007, I became Chief of Kennett Square Police Department. I live in West Grove with my wife, Lois. I have two daughters, one son and three grandchildren*. Chief Zunino requested Corporal William Holdsworth to be interviewed for The Story of Kennett: Shaping Our Future One Child at a Time.*

Background of Corporal William (Bill) Holdsworth: *Unionville, PA was my home town growing up. I graduated from Unionville High School in 1990 followed by attendance at Delaware Community College. I helped Kevin Coyle with his landscaping business during that time, and started my own landscaping business in 1992. I had two friends who had become police officers, and their strong commitment to this work sparked my interest. I attended the Police Academy in 1995 and was hired part-time by the Kennett Police Department in 1997. I kept my landscaping business for a while but after being hired as a full-time police officer in 1998, I wasn't able to keep up both jobs. I married Debbie in 2008, who had two children, Alex now 19 years and Alecia 17 years. We now have our two and one-half year old son, Nico added to our family.*

The mission of the Kennett police is to preserve life and property and to maintain a peaceful community. We have fully moved to community policing, starting with the leadership of Chief Albert McCarthy and continuing with the leadership of Chief Edward Zunino. This has made a huge difference in the reduction of arrests, drugs and gangs in the community. We get involved in the community and advocate keeping the lines of communication open.

The Kennett police have a great relationship with the youth as a result of our community presence. We stay connected with the youth through community programs and organizations such as Study Buddies, After-The-Bell, and The Garage Community and Youth Center.

We are pleased to work with Carter CDC/Study Buddies to host an annual National Night Out on the first Tuesday in August. National Night Out is an annual community-building campaign that promotes police-community partnerships and neighborhood camaraderie to make our neighborhoods safer and better places to live. We block off East Linden Street, and officers and youth make presentations and take part in activities. My favorite memory was when the students in Study Buddies made cards, similar to baseball cards, with each police officer's photo and a list of his/her personal interests. The students then made trades to assure they had the entire card collection.

∞

We have twelve full-time officers, three part-time officers, two parking meter officers and two administrative staff. One of the full-time police officers, Sarah Capaccio, is assigned to the Kennett school district full-time. This came about after the Kennett Square's police department and the Kennett Consolidated School District collaborated to apply for a state grant to fund a school resource officer. In 2014, we received the grant for $55,000 for the first year of the program and half that amount for the second year. To continue, the cost will be shared between the school district and the Borough of Kennett Square. Officer Capaccio works full-time in the district's two borough schools – the Mary D. Lang Kindergarten Center and the Kennett High School – under the command of the police department and in concert with the school administration. She also makes weekly visits to After-The-Bell at the Kennett Middle School. Previously, officers patrolled the schools regularly, but sporadically. Officer Capaccio's presence provides better security monitoring, the ability to address concerns proactively, and the opportunity to build positive relationships with the students.

We make regular friendly visits to The Garage Community and Youth Center in the center of town. Because of our interaction, the scene has really changed – from the students escaping out the back door when we arrived to them now coming up to us to have an interaction and even ask for a favor. Just last week, one of the students asked a favor. He wanted to surprise his girlfriend with an unusual and grand invitation to the

Kennett High School Prom. After receiving permission from The Garage administration and the parents of this student, we agreed to grant him his favor. Two police officers entered The Garage and went to this student and handcuffed him, telling him he needed to come with them. The student put up the normal fuss as we brought him to our police car that was parked out front. At this time, the girlfriend looked shocked and ran out after him, only to immediately see a huge sign that other students were holding up behind the car, saying, "Will you go to the prom with me?" This was definitely going the extra mile on the student's and police department's part, but I am sure it will be a memory that will continue to build a trusting relationship.

∞

To address the growing Latino population in the borough, we continue to try to recruit bi-lingual officers. Oscar Rosado was with us for eight years, and this year he became a Chester County detective, which is kudos to him, but sad for us. We have one part-time officer, John Ortiz, who speaks Spanish, and he also works for Kennett Township Police Department. We always want to have effective communication and try to accommodate a given situation. We will call on John Ortiz to help us out, or Oscar Rosado or even my wife, who speaks the local Spanish. It is difficult to use the Language Phone Line, because the accent and choice of words vary from our native resident's language.

We try to take every opportunity to educate the Latino residents about us being here to help them. La Comunidad Hispana has held several forums for Latinos to ask questions and become familiar with the Kennett police. Again, I recently participated in a panel discussion with three other police representatives at an EL Café, which was organized by Maribel Gonzalez from the Kennett school district. There are misconceptions about the police that we are trying to change. One of the questions I receive quite often is, "Is it true that you deport residents who do not have a driver's license?" I quickly respond by saying, "We are not the INS. If you are breaking a driving law, then we need to give you a ticket, just as we do with all residents." I emphasize that we invite residents to talk to us if they are having problems related to being victimized or have other concerns. The door is open for communication and mediation.

Yes, we ARE the town of festivals, and that is a good thing! Non-residents come join in the fun of a small town. In April, we have The Kennett Area YMCA Healthy Kid's Day along with an art festival; in May, we have Cinco de Mayo, The Kennett Run, and the Memorial Day Parade; in September we have the Mushroom Festival; in November we have the Holiday Parade; and New Year's Eve we have the Mushroom Drop. The cost of police and public works is covered by the respective festival funders. When large crowds gather, the police department is vigilant and needs to be prepared for anything. Gangs and drugs are always on the forefront, however at this time, most of the serious Chester County offenders are incarcerated.

In response to your question about looking ahead and what we see on the horizon, I say it could be anything. With some of the terrorist attacks, in various forms, around the country, our police department anticipates and prepares. We have active shooter training every year, when we participate in mock drills. The Chester County District Attorney's Office along with the Department of Emergency Services conduct these trainings.

Nine of us have been trained to participate on the Municipal Drug Task Force (MDTF). This group handles drug problems specific to Chester County. The MDTF is made up of police officers from local police departments, all with significant experience in drug investigations and with knowledge about local drug problems. The MDTF officers work with the DA's Drug Strike Force to take down local drug dealers and gather crime-related intelligence across Chester County. And, with the deployment of Narcan/Naloxone as an antidote for opiate overdoses, we have saved three lives in the past year. We also have the Take-Back Prescription Drug program because the drug addiction and misuse of prescription drugs is growing.

The Kennett police department works well with other area police departments. Kennett Township (which circles the Kennett borough) has recently formed their own police department, so we often work hand and hand. In closing, I would say that the Kennett police department is a great place to work. Chief Zunino strongly supports the community policing model, which makes our work more rewarding and productive. I guess we are all believers that this is the best way to stay a safe and peaceful community.

40

"Good people make bad decisions. It doesn't necessarily make them bad people. Therefore, even defendants deserve the courts' respect."

— Judge Maisano, presiding over the Chester County
Magisterial District in Pennsylvania —

Chester County Magisterial District Judge

Honorable Daniel J. Maisano

06/12/2016. *I was born in Wilmington, Delaware and lived in a single parent household until I was 12 years old. My mother then remarried a 2nd lieutenant in the Army, which afforded me the opportunity to be schooled in Italy for two years. On return to the US, I attended Salesianum High School for one year and then graduated from Dundalk High School, in Dundalk, MD. I received my undergraduate degree in Political Science from the University of Delaware in 1973 and I received my law degree from Delaware Law School in 1978. Even though I took and passed the Pennsylvania Bar Exam in 1979, I didn't practice law until five years later due to the economy and the glut of practicing attorneys. For the five years from passing the bar and starting my own practice, I owned and operated a real estate brokerage office in Delaware. Deciding that if I was ever going to practice law, it was now or never, I went to Media, Pennsylvania, the county seat in Delaware County, rented office space on a Friday, ordered my letterhead and business cards, and was practicing law by Monday. In 1989, I moved my law office to Marshall Street, Kennett Square, where I also lived. In 1994, I became the Magisterial District Judge for the Kennett Square area and served in that role until 2016. I am currently practicing law in shared facilities with my wife's business IKOR of Brandywine Valley. Recently I also began teaching my first law related course at Wilmington University with another course already scheduled for the fall. I live in the area with my wife, Patricia Maisano.*

My court, Magisterial District Court 15-03-04, has jurisdiction over Kennett Square Borough and Kennett, Newlin, East Marlborough, Pennsbury, Pocopson and Birmingham Townships. In the 22 years I served as an MDJ, my court disposed of over 100,000 matters. During my 22-year tenure, the district court was located on East Birch Street, North Broad Street and now it's located in New Garden Township next to the Penn National Bank on West Cypress Street.

As far as my interactions with the Kennett youth, I primarily heard court cases that dealt with truancy, followed by non-traffic offenses, involving disorderly conduct, trespassing, and under-age drinking. (Other than possession of a small amount of marijuana, drug cases were dealt with at juvenile court in West Chester.) The number of court hearings for juveniles was much less in my earlier years as judge, because the schools took on the responsibility of addressing many of the issues, such as fighting on school property and intoxication on school property, in house, without police intervention. This took a turn with the advent of the Zero Tolerance policies of the late 1990s; we saw a dramatic increase in citations issued to our youth and resulting appearances in court. The Kennett High School administration and the Kennett Square police chief made a wise decision when they placed a Kennett police officer on the school premises the past couple of years. This proactive form of community policing has dramatically decreased the number of incidents at the schools and reduced the number of citations issued to our youth on school property.

∞

As far as underage drinking goes, unlike West Chester with its university, Kennett has not had a lot of underage drinking cases. It is a tough offense, as Title 18, Section 6308 directs losing one's driver's license for ninety days, which ends up being more of a hardship on the parent than on the child. I am grateful for the diversionary programs authorized by many of the local police departments. Even though it is discretionary with the police officer writing the citation to recommend a diversionary program, the Kennett police officers seem to understand the value of this approach for first-time offenders. In place of losing a driver's license, the youth attends an Alcohol Awareness class sponsored by Council on Addictive Diseases in Exton, PA, or takes the Third Millennium on-line course, receiving a certificate of completion which the offender presents to the court along with proof he/she has completed 20 – 30 hours of court mandated community service. The Diversionary Program offers a better teaching lesson than following the book to the letter, because it allows the youthful offenders many hours to contemplate the cost of underage alcohol consumption while they are performing their community service project and/or attending the alcohol awareness classes, in person or on-line. Upon successful completion of the program, the citation is amended to a disorderly conduct citation or a borough ordinance violation citation which the offender then pleads guilty and pays the requisite fine and costs, thus avoiding the driver's license suspension.

The zero tolerance policy has been a challenge because along with it comes unintended consequences. In addition to a school suspension one also receives a citation for a violation of a borough ordinance or a violation of the Pennsylvania crimes code, which can negatively impact one's job prospects in the future, as well as qualification for college admission and financial aid.

As I hear court cases, I tell the parents accompanying their child, "Good kids make bad choices. It doesn't make them bad kids." The question being, "Am I learning from this mistake?" I also give a strong message to the youth standing before me. I am in a unique position to help a youth look at the long-term consequences of his/her decisions today. I recall one case, when I challenged a youth, who was continually being brought to court for "dumb stuff." I gave a harsh talk, asking him to think about his vision for his future 5 and 10 years down the line. Did he want to be sitting in front of me in handcuffs on his way to Chester County Prison or did he want to have a wife, children, and a nice home where they enjoyed family gatherings and could go out and attend their children's soccer games? I told him to go home and look at himself in the mirror and ask himself what type of future he wanted for himself and then start making the right choices to achieve that future. The choices we make today will have an impact now and many years into the future. Years later, this youth came to visit me at the district court and told me that he wanted to thank me. He said he was now married, had a couple of children and owned a home, and yes, he was going to his children's soccer games.

∞

In the case of summary violations like disorderly conduct, harassment and truancy, we welcome the opportunity, at the suggestion of the affiant, to allow a youthful offender to perform community service in lieu of having a conviction on his or her record that can negatively impact their life years in the future.

My main frustration with the system was always my inability to do more for those students who came before me with chronic truancy violations. Our options, as magisterial district judges, to deal with truancy are very limited. Truancy is, more often than not, a symptom of a larger problem or problems. It could be bullying at school, abuse, physical or sexual, a home or a mental illness issue such as depression or anxiety attacks. Failure to address these issues results in an uneducated, unengaged student whose career and income producing opportunities in life are severely limited. This may result in a young woman becoming financially dependent on her spouse and unable to leave a physically abusive relationship, especially where children are concerned. For the male, the opportunity to obtain financial security through the sale of drugs or other criminal enterprises becomes extremely appealing. In the end, we all pay more to incarcerate those criminals who have resorted to crime because they were unable to obtain gainful employment because of their lack of education. More resources need to be allocated to address the truancy issue so that our youth can graduate and compete in the job market with the best opportunity for success. That way, we all benefit.

As a judge over the last 22 years, I have tried to make a positive impact on my community. I have tried to impart the wisdom of my age to the youth that have appeared before me with the hope they can lead better, more productive lives without having to make many of the mistakes we, their elders, had to make. I have always tried to be fair and impartial. I treated everyone who came before me; witness, prosecutor, defense attorney, law enforcement and even the defendant with respect. Not everyone who commits a crime is an evil bad person. Like our youth, even adults sometimes make bad choices; it doesn't make them a bad person. There is the law and there is justice. For my legacy, I hope to be remembered as a jurist who knew the law and who applied the law, but who did so in a fair and just manner.

"Every child is a different kind of flower, and all together they make the world a beautiful garden."

— Author Unknown —

Historic Kennett Square
Mary Hutchins, Main Street manager

05/10/2016. *I was born and raised in Montgomery County. I graduated from Lansdale Catholic and then from Ursinus College with a degree in English. I was a para-legal for a short time and then moved into the journalism field when I worked as a stringer for the Perkasie News Herald, PA. My husband's job moved us to this area in 1988, and, soon after, I took a staff writer's job with The Kennett Paper. David Yeats Thomas was the editor and Jaime Blaine was the publisher. I eventually moved into the editor position and stayed with The Kennett Paper until 2000. After a short time with Suzi McCoy and working for her marketing firm, I was ready to move into a full-time position. I was offered the Main Street Manager position in 2001 for Historic Kennett Square, and here I am still excited about Kennett Square and committed to helping it move forward to its next edge. I am married to Bill and we have three daughters, Sarah, Mary, Lizzie and two lovely grandchildren Charlie and Eloise.*

Our Mission: To actively support and enrich community vitality and pride, to help preserve the historic district and small town atmosphere, to promote economic and positive, productive relationships within Kennett Square and the surrounding townships.

Historic Kennett Square is a Main Street organization. Main Street is a downtown revitalization model developed by the National Trust for Historic Preservation in 1980. Main Street is a comprehensive, community-based revitalization approach. Communities across the U.S. apply its four key components with great success:

1. *Design* means getting Main Street into top physical shape. Capitalizing on its best assets such as historic buildings and the traditional downtown layout is just part of the story. An inviting atmosphere can be created through window displays, parking areas, signs, sidewalks, street lights, and landscaping; good design conveys a visual message about what Main Street is and what it has to offer.

2. *Promotion* means selling the image and promise of Main Street to all prospects. By marketing the district's unique characteristics through advertising, retail promotional activities, special events, and marketing campaigns; an effective promotion strategy forges a positive image for shoppers, investors, new businesses and visitors.

3. *Organization* means getting everyone working towards common goals. The common-sense formula of a volunteer-driven program and an organizational structure of board and committees assisting professional management can ease the difficult work of building consensus and cooperation among the varied groups that have a stake in the district.

4. *Economic Restructuring* means finding new or better purposes for Main Street enterprises, helping existing downtown businesses expand and recruiting new ones, a successful Main Street converts unused space into productive property and sharpens the competitiveness of its businesses.

When I started with Historic Kennett Square, I went to training in Harrisburg for Main Street Management. I was fortunate to have David Teel, then the current borough manager promoting further PA State funding, which ended up providing Main Street funding for five additional years after being funded in 1986 for three years. We also had the building at 106 W. State Street, where I currently have my office. Now we continue onward as any other nonprofit. Our Annual Brew Fest provides one-third of our funds and, in addition, we are a line item in the Kennett Borough and Kennett Township's annual budget. We write and receive grants and have individual sponsorships. Our budget today is $460,000.

Soon after I started working for Historic Kennett Square, I joined the board's philosophy that it was important to have events that represented the whole community. I supported the beginning of the Cinco de Mayo festival, which was spearheaded by La Comunidad Hispana, and also the Martin Luther King (MLK) CommUNITY Breakfast, which was introduced by Mabel Thompson, a community leader. These events still continue and have grown. The Farmer's Market is another forum for community gathering of all walks of life and has been going strong since 2000. Historic Kennett Square also supports the Art Strolls on the first Friday of the month, the Memorial Day Parade, the Halloween Parade, and the Holiday Parade and carriage rides; all ways for families to come into town and commune.

In the past year, we have started Third Thursday, when we block off State Street and families come and dine and play in the square of Kennett Square. It is a delight to see young children riding their bicycles and enjoying the time with the larger crowd. The annual Brew Fest continues to be an event that brings visitors to our town, who participate in a responsible fashion. It has been the impetus for three breweries coming to town; they will bring in even more visitors.

There is a nice history of how our Kennett Square revitalization got started. First, The Kennett Square Main Street Association was incorporated in 1986. This organization was active for about three years. Michael Walker was president, Dave Torelli was vice president and Tim Umbreit was secretary/treasurer. Other board members included Wilson Whittle, Peter Temple, Neil Joines and Carol Merrick, among others.

In 1995, the Kennett Square Main Street Association was changed to the Kennett Square Revitalization Task Force (KSRTF), and in 1997, that organization bought the building at 106 W. State Street.

In February of 2000, KSRTF hired Doug Harris as its first coordinator, and he was charged with finding tenants for the building. Doug resigned later that year, and I was hired full-time in early 2001 as the executive director of KSRTF.

In 2003, the board of directors changed the name of the organization to Historic Kennett Square because "Historic" was the number one Google search for people looking for a place to visit.

My primary role as Main Street manager is to promote economic development. I have been a champion of the town since 2000, and I join others in believing that we have something unique here in Kennett Square that needs to be promoted. I really don't have to recruit new businesses coming into town. I have a waiting list of applicants, who would like to locate here in Kennett Square. Most of the applicants are dedicated business folks, who have developed a plan and are serious about creating a viable business. They also have a vibrant social media presence.

One of our talismans of success is how well Historic Kennett Square works with the Kennett Borough. I am considered a team member and actually they treat me like a de-facto borough employee. I regularly attend meetings as we jointly look at our plans for the future. Many developers or businesses will come to me first to explore an idea for a venture in town then I can be the intermediary for them at these meetings. Our goal is to meet the holistic needs of a small town. We still have several undeveloped properties that could meet some of these needs. Economically, we could always accommodate more restaurants, as we now are becoming a weekend destination dining town. We also are supporting Chester County's VISTA 2025, which will bring in more offices and businesses along Route 1 and will provide employment for those who would like to live in our family-friendly town. Socially, we also would benefit from affordable apartments for the single millennial who are working at the local businesses. Affordable senior housing is another need. We work well with Kennett Area Restaurant Merchant Association (KARMA.) My message continues to be: It is my job to get people to town, and your job as merchants is to get them to the cash register. Most of the businesses here are doing well and are enjoying the small town atmosphere.

What makes Kennett Square so special is that residents love this town. They support the town in so many ways on a daily basis. As I look around at other small towns in the area, I don't feel that same commitment that is expressed in this town.

∞

As we look at the future, there are several challenges we face. We will need to guide and manage the development to prevent over-crowding and sustain a balance of town accommodations. We would like to have more diversity present on our boards and in our leadership. We also will continue to face funding issues, as will most nonprofits in the area. I continue to attend training in Harrisburg with the PA Downtown Center Organization (PDC) and this is helpful in addressing some of these challenges. Recently, we contracted with an outside consultant to help us work through a strategic plan. It is so important that we are ahead of the stream of change and are instrumental in guiding that change.

If I had a windfall of money, I would enjoy starting an art and culture center. It would bring another dimension to town and could be a great meeting site for all aspects of community life. I have had community members approach me on this idea. It will take the right location and funds to make this happen, and a group willing to support it.

As for the youth that you are referring to in your book, I hear quite often that kids who have been raised in this town appreciate this town experience. There is a pride about being part of this community and yes, some come back and raise their kids here. It is a great family town!

"Adults are the first and foremost teachers of love, peace, truth, tolerance, happiness and spirituality to their children. No school on Earth can ever replace them."

— Robert Muller, recipient of the UNESCO Prize for Education in 1989 —

Borough of Kennett Square
Dan Maffei, borough council president

06/27/2016. *I was born in Philadelphia, PA and before school age, my family moved to Newlin Township, where I attended the Unionville-Chadds Ford schools through my graduation in 1988. I attended Penn State and enrolled in communications classes, but left when my father's friend, who was a landscape designer, asked me to help him with his business. I really enjoyed the work of developing landscape plans, so I continued working five years in his office. Realizing that I needed to understand more about plants to be a successful designer, I attended Longwood Gardens' Professional Gardener Program, a two-year diploma program in ornamental horticulture. Following graduation in 1996, I moved to the borough of Kennett Square and worked at W.D.Wells & Associates located in West Grove, PA for nearly fourteen years. In 2011, I started my own business, Maffei Landscape Design, LLC and have been able to successfully promote my business on social media and through customer referrals. I also teach as an adjunct instructor at Longwood Gardens for the same program from which I graduated and in their Continuing Education Department. In 2005, I was appointed to the Kennett Historical Commission, serving as the chair, and became acquainted with the borough council through the delivery of my monthly Historical Commission reports. I decided to run for borough council in 2009 and I continue to serve, currently as borough council president. I am happily married to Linda Irwin, a Kennett Square native, since 2001.*

The borough council provides general supervision of the borough. We set the legislative and budgetary environment that runs the town, speak as the voice of the community and set the tone for quality of life by developing and enacting strategic plans that are in the best interest of everyone who lives and works in the borough. The Borough of Kennett Square operates under the "weak mayor" form of government. There are seven council members and a mayor who are elected by the voters. The council votes to enact legislation and to oversee the business of the borough. The mayor does not vote on these issues, but may cast a tie-breaking vote. The mayor is the ceremonial head of the borough and oversees public safety and the police department. The chief administrative officer is the borough manager who is appointed by council and is responsible for the day-to-day operation of the borough. The manager oversees all of our business that is conducted through the following departments:

- Administration—including a bi-lingual and exceptionally friendly receptionist who makes a great first impression when entering the borough hall
- Finance
- Public works—including streets, water and sewer
- Police (The mayor and chief of police oversee the department, but the council sets the budget for this full-time force. We have patrol officers on-duty every day, at all hours of the day and night.)
- Codes/Zoning (Our codes enforcement officer is highly regarded as one of the most professional around.)
- Parking—including on-street parking, surface lots and a three-story parking garage

Our goal is to listen to the taxpayers and to insure that the borough's residents are heard and represented. We are fortunate to have a high level of communication and mutual respect among the council members. I decided to run for council in 2009, because the newspaper reports of council meetings were negative, highlighting a combative environment, and I wanted to change that. It is fine to disagree, but the process needs to be civil and respectful and I thought I could help foster a positive climate and focus on solutions. Upon swearing in to my first term I was elected as vice president by my peers and served with two strong leaders, David Miller and Leon Spencer, and learned from their experience. In my current role as president I am presiding over a unique situation in that we had a dramatic turn-over of council members between the fall of 2015 and January 2016. State election laws provide that an alternating two or three council seats would come up for reelection on even numbered years. This keeps a majority of the sitting council as experienced. In the fall of 2015 two members resigned, which called for interim replacements, and we were on a year when three seats were up for reelection. It takes a couple of years to become familiar with all the legalities, logistics and subtleties of this role and our new council members are working very hard in their position, and all the while bringing their fresh perspectives and life experiences to the table with new energy and new ideas.

We develop a strategic plan every five years and just completed one in 2015. The areas that we focused on are: borough services, effective government, partnerships, land use and planning, and finance. This plan sets short and long-term goals, identifies people responsible, and sets target dates for accomplishment. Through this plan, we keep the borough on track and provide a way of measuring success.

Council also adopts a comprehensive plan that is a detailed analytical and planning tool that guides land use and redevelopment decisions. This plan is developed through a cooperative effort with the Chester County Planning Commission and took about two years to prepare, which includes interviews and public participation activities. The result is an exhaustive report outlining specific, prioritized tasks that will lead to a healthier and more prosperous community.

∞

A new borough venture is the development of an economic strategy and implementation plan. In the spring of 2015, Historic Kennett Square, the borough's "Main Street" organization, applied for and was awarded a Vision Partnership Program grant from the Chester County Planning Commission. This grant, along with funding from project partners Kennett Township, Longwood Gardens and Genesis Health Care, allowed for the retention of a consultancy team to study seven focus areas in Kennett Township and the Borough of Kennett Square. These areas include: State Street corridor, Cypress Street corridor, Birch Street from Walnut to Broad Streets, Millers Hill, Ways Lane, the former NVF (National Vulcanized Fiber) industrial site, and the area west of Mill Road. When the results of this study are published in September 2016, we will have a better understanding of the market conditions that affect our town and which actions we should take as a council to respond to those conditions. This study may provide advice on such decisions as green space creation, types of housing that needs to be developed or the kinds of businesses that we should try to be attracting.

This year the borough council voted on forming an advisory commission on Latino affairs, a concept generated by the ad hoc Public Communications Committee. This commission will look at ways to better communicate with a segment of the population that has been generally disengaged from government processes. With approximately fifty percent of borough residents being Spanish-speaking, we understand that we must be able to communicate with this constituency, along with the rest of the community. Through a publicized application process, we appointed twelve members to the commission that will report to council and make recommendations on what we can do to better engage the Latino community.

∞

One of our greatest challenges is managing the increased development pressure within and around the borough. Kennett Square is becoming very popular as a destination for food, craft beer, shopping and culture and, because of this, there is rising interest in the creation of housing and other buildings. It is the responsibility of council to strike a balance between preservation of the qualities that made us attractive in the first place and finding ways to increase our tax base to mitigate the financial burden on our citizens. With the increase in service industries we will see an increased demand for housing that is affordable to entry-level employees of those businesses. Restaurants, shops, building trades companies, agriculture and tourism organizations would figure to grow with this expansion and they will require local workers who can pay rent or get a mortgage that is within their means. This issue is linked to the fact that the public transportation system in this part of the county is very limited. It is not practical for someone living in Philadelphia or Delaware County, where rents are cheaper, to commute to Kennett Square via car and there are no buses or trains linking us there. There is a bit of a "chicken-or-the egg" syndrome when it comes to attracting public transit to our town. The transit service needs ridership and high population density to justify its existence, and the town needs transit to enable commuters to come and help make our businesses grow, thus increasing density and potential ridership. In the interim we will have to rely on other transportation methods and create structured parking, while encouraging those who already live close to use alternative modes of transportation, such as walking or biking.

As for future challenges, I see the possibility of a leadership crisis due to increasing time demands being placed on folks through longer work hours, commuting, other commitments and other factors. The time commitment to serving on council and other committees is great, and many people cannot dedicate enough time to serve because they are at work or have other obligations. There are a number of vacancies on boards and we have many experienced folks who will not stay in their positions forever. We are looking to high school age citizens to step up in such ways as showing interest in our junior council member position, taking a leadership role in civic organizations such as Study Buddies, The Garage, Boy Scouts and Girl Scouts, YMCA classes and others. We seasoned folks can help by taking on a mentoring role and encouraging this participation. This kind of involvement at a young age will hopefully continue through the formative young adult years and result in a new generation of leaders that we can rely on when the current members retire!

When my wife, Linda and I moved into the borough, we did not have a crystal ball telling us Kennett Square was going to be the talk of the region. Now, looking back, we say to each other, "What a great move that was!" I believe that Kennett Square is a wonderful place to call home, and I am looking forward to an even brighter future.

"Let us put our minds together to see what we can build for our children."

— Chief Sitting Bull, Native American Chief of the Sioux tribes —

Borough of Kennett Square
Leon Spencer, mayor (1999 to 2010)

04/07/2016. In 1991, while an employee of State Farm Insurance Company, I transferred from the Ohio Regional Office to the Pennsylvania office in Concordville. It was interesting and amazing to me to move back to my hometown after being gone for over twenty years; things were much the same as I recall from my high school years. Stores were closed in the evening, so there were few cars parked along the streets in the business district, and loitering still existed along the corners of State Street. There appeared to be a lingering theme of, "There's nothing to do."

I found myself returning as a "naysayer" willing to complain about certain conditions in the town. It dawned on me one day that I needed to step up and be part of the solution. As a result, I got involved in government service. My introduction to the local elections came as a result of visiting the soccer field at Kennett High School one afternoon. I noticed that the coach had a strong resemblance to my high school physical education teacher, Mr. Ed Holcroft. Much to my surprise, it was he. He spotted me and welcomed me back to the community. At a subsequent game, I met Dr. Larry Bosley, who was the superintendent of the school district. He, too, was very welcoming and showed an interest in my return to Kennett Square and to my high school alma mater. In the aftermath, we engaged in several conversations, one of which included an invitation for me to consider serving on the school board. I viewed that as an opportunity to make a difference and decided to run for the position. Encouraged by the district's commitment to the arts and to maintaining a solid educational curriculum, I ended up serving on the board for almost six years.

I have vivid recollections during my tenure as a school board member of the many concerns about the growing number of Latino students in the district. There were those who believed that non-Spanish speaking students were not getting the classroom experiences they deserved. Through the process, it became quite apparent that those fears were not justified. Latino parents sought to do all that they could for their children and the educational community was committed to making sure that all students received the optimal learning experience possible.

Further resistance to the growing Latino population became evident while serving as the Kennett Square mayor. A resident approached me one day with the fiery question, "What are you going to do about those Mexicans! They are crowding our schools, causing trouble and taking over!" I looked that person straight in the eye and said, "I am going to love them unconditionally!" I also offered the thought that we are all breathing the same air!

∞

It was the perceived failure to respect those of Latino culture that spurred my interest in taking a special stand. I felt the need to support those in my community whose last name ended in "z," many of whom worked in the mushroom industry. As the volunteer mayor who worked full-time at the Tatnall School in Wilmington at the time, I was privileged to have a two-week spring break. In 2000, I spent one of the weeks working in the mushroom industry. Jim Angelucci and Don Phillips consented to allow me to work at Phillips Mushroom Farm. What an eye opening experience that was! The first day, I spent eight hours picking mushrooms. I wondered, "How do they do this day after day?" Day two, I arrived at 4:00am for the filling process as trucks from Laurel Valley Farms shipped in conveyor loads of manure-laden compost. Armed with pitch forks, we spread the mix on top of the boards that were used for growing. The smell was disgustingly pungent! We worked straight through until 1:00pm. Again, I wondered, "How do they do this day after day?" The third day was spent in the packing room, and when a bell rang every twenty minutes, we changed packing stations. Despite the "movement," the task quickly lost appeal. "How do they do this day after day?" The fourth day was truly interesting! Donning lab coats and related sterile gear, we spent the day doing spore research. Day five, my final day, was spent in the shipping area. From a warehouse setting on the second floor, orders were filled by transporting large bags of mushroom products by hand trucks to two large holes in the floor at the end of an aisle. They were then dropped to two men below who would stack them into skids. "How do they do this day after day?" The week at Phillips was one of the most rewarding of my life! It helped me to appreciate the magnitude of the labor provided by those who work in the industry that puts Kennett Square on the map.

∞

Real communication, when one listens and takes in what is being said, is so essential to living together in a diverse community. I was especially appreciative of the Kennett High School Unidad students, who put the effort into communicating with their families and neighbors when there were complaints about laundry being hung out on front porches. The students explained the expectations, and the families responded affirmatively because they said they wanted to know what they needed to do to be accepted community members.

I guess I always tried to give a higher level message and take the higher road. It is what I had been taught at home and in my faith community. I was ordained an elder in the Presbyterian church and learned how important it is to "keep the faith" as life poses us with challenges. I also hold the fundamental belief that there is good in all people, and that although I may dislike a person's behavior, I am always called to love that person. Respect is the key value that I try to hold at all times.

Thankfully, I really haven't been subjected to prejudice during my lifetime. I grew up in a neighborhood that was mostly white, and I didn't think anything of it. I was encouraged and supported at school to develop my musical and leadership talents even though I was a minority. The local black community showed the greatest prejudice towards me, asking me why I talked "like the white kids," or "acted like them." My response was consistent. "I live in a big world, and I want to experience the beauty of it all!" The only time that I can say that I experienced myself as "colored" (which is the name they called us back then), was on Sunday morning when I attended New Garden UAME Church on East Linden Street, Kennett Square, which was attended only by black community members, and when I went to the black barber on State Street. (Outside of this Kennett area, Ohio is where I felt community prejudice when I rented an apartment with white classmates in an all-white neighborhood.)

Kennett Square schools were integrated in 1956 when I entered Kennett Elementary School, which was showcased in a Maryland newspaper as one of the first integrated schools in the area. This course of action was thanks to Superintendent W. Earl Ruppert and the school board.

As mayor of Kennett Square, I had very little authority because I had no fiscal responsibility. My primary role was to oversee the police department. During the early 2000s, I saw an ongoing decline in the number of juvenile delinquents, and I attribute this to a strong police force who worked with the kids and the many after-school programs that were taking place, such as: the YMCA, Study Buddies, After-The-Bell, The Garage Community and Youth Center, efforts from the school district and more. Kids are basically good, and, when they have an opportunity to do good things, they stay that way!

I am not a micro-manager, but when I was overseeing the Kennett police department, I made the effort to spend one-on-one time with each police officer. I rode the beat to gain a personal experience of their job and the situations that they encountered. I wanted them to know that I sincerely respected their role in the community.

∞

In 2010, Matt Fetick approached me and said he would like to run for mayor of Kennett Square, but he would only run if I was stepping down. I personally don't like life-long politicians in one stint, so I decided that it was a good time for me to step down. I might add that Matt Fetick is doing a great job and is a great listener. I took one year off from a civic role, then ran for Kennett borough council, with a win in November 2011 and completed my four-year term in December 2015; serving two years as president of council. We are a borough of 6,500 residents, comprised of 60% Latino, 29% Caucasian, 5% African American, and the rest categorized as "other." The government officials that we have in place are solid, genuinely good people who are committed to the community and are not over-paid. Borough Manager Joe Scalise, who was appointed from within Kennett, is an outstanding example of the above qualities. He has been working for the borough since he was 19 years old, which exhibits a real commitment to the town.

As I reflect on some of the issues that the borough currently faces, I come up with these items:

- People want to move to Kennett Square; it is now the place to live. Can the infrastructure endure the growth?
- As we continue to evolve and change, can we respect the longtime residents of Kennett Square?
- How do we deal with the affordability of rental and homeowner properties? And, I would say, we are not an over-taxed town.
- We added a junior council person on council as an honorary member. As he graduates, my hope is that we continue to bring another youth on board in this civic role, not only for the youth's sake, but also for the health of the community.

Some of the most essential elements that will continue to keep Kennett progressing are:

- Safety First. I want to feel comfortable with the thought that anyone can jog any time of day or night around the town and feel safe.
- The town must be user-friendly by offering places to park, places to shop and affordable places to live.
- We need to be known for our respectfulness. Let's be known as "The Golden Rule Community!"

As you probably can see, I think Kennett Square is a pretty wonderful community. A group of key leaders meet every Thursday early in the morning to pray together for the community. This united group understands that there is a God that is overseeing the "Uncommon Results." This is certainly one of our underlying strengths, along with the hosts of community members, who rise up to meet a need, which has happened with the development of the many youth programs. Family Promise is the most recent example of addressing the need to help homeless families. Yes, we are a community that works together!

"We owe our children, the most vulnerable citizens in our society, a life free of violence and fear."

— Nelson Mandela, former president of South Africa —

Borough of Kennett Square
Matt Fetick, mayor

04/27/2016. Chester County has been my home since I was 4 years old. I'm a graduate of Downingtown schools. Following high school, I became an EMT and eventually went to the Police Academy upon my appointment as a police officer in West Chester where I served for 7 years. After leaving the police department I began a career in real estate that now spans Pennsylvania, Maryland, Delaware and London England; and currently lead a nationally ranked and recognized real estate brokerage. My partner, David and I have a new son, Oliver.

My role as the mayor of Kennett Square is to assure public safety through overseeing the Kennett police department and to be a voice of the people. As the elected executive, my responsibility is to sign or veto the legislation that the borough council proposes. When community concerns are not being addressed, I bring them to the table and become an arbitrator of discord. I also participate in and foster activities that enhance the economic, social and environmental well-being of the town and residents. When people need help accessing government services, I help direct them to the right point of contact.

Kennett Square has over thirty nonprofits and many community-wide festivals and events. Many hours of my volunteer role as mayor are spent attending community affairs and fundraisers. As the official spokesperson for Kennett, it is my role to endorse and validate the resources that these events bring to the community. The nonprofits are providing services that the government doesn't cover, and the community events are bringing pride and revenue into the town. These organizations appreciate the validation of support from the mayor's office, and I make it a priority to be available whenever possible.

After I became mayor, I was invited to a Historic Kennett Square meeting and was asked what my vision was for the town. I told them I did not come with an agenda; rather my aim was to help them achieve their vision. I chose to run for mayor so I could utilize my skills as a former police officer in the mayor's role in overseeing the police department. It is a good use of my skill set. It was important that the timing of seeking the position was right, and that I did not compete for the office with the previous mayor, Leon Spencer. I wasn't interested in campaigning for office; I just wanted to serve the community.

∞

Kennett Square is the ideal small town USA. We do so many things right. We have an efficiently run government with a balanced budget. Also, our strength is in our diversity expressed socially, culturally and economically. We have homes for high income families within blocks of low income neighborhoods. We have the opportunity to share resources and have a visible reason for volunteerism. There is a culture of community service in Kennett Square. Many of our residents serve in different organizations from The Garage Community and Youth Center to the Kennett Senior Center. There is an opportunity for anyone who wants to get involved.

On the History Channel, I have been watching *The Men Who Built America,* which highlighted how large corporations have been an important element of a healthy economic community. Historically, the mushroom industry has done a great job in providing resources for the community. With the growth of other businesses such as Genesis Healthcare and Chatham Financial, we are seeing corporate involvement in the community continuing to grow. These industries have invested in the town financially big time, and this helps build a strong economic base. Our town would suffer if large businesses left.

As for our present challenges; the town currently has three major properties that could bring in high density housing, for both rental and ownership. We could be reaching a tipping point of having to expand our water, sewage, and underground pipelines and infrastructure. An increase of restaurants with liquor licenses may require hiring another police officer. And, we want to have adequate restaurants for visitors coming to town; nothing is worse than traveling to a destination site to find "no room at the inn." Last Saturday, all of our restaurants were full at 6:30 pm when I wanted to dine in town with my family. This is good news at one level and a challenge at another. It seems we are currently on the path of moving Main

Street as far as Mill Road, which is another way to expand and grow.

Property taxes continue to be a point of concern for residents. Many of the new residents support the idea of moderate tax increases to support infrastructure and services. However, longtime residents are concerned about being taxed out of their homes. Finding this balance between investing in our town and not pricing residents out is a challenge that we will continue to face.

Often times I will hear the concern about creating more affordable housing. This is a complicated issue. What is affordable? Homes are affordable to the person who purchases them. I think the question that is being is asked is to make sure that we have workforce housing. We can't control what type of homes and price points that developers propose for land they own. However, we can implement strategies that encourage work force housing.

We are very fortunate to have an excellent working relationship with Kennett Township, which circles our town. We are able to share resources in times of emergency and with planning. Our police and fire departments work together as well as our municipal managers.

As mayor, I don't establish benchmarks per se, but I do engage in an annual reflection process about how Kennett Square is doing. My first reflection deals with how well we have provided the core public services, i.e. police, fire, EMS, water, sewage, trash removal, and public facilities and asking what adjustments need to be made. I also like to look at how the nonprofits have done. The information I want to understand and assess at the end of the year is who is being served, what is being done, and how is "the serving" being accomplished by the agencies. My assessment also gives me more information about the town.

As for running for mayor another term, I will serve in the capacity my neighbors want me to. I want to be involved in serving the community, but at a very local level where the problems and solutions are more tangible. On a daily basis, I am approached by residents with a question or concern, and it is satisfying to be of help and to be able to find answers. I enjoy the relationships and the ability to make a direct impact on our community, which would not be possible to this extent in other statewide elected offices.

45

"We owe our children, the most vulnerable citizens in our society, a life free of violence and fear."

— Nelson Mandela, former president of South Africa —

Youth Story – Leading a Cause
Kelsey Logan, graduate of the Kennett Area School District K-12 program

12/03/2016. *I started my education in Kennett at Our Small World, a pre-school program, at 3 years old, and then went on through the Kennett public school system. My mother, Dr. Connie Logan was a math teacher who wrote the first grant that brought WIN, the Walk in kNowledge program supports the Hispanic population going on to college and further education. My dad, George, worked in Product Development for DuPont. I graduated from Kennett High School in 2003, went to Penn State, majoring in psychology and then got my masters from George Mason University in organizational psychology. I worked for a number of companies after graduate school around the Washington DC area and then went on to Australia with Deloitte, a consulting company, where I met my husband and started a family. Our son will soon turn one year old.*

The best part of growing up in Kennett was my ability to explore with my brothers. There were a lot of exciting things to study and learn about. I especially liked to swim and spent my summers in a pool, going on to swim for Kennett High School. I was also in the Rotary Interact Club that was sponsored by one of my greatest teachers, Mr. Duffy, which got me into volunteering.

My life came to an abrupt halt in 10th grade when my brother, Cameron, was hit and killed by a drunk driver during his senior year. He was something of a golden child, and his death affected so many lives. The community really came together for me and my family. I even recall the kindness and understanding of the postman, as he delivered the cards of sympathy with such empathy.

I didn't want Cameron to die in vain from a senseless tragedy. I decided to take this preventable and life-changing event and turn it into a cause that would keep others from experiencing the same pain that my family had to endure. I threw myself into Mothers Against Drunk Driving (MADD). All through high school I volunteered as a speaker and worked to expand awareness. Now, one of the most active programs in the local schools is an After-Prom-Party to give the kids something to do all night, and keep them off the roads and out of trouble.

In college, I became active in the Penn State Dance Marathon (THON) for the Four Diamonds Fund which raises money to conquer childhood cancer. In my first year, I raised $10,000 and danced in Thon. In my second year, I led my sorority's participation, which raised $208,000. I'm proud to say that last year Kennett High School had a dance marathon fundraiser for the Four Diamond Fund and raised $26,000. This year Mr. Duffy's daughter is on the committee, and their goal is $68,000.

I will always appreciate being raised in the Kennett community, and I look forward to passing on what I learned to my children. Fifteen years onward, we still have a fundraiser for Cameron every year and the money goes towards scholarships in his name at Kennett High School and Salesianum School, a Catholic high school in Wilmington, Delaware.

46

"While we try to teach our children all about life; children teach us what life is about."

— Angela Schwendt —

Kaolin Mushroom Farms, Inc.
Mike Pia, co-owner

05/16/2016. I was born and raised in Kennett Square and attended Kennett schools. I still live in the area with my wife Nancy. We have four children, four grandchildren and one on the way.

The story of Kaolin Mushroom Farms starts with my grandfather, John Pia. He was born in 1894 in a small village near Asti, Italy and at the age of 16 years old, immigrated to the United States working first in New York restaurants as a dishwasher and waiter, and then moved to Ontario, California to work for a winery. After a few years he missed his family in Italy and decided to visit them. Upon entering the country, he was immediately drafted into the Italian Army where he spent five years. After his service, he returned to New York, where he met his future wife, was married and returned to California, eventually having three children there. When the depression of 1929 hit, the wine industry was decimated, so he moved his family to Chester County where his brother-in-law had a friend who owned a mushroom farm and was in need of laborers. He learned about mushroom growing by working in the business and in 1932, he rented a small mushroom farm, bought some cows and went into business for himself. In 1941, to help support his family, he began growing tomatoes as a sharecropper for the Campbell Soup Company. His son, Louis Pia, my father, started working full-time in the family business in 1945. In 1950, Louis began to formulate a new type of mushroom growing substrate (the composted food base for the crop) that had been developed by a professor at Pennsylvania State University. It was so productive that other local growers began asking him to formulate some for them and this soon became the family's main revenue source.

In the mid-1970s, John and I began to work full-time in the family business. In 1983, our family switched its focus from composting back to mushroom growing when we purchased the largest site mushroom farm in Chester County from a subsidiary of the Clorox Company. John and I assumed ownership and control of the company in 1987. John manages our sales and distribution and I run our growing and composting operations. We are a fourth generation family-owned business, with our sons, Michael Jr. and John Jr., presently work in the business. John and I still run the day-to-day operations and have not yet begun to transition the business to the next generation, but they are definitely interested in that opportunity.

When the mushroom industry began in Chester County, the labor force was made-up predominately of Irish and Italian immigrants who eventually went on to start their own businesses. Today we are seeing a repeat of the generation entrepreneur pattern, with some Mexican mushroom workers moving forward and starting up mushroom farms themselves; there are over a dozen Mexican-owned farms in the area today.

∞

Kennett Square was a good location to establish a mushroom industry. Kennett has proximity to major metropolitan areas. In the beginning, there was no refrigeration for shipping; local growers could ship by train to Washington DC, Philadelphia, New York and Boston, and still deliver fresh in one day. In addition to our headquarters at 649 W. South Street, we now have mushroom farms at 339 East Baltimore Pike, (West Grove farm); 129 Starr Road in Avondale (Alpine Farm), and 6638 Limestone Road (M& J Farm.)

Kaolin Mushroom Farms Inc. is the fourth largest producer of mushrooms in the United States, growing nearly 60 million pounds annually. Pennsylvania and Chester County represent 63% and 43% respectively of the total Agaricus mushrooms produced in the United States.

We have a full-time workforce of nearly 1,000, of which 40% are harvesters. Women compose about 20% of our workforce – fewer in harvesting than in the packing area. Our days typically start at 5am and can extend into late afternoon if there still is harvesting to complete.

We have continued to pay the harvesters by piecework. This means, that workers are paid for the quantity of mushrooms they pick; faster harvesters can earn more than double the average earnings. As a trial, when we began growing portabella mushrooms at our smallest farm, we decided to pay by an hourly structure. The larger portabella mushrooms require careful handling and adequate time to fully grow and we thought this approach would be the best way to maintain the quality required by our customers. While our quality was very good, productivity was low so we kept the hourly rate but introduced a piece rate bonus. We were very pleased with the results, which were that harvester's earnings increased considerably, the Company profited by needing fewer workers, and product quality didn't suffer at all.

The vast majority of our Mexican workers came from Moroleon, Guanajuato, Mexico and, even though it wasn't an intentional plan, I'm told that most of Kaolin's workers are related to the original Zavala family. We now are seeing the second generation applying for work here, some being college graduates and working in professional human resource or business positions. Because we are a large company, we are fortunate to be able to offer many opportunities to promote from within. When someone shows initiative in advance, we work with him/her to help them do so. At times, this results in the person moving on to another business or another kind of work outside of Kaolin, nevertheless we believe strongly in providing opportunities to those who desire them. Elaine Marnell, who speaks Spanish, has been our labor relations director since 1993. One of her roles is to create relationships with the employees and encourage them to pursue opportunities.

∞

Immigration issues need to be solved nationally. It helped in the mid-80s to have amnesty, because families were able to join their spouse/father in the area and make a life for themselves. We helped a couple hundred employees apply for their green cards and helped them in the process to bring their families to the US legally. Years ago, we made a conscious decision to hire only documented workers and to be stringent about this practice. Just this past year, we were visited by the INS and received a clean record. However, our country needs to face up to the fact that the Mexican migrant is supporting the US fresh food economy, and we need to develop realistic and sensible solutions for the undocumented workers. We can't consider drastic approaches like threatening to ship long-time undocumented residents back to Mexico; even if it were a possibility, which it is not. A solid immigration process and policy needs to be laid out that recognizes our dependency on the current Mexican workers, and then we need to develop stronger regulations for the future.

American workers do not want to work in agriculture. We have recruited far and wide and the message we always receive is that the Americans will not get involved in this kind of work. Most of our workforce comes from an area of Mexico that makes clothing. Some theorize that these workers are agile with their hands because of this background, which serves them well for harvesting mushrooms. I'm not sure if that's the reason, but I do know that as an employer, I feel very fortunate to have the workforce we do. Our employees consider agricultural work to be honorable, and while there is no doubt it is hard work, it is work they are justifiably proud to do.

∞

Our company has had challenges in the past, one being when the company became unionized. Prior to purchasing our Kennett farm in 1983, we had twenty employees. In ten years, we grew to six hundred employees. We added many new supervisory positions to handle the rapid growth, however, we were not on top of our game in the area of providing training for those supervisors. Some were disengaged with the workforce and unaware of issues that were important to the workers. As a result, some workers became disgruntled and felt their voices were not being heard, so in 1993 they chose to vote for a union to represent them, and that election was ratified in 2000. In 2014, over concerns that they were not benefiting from the union contract and there were rumors of misuse of union dues, one of our employees started a petition to decertify the union. This soon led to a decertification election where employees voted overwhelmingly to disband the union. This was one of the only decertification elections conducted by the PA Labor Relations Board, who had jurisdiction over our union. We are pleased to know that our workers feel satisfied with how they are treated by the company, and how we help to meet their needs.

We also have gone through the years of adapting to OSHA and food safety standards that were historically focused mostly on manufacturing and food processing. Food safety standards in particular are much more stringent and of course we receive regular audits from several different food agencies. We've received a superior rating by the Global Food Safety Institute each year since 2004, and we are constantly training our management to help us stay in full compliance.

One of our greatest challenges today is recruitment. Affordable housing nearby our operations is very difficult to find, therefore transportation for employees living a distance away is a problem. To deal with the transportation issue, we started running buses from Wilmington, Delaware to Kennett and back. We attempted to provide round-trip transportation between Lancaster, Pennsylvania and Kennett, but we were unsuccessful. We are trying to be creative around how to recruit harvesters. We have an outreach to high school students, who would like to work on week-ends and make some extra money. In West Grove, we are starting the work day at 7 am, instead of 5 am at the request of those harvesters. We have had to make changes in our infrastructure, because we need to be able to transport our product at a certain time each day; however, we have seen a 15% increase in productivity with these workers, who are now better rested. While we are starting two hours later, we are finishing almost at the same time as we did prior to the time change. We will continue to work towards implementing favorable working conditions to accommodate our workers and to try to attract more employees.

We would like to recruit more women and are exploring ways to address child care and other obstacles for women working in our industry. The first women harvesters that started at Kaolin had a challenge working in an all-male environment, but they certainly led the way for others. We also are fortunate to have long-term employees who are a support to the new employees.

The mushroom business is a high volume, low margin commodity business. When costs like oil and transportation are down, our profits are enhanced, but the biggest factor in our business is the productivity of the crops. Our profitability is directly related to how well we produce, so there is a constant focus and attention to detail on all matters that impact our crops.

∞

Two hundred years ago, 90% of Americans were farmers. They had a clear concept of the nature and importance of food production. Today, less than two percent of American citizens are farmers. Every year, laws are passed that make farming as an occupation more and more difficult, and since laws are brought about by public pressure and influence, the need for farmers to communicate is more important now than ever before. To increase understanding, we as farmers must continually educate people in our respective communities about what we do behind the scenes and promote our contribution to our community and to society in general.

We would like to expand our mushroom business, and this will likely bring in more employees into the area. We need affordable housing beyond the Kennett borough, as the borough is nearly saturated and the cost of housing is high. Yes, more students resulting from those new employees would have an impact on the schools. On the other hand, our business provides an economic base for the town.

Kaolin Mushroom Inc. takes on a conscientious responsibility towards its employees and the broader community. We provide support and cooperation to the community including to local nonprofit agencies, because we understand that they are providing some of the services that our employees and other residents utilize.

When I reflect back over the years, I can see that flexibility and a willingness to change with the times, has been our strong suit in staying a successful business. We have always been on the cutting edge of new ways to improve what we do. We were the first mushroom farm in North America to conduct our compost operation completely under roof, because we knew that odors from the traditional method of outdoor composting would eventually not be tolerated by residents.

We started our business growing and selling white button mushrooms but eventually expanded to selling nearly all cultivated mushroom varieties. A few years ago, we began mushroom freezing and processing operation to diversify into other markets. When more attention was being paid to the portabella mushroom, we increased that production. We continue to draw on technology and science, which improves our efficiency. Who knows what the future brings, but we do plan to be around for a while. We will work through the challenges as they present themselves.

"Above all we need, particularly as children, the reassuring presence of a visible community, an intimate group that enfolds us with understanding and love, and that becomes an object of our spontaneous loyalty, as a criterion and point of reference for the rest of the human race."

— Lewis Mumford, philosopher and urban planner —

InterGen Kennett Community Coffee Klatch
Joan Holliday, co-founder and community organizer

Kennett Square has learned that community life becomes vibrant and dynamic when it provides an ongoing process for communing intergenerationally. For over two years, a Thursday morning intergenerational Coffee Klatch takes place at a central gathering place in town. The invitation: "Come join a circle of community folks of all ages and have conversations that cross-fertilize and bring to life the experiences of different ages."

Roberta Eldridge, volunteer facilitator, arrives early and ensures that the tables are assembled in a round format with coffee available. As old and new members arrive, she welcomes them and leads introductions and asks for community announcements. After this time, attendees have one-on-one interactions or bring up a group discussion for all to engage.

College youth, who are learning about psychology or sustainable agriculture, will share some of their learning and passions. The senior folk ask questions of interest and then share a story that relates to the subject. There may be a mother with a small child entering the circle and passing the child around to have one-on-one interactions with a community member. Seniors bring photographs and exhibits from their past and younger generations hear about the life from a different era. Adults, who are taking a break from their job, come to learn about what is happening in town and to share some new effort that they would like the community to know about. The possibilities for interaction are endless! It's the space that is needed, and the Kennett community has learned the importance of sharing time together.

Recently, Mary Ann Piccard, one of the seniors, came to the Community Coffee Klatch with a passion about bringing an artisan market to town. She spoke about her past and how meaningful it was to enter a center where she learned pottery, painting and even hand crafts such as knitting and crocheting. Having an arena to share her idea helped spark the interest in others, and now there is a town group forming to explore the idea. Best of all, it looks like her idea has come at a perfect time with plans for new town development on the table.

InterGen is learning to value and promote the core processes of each phase of life – the child, teen, adult and senior. Each has an essential process to contribute to ongoing community life, and instead of isolating ages from each other, we are looking at ways to help all generations creatively interact.

The child phase of life makes life whole. Children promise all generations hope – a new slate reflecting the whole cycle of life – children make life whole. In the many interviews of how the Kennett area community is focusing on the kids, the many programs, in turn are providing opportunities for all generations to interact. There are endless stories of how adult and senior volunteers, working with children, leave with a delight in their hearts and a feeling that they received more than they gave – the experience of wholeness.

The teen phase of life makes life real and causes our community to stop and respond to the question, "What is 'real'?" Community life may have been going about in an established fashion, and then is given pause for reflection, when a teen confronts the current system. How refreshing and yet challenging for the established culture to stay present to this process! Bringing teens to the center of town and asking them to get involved through identifying causes, joining a volunteer effort or sharing their views opens up the opportunity for our community to explore and experiment.

The adult phase of life makes life fruitful. This phase keeps our economy running and community growing. There are many steps that precede this phase; a healthy upbringing; a meaningful educational experience and a sense of one's own talents to be shared with society. The maturity of this phase of life carries the weight of life. Adults are regenerating the community with children; serving in jobs that provide products and services, and are guiding the future with policies and governing practices. Our American culture focuses on this phase of life and reinforces its value as primary. In many ways, it is up to this generation to see the value of the other phases of life and build-in mainstream processes that utilizes the assets of each age group. Daycares in a workplace helps bring in a youth energy that can lighten-up the intensity of the production mindset and bring perspective. Creating business internships for teens, as they are exploring their future careers can bring a fresh pair of eyes to the scene. And, valuing the experience of seniors through inviting them to become board members and advisors will be helpful in integrating successes from the past into the future.

The senior phase of life makes life wise. Last, but not least is the senior phase of life, which helps make life wise. Through life's experiences, and with a view of the end in sight, there is a reflection process that can be shared with the younger generations. Other cultures around the world have given respect and honor to this phase; we Americans are still learning the gift of a senior. Unfortunately, a trend we have in our country is one of seniors moving away to a retirement community, where they do not interact with the mainstream. They create their own community of seniors and appear happy among themselves, but the larger community loses a tremendous resource. I also question if the senior truly completes his/her life with this model, because an essential process for this phase of life is to hold the past, present and future in one's mindset.

Our Kennett area community is recognizing the need to be intentional about bringing together different generations. We see the value in breaking the common trend of age compartmentalization. One of the local retirement communities and the broader Kennett community are learning how to "bridge" generations by creating opportunities for interaction. For example, students waiting to be tutored in English as a Second Language are now being matched with seniors at Kendal Communities. This has brought new conversations, interests in another culture, and recognition of a community need. After-The-Bell is transporting youth to the same location where youth are learning how to make pottery with the seniors. On the other side, Kendal residents are realizing that they can travel the few short miles to Kennett and are welcome at a Bridging the Community meeting or the Kennett Community Coffee Klatch, where they can become integral to a community process. The magic and dynamism of inter-generational interactions is "real" in all of these examples, which tells us that we must continue to be intentional about making this happen more broadly and in greater depth!

Common
Themes

"All for one and one for all, united we stand and divided we fall."

— Alexandre Dumas, *The Three Musketeers* (1844) —

Youth Program's Common Themes
– the Elements of Success –
by Joan Holliday and Bob George

As we've interviewed and reflected on the many Kennett Square community educational and mentoring programs for the youth, we are picking up some common themes that run through all the programs. These may give us some clues about contributing factors, which make Kennett Square being "all about the kids" distinctively successful. These common themes are:

Kennett youth programs focus on youth's potential and provide whatever supports that are needed to reach their potential. The interview with Sarahi Zamores, a migrant to the United States in middle school, certainly highlights how her mentor "walked the walk" with her and believed in her potential to attend a highly rated four-year college. Sarahi achieved her dream and now believes in helping others reach their potential through participating as a volunteer in the very program that helped her.

It is worth going back to some of the interviews and pulling out the explicit reference to "developing youth potential. Young Moms' mission statement is: "To empower teen moms to reach their potential as women and mothers." After-The-Bell addresses the risks that youth face in middle school years and provides a safe and engaging after-school program to help develop youth's potential. The Mission Statement for Together for Education speaks about the partnerships that it facilitates to help children reach their greatest potential in the Kennett elementary schools. The vision of focusing on potential prevails, and a broad range of supports are provided.

Kennett youth programs and the school system address the uniqueness of each child/student and adjust the programming and teaching to the individual – regardless of the level of challenge. In the Study Buddies after-school program, the overall objective is to educate and care about the whole child – academically, physically, socially and emotionally. They are not just an education organization, but a grassroots effort that is rooted in the neighborhood. This means that each child is addressed holistically and provided the resources they need.

Head Start addresses the subject of focusing on the individual in their Mission Statement: "To provide comprehensive, high-quality early childhood services to ensure that children and families can achieve individual success." The Maternal & Child Health (MCH) Home Visiting Program, as well as the Family Center refers to the importance of building relationships, which starts with valuing the uniqueness of each person and family that they serve. And a beautiful reflection that highlights the point of being valued for being oneself can be found when Patty Hillkirk, director of Camp Dreamcatcher for HIV infected and affected youth, refers to something a camper stated in her evaluation; "I had somebody I can talk to and learned that I'm always going to be perfect just the way I am. "

Since 1978, the three superintendents from the Kennett Schools speak about the importance of focusing education on the success for each student and partnering with additional community programs towards this goal. Past superintendent Dr. Larry Bosley states, "Why not cooperate with the community? They are sharing the same vision that I had; 'Kennett is about each kid – It is our gospel!'" Dr. Rudy Karkosak, past superintendent, tells us about helping the community establish The Kennett Education Foundation to provide scholarships for students who did not have the means for higher education, but displayed good skills and a dedication to continue their education. Dr. Barry Tomasetti, the current superintendent, sums up his interview with, "The Kennett community, which includes the school system, provides every student with the hope that they can succeed in life. Our goal is to provide the type of learning opportunities to make this hope for success a reality."

The school's strong partnerships with after-school and in-school programs, and their willingness to host Walk In kNowledge (WIN) in high school, After-The-Bell in middle school and Together for Education in the elementary schools is testimony to the commitment that no child will be left behind!

Each program has been started in the past twenty years, so the ongoing effort is close to the "founder's" passionate vision and mission. The current programs are still experiencing the heartfelt work that preceded it, and the new executive directors are cut from the same cloth as the previous directors. Going the extra mile seems to be the norm, rather than an exception. This is strength for today; however, there could be a concern for the future, when the experience of the program's creation is far from view. The hope lies in the current practice of recognizing the history of success and in seeking future leaders, who share the sustaining values of the program.

Each program director articulates how they continue to creatively evolve and meet the presenting needs in their programming and move to the next cycle of growth. This common theme continues to repeat itself throughout the many programs. YoungMoms has moved into offering a YoungDads program, realizing that the young mother and child are part of a larger family system. Mothers and fathers working in concert on parenting approaches and sharing common goals and dreams for their child will certainly help contribute to the health of future family life. The Garage Community and Youth Center has replicated their Center in another area of Southern of Chester County. They saw the need that they were meeting and stretched their wings to make this happen. Path Stone Migrant Head Start has added a Kindergarten readiness class this year. Beyond the excellent programs that currently exist, the need for this later child development intervention is high, and Migrant Head Start took on a natural extension. The strength of looking at what comes next to meet emerging needs keeps Kennett's youth programs on the forefront.

There is a pride about each program and being part of the collective Kennett Square community. I am not sure how one instills pride in an organization, or town, but it seems to be a prevailing experience in the Kennett area. Each program seems to be small enough that employees and volunteers are able to hear the stories of progress throughout the years. The town has taken the risks to grow and the community continues to create events that give the town a "small town feel." The current Beer Garden has been controversial, yet it is turning out to serve as another arena to "be community". The town has also fought to keep the library in town, which looks like it is going to happen. This will offer the opportunity to consolidate other town services within new construction. Kennett Square has been named among the Pennsylvania's "Most Beautiful Towns" in 2015, and it was also named the "Coolest Small Town in America" in 2010. When a Budget Travel article asks, "How does a town pack in more personality than cities triple their size? How?" We read the author's response, "It all comes down to the people."(Budget Travel LLC on-line; "The Coolest Small Towns in America: Kennett Square" by Nicholas DeRenzo, Tuesday, August 24, 2010)

There is a diversity of funders and volunteers for each program. Bridging the Community has been promoting volunteerism since 1997. One of the prevailing principles is; "Each person has a community role to play." This means every person must become involved regardless of position, title, age, race, ethnic background or economic status. This principle has empowered many community residents, who would not have gotten involved in the past because of overt or subtle community restraints. Study Buddies is a great example of church leaders and street residents recognizing that they had an outreach role to play in the broader community and the spirit of volunteerism grew! The majority of youth programs depend heavily on volunteers to implement their programs. Bridging the Community, along with service clubs and churches, have inspired them and supplied them.

The Longwood Rotary deserves recognition for supporting many community projects through volunteerism. This is a service club, which promotes, "Service above self." Every week the group gathers to learn about needs in the community and in smaller groups go out and complete extensive projects. As with Bridging the Community, participating in a group energy that is focused on making a difference, keeps the effort moving and growing.

All the youth programs have fundraisers. This has been an opportunity for community members to learn about what each program is accomplishing. It is always amazing to experience the level of financial support that is given from all levels of the community. One of the practices that has encouraged involvement from all community members starts with someone with financial means, purchasing a group of tickets for an event, then donating them to those, who would find purchasing a ticket a hardship. The ticket recipients then offer their financial contributions on a sliding scale. This helps bring together a broader spectrum of the community and encourages volunteerism and financial investment from each and all.

Charitable foundations seem to have an affinity for funding programs that have a passionate mission behind the effort and a measurement of the positive outcomes throughout the years. The Garage Community and Youth Center recently won a three-year, $135,000 grant. Executive Director, Kristin Proto, in a *Kennett Paper* newspaper article on July 15, 2016 explains; *"It's the biggest grant we have ever received, and I think it's a testament to all the work we have done for the kids over the years."* Proto continues by saying, *"The Garage was selected for being a high-quality, effective out-of-school-time program that strengthens academic achievement, successful engagement in school and post-secondary success for disadvantaged youth."* Carter CDC recently received a $20,000 grant from Longwood Foundation Inc. with the compliments that this group is doing meaningful, grassroots work that will help make the greatest difference.

Community-based child support is provided through a continuous and seamless stream of programs from prenatal through high school graduation and beyond. In identifying the youth programs that serve the Kennett area to interview for this book, it was satisfying to see that there are a number of efforts that support each phase of a child's development. There is a Kennett culture that is intentional about building strong relationships with the youth and this means that if there are some areas that need to be expanded or newly developed, it will happen!

These are the most outstanding themes that come to mind when reflecting on the interviews. Some of the tenets may be ones other communities subscribe to; however, it is the whole package that makes the difference. Underlying all of them is the tremendous commitment of leadership by employees and volunteers to the development and care of the child; this is the over-riding element of success.

Volunteers

"The miracle is not that we do this work,
but that we are happy to do it."

— Saint Teresa of Calcutta, Roman Catholic nun and missionary —

Volunteerism is Integral to the Kennett Culture
by Joan Holliday

Kennett Square-wide volunteerism is a concept that was revitalized twenty years ago. Up to that time, volunteering took place through service clubs or church outreaches in which they were supporting a particular mission, but not promoting community-wide volunteering. In 1997, Bridging the Community's bi-monthly meetings created an energy field that promoted volunteering as the means for achieving a town vision, Kennett Square: "Every day a better place to grow up in and grow old in." With a vision and guiding principle of "coming from the heart" in place, not only did a community member sign-up for existing volunteer opportunities near and dear to his heart, but Bridging the Community created the impetus for sharing dreams and actualizing grass root volunteer efforts to improve the town. Indeed, a town volunteer movement was started and this movement continues today!

The profile of a Kennett volunteer has many faces. Following are some of the ones that stand out in my mind.

A Kennett volunteer is a retiree who is looking for a way to share seasoned talents and make a contribution. In most cases, this volunteer wants something ongoing that is mutually rewarding. Mentoring/tutoring roles; home repair; gardening projects or board and/or committee work are common areas for volunteering. Although there are many committed and helpful volunteers that come from this segment of our community, one particular senior volunteer is worth mentioning. Anne Humes started volunteering twenty years ago in our community. She was an original member and is a regular attendee of

Bridging the Community meetings where she stands up and shares lively photographs that showcase her volunteer involvements. She encourages others to get involved and participates in new volunteer efforts on an ongoing basis. Anne, who is approaching ninety years old and is still going strong, has become our town's volunteer mascot.

A Kennett volunteer is a youth who is looking for an opportunity to step out into the broader community and spread his/her wings. This youth many times "catches" the spirit of volunteerism and continues to evolve and expand the role; this is the case with Lindsey Pugh. As a high school student, she started to tutor in one of the Study Buddies after-school programs. She became hooked and brought both of her brothers into the process after she graduated. This family provided faithful tutors for Study Buddies over a span of six years. Lindsey went on to college and came back and worked in Migrant Education, voluntarily starting a soccer club for Latino boys as a gang prevention strategy. From there she moved on to law school and has come back to serve as a law advisor on a board that supports a Study Buddies process.

A Kennett volunteer is a youth who is looking for an opportunity that will provide the experience in a career he/she may be pursuing. Nancy Ayllon stands out as a youth who was seeking experience in law and decided to work right in her own back yard where there was a tenant/landlord/town conflict. With the help of the code enforcement officer and a Latino social service agency, Nancy and her peers took on the role of educating the Spanish-speaking apartment residents of the rules of their housing development, as well information about the unspoken community norms that facilitated integration into the larger community. She served as a reconciler and enforcer of the law and won a countywide award for her youth leadership. Recently, Nancy has graduated from law school and is engaging in a profession that will continue to help first-generation immigrants.

A Kennett volunteer is a person in the mainstream of life, who wants to actualize a dream project and is looking for like-minded persons to help develop this dream. A neighborhood street was revitalized and transformed thanks to Theresa Bass and other community residents. She expressed this dream and invited like-minded volunteers to join her. Together, they helped bring in state and local grant funds that turned a drug infested street into a family-friendly neighborhood. Another example of this type of volunteer happened in March of 2008. Kennett Middle School students' dream of creating a community garden was brought to a Bridging the Community meeting by their teacher, Susan Metz. In a matter of no time, sixty raised-gardens in our local park were constructed. They were producing wonderful vegetables that same year and continue to thrive, supported primarily by community volunteers.

A Kennett volunteer is a person who is willing to support a defined community event or fundraiser. These volunteers come from every age group and see an opportunity to help out within a prescribed time frame. Some of these volunteers are living very busy lives or others are testing the volunteer waters. Others enjoy the community camaraderie during their committed time and decide to get involved in other ways after the event. Some of the youth programs offer opportunities to get involved in a short time frame, which helps this volunteer experience the freedom of helping out without a long-term commitment. The Garage Community and Youth Center comes to mind as a large group of students participate in the walk every year on the National Hunger and Homelessness Awareness Week.

A Kennett volunteer is a person working within an agency, who sees the value of volunteering above and beyond one's assigned job to advance the community. One community person that comes to mind is Jeanne Searer who held the job of volunteer coordinator at the Kennett Area Senior Center. She came to a Bridging the Community meeting as part of her job, but then understood the value of promoting volunteerism for the entire community and started coming on her own. Since she left her job, she has been helping facilitate the Bridging the Community meetings and is involved in many community outreach efforts, especially promoting Latino community involvement.

A Kennett volunteer is a person who is motivated by his/her religious beliefs and looks for opportunities to join efforts or initiate a grassroots effort. The Borough of Kennett Square, which is one square mile, has fifteen churches and counting. Starting from the earlier times of the Quakers, who were leaders of the Underground Railroad, the town of Kennett has had religious volunteers putting into action their spiritual values. Several of the youth programs we interviewed came out of this fabric and have the ongoing support of church volunteers. In turn, these volunteers attend Bridging the Community meetings to promote their mission and meet like-hearted community members who join their efforts. Jay Malthaner, the founder of Good Neighbors Home Repair, is a shining example of one who built an organization founded on the Christian commandment of "Love thy neighbor." Jay has recruited hundreds of volunteers under the umbrella of this mission and has extended the invitation to youth who are willing to use their summer vacation to help out.

In tallying up our volunteers, Kennett has over 2,000, and some of them are almost full-time. Assuming the average volunteer time is only two weeks a year, the financial benefit would be forty hours at eight dollars an hour times 2,000 people totaling over a half million dollars. In Kennett, much of the time involves teaching and tutoring children, which has professional value, which in turn doubles the financial benefit to the town.

Two interns, Lucas Freire and Wesley George, contacted the organizations that were interviewed to obtain data about the number of volunteers they involved in conducting their programs. Following is the volunteer data report from the organizations:

Interviewee	Organization	# of Volunteers
Joan Holliday	Kennett Community Coffee Klatch	4
Kristin Pronto	The Garage Community and Youth Center	282
Linda Mercner	YoungMoms	80
Kathy Do	After-The-Bell	179
Loretta Perna	Walk In kNowledge (WIN)	12
Bob George	Kennett Education Foundation	32
Joan Holliday	Bridging the Community	4
Patti Hillkirk	Camp Dreamcatcher	300
Sam Heriegel	Together For Education	40
Doug Nakashima	Kennett YMCA	472
Melanie Weiler	Kennett Area Community Services	75
Mary Hutchins	Historic Kennett Square	15
Jackie	Tick Tock Early Learning Center	12
Alisa Jones	La Comunidad Hispana	10
Maritza Rivera	The Family Center, MCH	16
Tamara Acuna	Kennett Head Start	40
Patricia Quynn	Family Literacy/Even Start	3
Carrie Freeman	United Way of Southern Chester County	241
Maria McDonald	Chester County Futures	56
Jay Malthaner and Bob Johnson	Good Neighbors and Good Neighbors Youth Camp	80
Clarke Green	Boy Scouts of America (3 local troops)	80
LaToya Myers	Study Buddies/Carter CDC	15
	Total Volunteers	**2048**

Volunteerism is clearly an integral part of the Kennett culture. Just looking at the number of volunteers is testimony. Speaking as someone who has been part of this community-wide movement, I continue to emphasize that volunteerism needs to start from a caring interest and motivation beyond one's personal life. When this happens, there is a corner that is turned and there is no going back. "Coming from the heart" has infinite returns and so the circle of giving continues!

Volunteers in the Future

My experience has been one of creating a Kennett Square environment that promoted volunteerism through Bridging the Community. I also am aware that, in recruiting volunteers, it is helpful to understand general underlying values and motivations of different age groups that were molded and shaped by their life experiences. In 2007, Peter Brinkerhoff, the founder of Corporate Alternatives, published <u>Generations: The Challenge of a Lifetime for Your Nonprofit</u>. In this book, Brinkerhoff concisely presents his research on how the current generational shift will impact every aspect of the nonprofit world. Below is his summary of the general characteristics of the three generations that will make up the volunteer bank in the next twenty years.

<u>Baby Boomer</u>

Born: 1946-1962

Size: About 80,000,000

Key Events: Grew up in an era of huge social change and wealth. First generation in 200 years to rebel against their government. Virtually every social, scientific and cultural institution underwent major changes during their adolescence.

Key Values: Sense of entitlement; optimism; competition; focused on their careers; endless youth; cynicism about institutions.

Critical Technological Change in Their Lives: Television

Motivators: Their value to the team; their ability to improve services; being needed; public recognition; helping to change the world.

<u>Generation X</u>

Born: 1963 – 1980

Size: About 45,000,000

Key Events: Have worked in the shadow of the Baby Boomers. End of the Cold War. Beginning of globalization.

Key Values: Independence, self-reliance, stability, informality, fun

Critical Technological Change in Their Lives: Personal computer, cable TV & video games

Motivators: Value of independent thinking, value to the organization, work-life balance

Millennial

Born: 1981 – 2002
Size: 80,000,000
Key Events: First generation to be born in a truly diverse, high-tech society with a global perspective.
Key Values: Work-life balance, confidence, social commitment, complete comfort with technology, networking, realism, being well-informed, time management
Critical Technological Change in Their Lives: Connection of the Internet affecting every aspect of their lives. Rapid pace of technological innovations.
Motivators: Doing things in groups; recognizing the need for their new perspective and ideas; making a real difference for the community.

As I reflect on the nature of key values and motivators for each of the above three generations, I have come up with the following thoughts and questions:

The Baby Boomer generation has had its first wave of retirees. There is still hope that this group will have the motivation to carry forward their values of "wanting to help change the world" and "being needed." I believe that recruitment for serving on boards and purposeful volunteering will peak their interest. At the same time, the latter part of this generation now has less certainty about comfortable retirement due to corporate downsizing and change. Recently, the Kennett area has experienced substantial downsizing and major corporations moving out of the area. This change has recently affected the United Way of Southern Chester County contributions and may affect the time to volunteer, as well.

The Generation X group seems to be carrying on the work of the world economy. Because "work and life balance" is a motivator for this group, the hope is that employers of large and small businesses will make it part of the culture to participate in "community volunteer days." In the Kennett area, in particular, realty companies and banks, participate in MLK Volunteer Day and Make a Difference Day. One financial corporation has even gone beyond the designated days and has made volunteering part of the culture during the workday. More of this would help keep community volunteering alive and well. Volunteering is "fun," which is a key value for this group. 5-K runs, fairs, festivals and creative events may peak the volunteer interest of this group.

The Millennial Generation has motivations that provide much hope for future volunteerism. In a general sense, this generation wants to "make a difference in the world" and be "valued for their new ideas." Some of our current nonprofit efforts need to be examined, adjusted and even changed to serve their articulated mission, so let's draw on this generation to give us insights and a lift. Providing technological expertise, along with innovative applications, will be a great contribution. And, when organizations become myopic, let's ask the millennial to help us keep the global perspective.

At some level, most people recognize that they are a part of a circle broader than their own personal life. We live in a world where technology can make global connections in seconds. So, the awareness is there, it is the *motivation* and *values* that need to be uncovered when making a volunteer appeal. These are the spiritual roots that bring a deeper satisfaction and meaning to one's life. I personally believe that love of self and neighbor are one package to have a fulfilling life, and you can't have one without the other. Just ask the smiling Kennett volunteer!

Stress Test

> **"Our ability to reach unity in diversity will be the beauty and test of our civilization."**
>
> — Mahatma Gandhi, peace activist —

The Stress Test
by Bob George

When you have a stress test during a medical check-up, you receive information about your heart health. I love tests and measurements, so let's do a stress test on Kennett.

James Fallows, the National Book Award winner, wrote an article in the March 2016 edition of *The Atlantic*, "Eleven Signs a City Will Succeed," as part of a series of articles about a 54,000 mile journey around the country he and his wife took in a single engine airplane. Mary Hutchins, executive director of Historic Kennett Square, brought the article up when we interviewed her about Kennett and the importance of Kennett having a "downtown". So, what are the signs of a healthy city that Fallows and his wife found on their tour of our country, and how do we measure up to their benchmarks? Will Kennett be seen as a successful city with this set of metrics? By looking at these 11 signs we can get some kind of feeling of how we are doing with other communities around the country. We will give each sign a score from 0 to 9, where 0 is a complete failure to show that sign, and 9 is a completely successful implementation or accomplishment of that sign. Any city that has a rating of 90 or above will be rated as an "Excellent American Community."

Sign #1: Divisive national politics seem a distant concern.

"… overwhelmingly the focus in successful towns was not on national divisions but on practical problems that a community could address. The more often national politics came into local discussions, the worse shape the town was in."

Here I have to provide full disclosure. I am one of the two Democratic committee captains in my precinct. I am anything but an unbiased observer of the national political scene. However, I'm also an engineer, an industrial economist, a business person, and an ex-Naval officer that was hired by DuPont to get things done. The reason I am devoting so much of my time to this project has a lot to do with how our national and state political systems have allowed the systematic deterioration of the middle class and the country's safety net. For the past three years I worked the polls at West Marlborough, the heart of what they call "mink and manure" country. This is where Katharine Hepburn wanted Jimmy Stewart to go to write his book in *The Philadelphia Story*. This is horse country, full of old money and long-term Republicanism, but not an ounce of animosity. The people who work in the barns and for the veterinary school are probably not in the same political party as those living in the big houses, but they all get along well. They may be following Thomas Jefferson's quote; "I never consider a difference of opinion in politics, in religion, or philosophy, as a cause for withdrawing from a friend."

∞

During the 2016 primaries there was a lot of different voting, but no sign of Trump divisiveness or even the heated competition between "Feeling the Bern" (Bernie Sanders) and Madam Secretary (Hillary Clinton.) There was only one presidential sign that I saw out front at a polling place, and that was for Kasich. Most people in Kennett don't wear their politics on their sleeves. Some feel more strongly than others, of course. But this is considered the suburbs of Philadelphia and the type of people that live out here can actually make a major contribution to picking the president. It is the Soccer Moms of the Philly suburbs whose votes swing to whomever they feel is best for the country as they see it at the time, that can tilt Pennsylvania from red to blue. This area offsets the balance that was best described by James Carvell, "Pennsylvania is Philadelphia and Pittsburgh with Alabama and Mississippi in the middle." This year, 2016, is not your father's political campaign with blue collar workers voting red. But even though every Chester County precinct except mine voted blue, the middle of the state that was feeling the loss of good jobs turned the state red.

As further evidence of the area's focus on local solutions rather than national divisive politics, take an example from our own experience at KACS. We were looking at expanding our food cupboard into a connected building next door. After applying for grants, we were awarded $80,000 towards the expansion, but it came with some politically loaded contingencies. This included a requirement that union workers completed the work that the new building would need to be fit for use. This basically added $40,000 to the cost of doing the work, totaling about $120,000. If we had non-union workers do it, the cost would be about $80,000, with the possibility that the work would be just as good. To some people involved at KACS, this was just government interference and their gut reaction was to reject the grant. However, the focus was always on practical solutions and what was best for the community. With the grant, we needed to raise $40,000 to get the new expansion. Without it, we needed to raise $80,000. We accepted the grant. It was never brought up that the difference in the cost of using union labor and non-union labor was largely in the cost of benefits which is what separates our food cupboard clients from the middle class people who don't need our help.

No one cares whether a volunteer is a Republican or a Democrat and school board candidates cross-file with both parties. In the 2016 primary, a candidate for the state legislator ran on both the republican and democratic tickets.

Score: 9/9. Kennett did not let divisive national politics get in the way of getting things done.

Sign #2: You can pick out the local patriots.

A standard question we'd ask soon after arrival was "Who makes this town go?" The answers varied widely. What mattered, though, was that the question had an answer.

This is very true of Kennett. In the introduction I mentioned that everyone knew it was Joan who would best tell Kennett's story. But if you asked, "who makes this town go?," the answers would depend on who you ask. The reason that everyone having an answer to this question is a good sign, is that it shows people's commitment to the town, their ownership of making it a great place to live. The variation in the answer is a function of their experience, passions and with which processes they interact. If you ask a senior person who knows the town, maybe he/she will say Marshall Newton, who passed away but left the legacy of the YMCA Good Kids and After-The-Bell. The young families who are tied into the system might say Rudy Karkosak, the retired superintendent of schools who is chairman of the board of After-The-Bell and the Kennett Education Foundation. Those concerned with the safety of the kids might say Chief McCarthy. And if you care about integrating the Hispanics into the system it may be Loretta Perna, who leads the WIN program at the high school. But if you're a merchant or professional in the downtown area and remember 20 years ago when Kennett was pretty much the post office and the library, you may look to Mary Hutchens, who leads Historic Kennett Square that has brought so many great restaurants and businesses into town. Or, it may be Mike Walker who brought his company, Genesis, into town; and with it jobs, office buildings and people who needed a place to eat lunch during the week. Or, it may be Mike Bontrager whose company, Chatham Financial, coordinates and funds a mentoring program, Together for Education, a nonprofit to support the classroom. He's also integral in the support of The Garage Community and Youth Center after-school program.

If you're a teenage mom who is having a baby before you are ready, you probably think of the public health nurse Joan Holliday who has helped set up a whole safety net for you that gets you on your feet, helped you finish your education and go out into the world.

Kennett runs a lot of processes and no one person touches them all. But people gravitate to what they know and can do best and for every process there is usually someone you can look to for leadership. Someone has said, "This is how I see what our world can be; let's make it happen."

Score: I would give Kennett a 9/9 for being able to pick out the local patriots.

Sign #3: "Public-private partnerships" are real.
"…in successful towns, people can point to something specific and say; This is what a partnership means."

We talked about how Chatham Financial, a private company, funds the Together for Education nonprofit to support the classroom in the local public schools. But it happened way before that. And it isn't just the private sponsors of the Kennett robotics team who are state champions and compete in the world championships, or the DuPont Company's education liaison Randy Guschl who helped the Kennett Education Foundation put together a sustainable model. Long before any of that, at the turn of the century (1900s), Kennett knew it needed a new school building and legend has it that it planned to pay for it through new real estate taxes. One of the locals, Pierre DuPont, really didn't like the idea of having to pay taxes on his Longwood Gardens estate. But when he found out the need of the community, in 1921 he donated the whole school and when it was built, it was the largest consolidated school (K-12) in the United States.

Another example of these partnerships is the After-The-Bell program at Kennett Middle School. The school allows a nonprofit organization, The Kennett After-School Association (KASA), to offer activities to students on the school premises after school hours are over. KASA is run by volunteers, but funded both by private donations from individual and corporate donors and via public grants.

When I graduated from Kennett in 1964, Mr. DuPont and his Longwood Foundation had given more money to the Kennett school system than to the state of Pennsylvania. And that connectedness between private and public entities still exists in the programs and organizations that support the kids in our community today.

Score: So the Kennett community is a 9/9 today because the local industries like PECO, Chatham Financial and DuPont know how much their employees depend on their hometown, and how they must help the town thrive.

Sign #4: People know the civic story.
In 1866, Bayard Taylor, an American poet, writer and diplomat, wrote a novel called The Story of Kennett. Although the story was fiction, Taylor accurately depicted the Quaker lifestyle (he was born to Quaker parents), the intellectual and physical

landscape, and the current trends in America. There are still strong Quaker roots in the area that lend to the local identity. This is a wonderful page turner with a very colorful depiction of the town.

For a long time, Kennett has been known as "the mushroom capital of the world," and still provides the nation with a large portion of its mushrooms. We have a number of places to go and learn about growing mushrooms, and we even have a mushroom museum included at the local Mushroom Cap. The story of Kennett has morphed and changed over the years, as with all places. There has been a resurgence in vitality that is palpable to people who have lived there for some time. It is a town with a history (albeit a vague one to the millennial generation) that has seen times of dearth and has come back from it. Now, it is seen as a great place to live and raise a family, which doesn't shout exciting to millennials.

This entire book is about that community and how it works today. We are getting the story out and the volunteers in the town are often hardwired to the story. There are healthy service clubs that keep the civic story out front. In his article, Fallows talked about towns that were big enough to do things. The smallest city he mentioned was Sioux City, Iowa and that is the same size as the Kennett southern Chester County region. The identity of the town and southern Chester County is well established.

Score: Nearly 50 people have come forward to tell the Kennett story and share their part of our civic story. 9/9

Sign #5: They have a downtown.

There is no doubt about it; the downtown is the glue that holds Kennett together. Where else would you go to watch your kid's high school band or the Girl Scout troop walk in the Memorial Day parade? Or, for New Year's Eve, to watch the Mushroom Drop …that is a real thing. (Did I mention we like mushrooms?) Fallows mentions over 2,000 downtown revival projects coordinated by the National Trust for Historic Preservation. Kennett is one of them.

Fifteen years ago, one of the doctors in town said that in 20 years the only thing left in downtown Kennett would be the library and the post office. But look at where we are today. We now have some of the best dining and great events in southeastern Pennsylvania.

Score: Kennett's downtown is a destination. 9/9

Sign #6: They are near a research university.

"Research universities have become the modern counterparts to a natural harbor or river confluence. In the short term, they lift the economy by bringing in a student population. Over the longer term, they transform a town through the researchers and professors they attract."

The University of Pennsylvania's veterinary school has a campus just three miles from town and is world-renowned for its large animal hospital and research center. It even has its own reality TV show on "Animal Planet" starting in 2016. Their teachers are tied into the community and the students always find the best new restaurants. The high school has a partnership with universities (West Chester University is 11 miles away) to continue the studies of exceptional students after the AP classes run out. My son took engineering calculus at the University of Delaware (14 miles to the south) in high school. KACS uses West Chester University for research projects on hunger and homelessness and the graduate students as interns.

The greatest influence over the years has been the DuPont Experimental Station with over 3,000 technicians, engineers and scientists. When I was growing up, 35% of our church congregation had PhD's. The Experimental Station is just 14 miles away and is being phased out as DuPont's corporate structure is downsized and the researchers lose their jobs. However, the colleges are growing. Historically, the high school has always had children of world-class researchers, marketers, salesmen and engineers in every graduating class. That may be changing. We will see how those global changes will affect the regional infrastructure.

Score: We will give it an 8/9, not for where it is but for what is on the horizon with the loss of a robust DuPont Experimental Station working on solving the world's materials problems and how to feed 9 billion people.

Sign #7: They have and care about a community college.

"Just about every world historical trend is pushing the United States (and other countries) toward a less equal, more polarized existence: Labor-replacing technology, globalized trade, self-segregated residential housing patterns, the American practice of unequal district-based funding for public schools. Community colleges are the main exception, potentially offering a connection to high-wage technical jobs for people who might otherwise be left with no job or one at minimum wage. Nationwide, only about 40% of those who start at a public community college finish within six years. But we saw a number of schools that were clearly forces in the right direction."

Delaware County Community College (DCCC) serves Delaware and Chester counties with three locations in Delaware County and six in Chester County. Almost two thirds, 62%, of their students transfer on to a four-year school program. It has been named a "Great College to Work For" by the Chronicle for Higher Education for the seventh year in a row in 2016. With about 45% of the student body identifying as non-white, it has a strong diversity program with an Institutional Diversity Committee comprised of professors, vice presidents, directors and administration personnel all representing their perspectives of what diversity means to them.

There is also the Brandywine campus of Penn State University where kids can commute to and from their home for two years before they go up to the main campus in State College, PA. This saves the student well over $30,000 in what can become crippling student loans. It is one of the top five schools that Kennett and Unionville grads go to after their senior year.

Technical education is becoming a bigger part of the options for the students. Some of the best and brightest kids are tied into this education process, which offers technical programs such as HVAC, plumbing, dental hygienist and automobile mechanics. A good friend who retired early from DuPont decided he always wanted to work on cars so he went back to school for automotive repair to learn and do what he loved for a living. His comment about his experience was, "This is really hard." Modern cars have more lines of computer code than the space shuttle. The high-end car designs are not that far from a driverless car.

Score: There is opportunity for better partnering here. Even though DCCC is number one for grads of Kennett with 12% matriculating into the community college and in the top 5 for Unionville there is a feeling that it is being underutilized. More effort can be put into improving the relationship with the high schools and the community college to reduce the number of graduates that don't advance beyond high school. This outcome would provide measurable benefits in pay and employment to the grads. 7/9

Sign #8: They have unusual schools.

Early in our stay, we would ask; "What was the most distinctive school to visit at the K-12 level?" If four or five answers came quickly to mind, that was a good sign. The common theme was intensity of experimentation.

As you can see from the heart of this book, with Study Buddies, the WIN program and After-The-Bell, the school district is working hard at collaborating with community partners to support their students. I have even talked to my siblings, all of whom went through the system, into awarding the graduating senior that demonstrates the most creativity and innovation with a statuette and a small grant. The Kennett Education Foundation challenges the teachers to come up with innovations in teaching and awards tens of thousands of dollars in grants every year. Mr. Shawn Duffy, the high school social studies teacher, is starting an investment club this coming year, with the dividends coming back to the Kennett Education Foundation. But it is not just Kennett, most of the schools have around 20 advance placement classes and still maintain a strong music, sports and extracurricular schedule for their students.

Score: The school district has a mindset to increase the number of graduates who proceed to advanced education after high school. 9/9

Sign #9: They make themselves open.

"The anti-immigrant passion that has inflamed this election cycle was not something people expressed in most of the cities we visited. On the contrary, politicians, educators, business people, students and retirees frequently stressed their communities were trying to attract and include new people. Every small town in America has thought about how to offset the natural brain drain that has historically sent its brightest young people elsewhere. The same emphasis on inclusion that makes a town attractive to talented outsiders increases its draw to its own natives."

Again, the reason we started this book was because Houston, Texas thought we had something to share on how to help immigrants integrate. One of the graduates is interning in the Atlanta, Georgia mayor's office to help them become a welcoming community. It turns out immigrants have just been a part of the normal churn that keeps our community healthy. The ability of immigrants to come into the community, establish a support network and then expand into the business community creates some of the very things that keep the town such a nice place to live. We aren't stuck with just a Taco Bell and McDonald's. We enjoy a variety of restaurants offering Italian, Asian, Mexican and local cuisines and located on the main street of Kennett Square.

But even before this recent immigration influx, I remember seeing a Maryland ad with a picture taken around 100 years ago of a diverse Kennett classroom with the caption that warned Maryland not to follow Pennsylvania's path and mix the races. Today, a number of Kennett area residents can't wait to show off the hidden rooms in their old houses that were part of the Underground Railroad. Kennett has always had more openness than most communities. I think it has a lot to do with the Quaker influence.

Many of my classmates were able to stay in the area because there were jobs available to them. Kennett is in the greater Philadelphia metropolitan area and the fact that there are jobs both in the immediate vicinity and the greater area, means there are opportunities for people in the community to find jobs that are a reasonable commute away. And our mushroom industry is just one example of the job network available to immigrants looking for "starter" jobs.

The planning commission for the town is actively working on the strategy of how to keep the economic and social systems healthy and open to both young professionals and families in need. It has not always been so smooth. A great leader in town, Dr. Leonard Kanofsky, saw the need for more low cost housing in Kennett in the 1970s, and he went out to develop it. In the end, he came back very disappointed with the community. I think he came face to face with NIMBY (Not In My Back Yard).

And lastly, remember our friends in Houston, Texas whose questions got us to thinking why Kennett does so much better than they do. I am sure there are many reasons for it but the short answer is that 80% of the kids in the Houston public school system are economically disadvantaged but 50-60% of the white kids go to private schools. And if all of the kids went to their own public schools, only 40% would be economically disadvantaged, about the same rate as Kennett. But then if Unionville and Kennett were combined with the private schools there would only be 15-20% economically disadvantaged.

Since the 1970s, we have grown the amount of low cost housing, improved the attractiveness of our downtown and now low-resourced students make up 40% of the student body, with some neighboring schools under 10%. **Score**: 9/9

Sign #10: They have big plans.

"If I see a national politician with a blueprint for how things will be better 20 years from now, I think: "Good luck!" In fact, few national politicians even pretend to offer a long-term vision anymore. When a mayor or city-council member shows me a map of how downtown residences will look when completed, or where the new greenway will go, I think: "I'd like to come back. Cities still make plans, because they can do things."

Kennett has a history of excellent planning and execution. Just look at the last 20 years of change that has transformed the borough of Kennett, integrated the township police with the borough's and made the downtown a destination for people all over. But, do we have a blueprint for the future? Not yet. We do have a high-end strategic plan being developed as I write this. We are just getting our arms around the library. The head of the borough council is a trained Longwood Gardens landscape architect and has an image in his mind of how the town should grow, but it's not on paper. The recommendations from the consultants give a set of options for each part of the town and guidelines to where we can apply resources. But a lot more work has to be done before we have a vision of the future for the town. And the council has to respond to what the builders want to do, so you can't be too prescriptive. I look forward to seeing the city plan that evolves with help from a professional staff to build a 20-year plan that addresses available resources.

Score: The plans are coming, but until they are processed and modified to fit the town, we get a 7/9.

Sign #11: They have craft breweries.

"One final marker, perhaps the most reliable: A city on the way back will have one or more craft breweries, and probably some small distilleries too. A town that has craft breweries also has a certain kind of entrepreneur, and a critical mass of mainly young (except for me) customers. You may think I'm joking, but just try to find an exception."

Following is an article from the local newspaper on the subject of beer and craft breweries.

Daily Local News POSTED: 04/10/16, 6:34 PM EDT

KENNETT SQUARE >> Mayor Matt Fetick doesn't mind at all if people refer to Kennett Square as a beer town.

In the past couple of years, council handcrafted an ordinance permitting craft brew operations, which paved the way for Victory Brewing, and Kennett Brewing Co. A new pop up European-style beer garden got approval to begin operations on Birch Street this summer. And at the New Year's Mushroom Drop a few months ago, officials gave the approval for beer to be offered for the first time.

And then there's the Brewfest, where tickets sell for up to $75, Winterfest, the Mushroom Festival, a Victory Brewing Co. Street Party, Cinco de Mayo and even the Kennett Run, where brew flows freely for anyone over age 21 after the race. Brewfest and Winterfest attract thousands of people, and those events are typically always sold out. Beer stations were even set up for last year's Music in the Park, a music series at Anson B. Nixon Park featuring local talent that has become extremely popular.

"We get a lot of criticism that there is too much beer in town," Fetick told members of the Longwood Rotary Club. "But here's the thing —we make no arrests. Zero. We have not made an arrest at the Brewfest in the past seven years."

Kennett Square's Ethan Cramer, who lost a relative to a drunk driver, often offers commentary about the perils of drinking events before he votes. Earlier this month, he voted to approve the Kennett BrewFest Oct. 1, after gaining assurances the event would be well policed and a designated driver program would be offered.

But the BrewFest is Historic Kennett Square's major fundraiser, and it raises tens of thousands of dollars from the single event. Historic Kennett Square helps to promote the town, and stages other events to attract people to Kennett Square, a town that's home to just over 6,000 people. Council members are quick to point out that Historic Kennett Square is one of the main reasons vacant storefronts are virtually non-existent.

"This is not college-town drinking," said Fetick, a former West Chester police officer for nearly 10 years. "There is responsible drinking (at the festivals and events). Quite honestly, I don't care if we become known as a small brewery town and as a destination for people to come and drink beer. As long as it is done responsibly, I am in support of it."

"We haven't had to add one police officer – not one; and not one dollar spent because of any (beer) event," Fetick said. "As a former West Chester police officer, working in that town with 27 liquor licenses just in the central business district, I know what drinking and carrying on is, and we don't have that problem." (Fran Maye)

The article from the *Daily Local News* says it all. The town is actually a little defensive about how healthy it is about taking advantage of the new beer craze. I was especially impressed that the new beer garden is focused on the family. **Score:** 9/9

In summary, Fallows provides a broad spectrum of what a healthy modern city looks like and though Kennett is smaller than a typical city, it measures up well with a rating of 93 out of 99. It is healthy, but past performance is no guarantee of future results. We need to fight entropy and continue to invest in our community to keep Kennett achieving its goal of being a place you can live well and raise a family, no matter how much money you make.

Thinking Hats

"When you're a carpenter and your only tool is a hammer, your whole world looks like a nail."

— Abraham Maslow, American psychologist and author —

Thinking Hats
– On Thinking About Kennett –
by Bob George

The Maslow quote rings true to anyone who ever worked as a consultant. As Joan and I have tried to get our arms around this community that is Kennett, we have used the tools we are most familiar with: interviewing, benchmarking for best practices, and gap analysis. Joan is well versed in organizational effectiveness from her years of leading community efforts in the public health arena. I have worked on hundreds of benchmarking and performance improvement projects at Penn State, the Navy and DuPont. There are tools available that can help you think about a subject holistically. "Six Thinking Hats," developed by Dr. Edward de Bono in 1985, became one of the standard tools of performance improvement. It is this set of tools that we will use in this chapter to analyze and structure our thinking about Kennett. What the thinking hats do is force you to look at your subject with different kinds of thinking, from different angles and there are usually some revelations.

1. **Blue Hat** thinking focuses on the thinking process and how you go about the next steps and plans.
2. **White Hat** thinking looks at the facts and data; at what you have and what you need.
3. **Red Hat** thinking focuses on how you feel about it; your gut instincts and intuition with no justification needed.
4. **Yellow Hat** thinking highlights values and who will benefit. It is optimistic about why something might work.

5. **Green Hat** thinking is focused on creativity and investigation of all the possibilities, alternatives and new ideas.
6. **Black Hat** thinking asks hard questions: what could go wrong, why won't it work? It is practical and realistic, looking to see why something won't work.

Blue Hat thinking on the thinking process that went into this book and this chapter will share the insights and fill in some of the gaps that have been left open. We won't bore you with all the planned meetings, the dead ends, missed deadlines and rewrites. Just realize that it may be true that nothing worth doing is ever easy. But that doesn't mean it can't be rewarding.

White Hat thinking provides a look at the data describing the make-up of Kennett. (Refer to the Kennett by the Numbers chapter.) It shows what we know about the demographics of the town, the statistics on graduation rates, employment and labor information, level of poverty, income levels and residential breakdown. We thought that this part of our project would really be easy, but good data is hard to find. We have the regional economic development plan, but much of that is about real-estate.

Red Hat thinking is a focus on how you feel and what your gut tells you. Joan and I talked about how we both felt that the story of Kennett was "about the kids." It seems that there is an underlying belief held by the volunteers, leaders and the community as a whole, that if we "get the kids right" then a lot of other stuff will fall into place. We also want the book to be a celebration of the successes of these programs, with stories that show how they are authentically meeting the needs of the community's youth.

Yellow Hat thinking is about the logical positive view which permeates all of our thinking on the subject. What is Kennett doing to get these results? How do the different classes and cultures meld into a successful process? We peeled back the layers of the community and found thousands of people making a difference. At the conclusion of the 2014-2015 school year, the United States achieved a new record of graduation rates in four years from high school—83.2%. This is up from 79% four years earlier. Positive results like these touch our hearts and reaffirm all our work and hopefulness for the future of our country.

Green Hat thinking is all about creativity. This type of thinking was responsible for the creation of the chapters on Common Themes, A Path Forward, and The Stress Test. One of the interviewees brought up the James Fallows article in *The Atlantic* that talked about how important a downtown was to a community. Mary Hutchins of Historic Kennett Square pointed out that our youth programs, many of which are located downtown, were enjoying their success in this area. So we took Fallows' questions about what makes for a successful town and applied them to Kennett. We figured that if you can apply a stress test to a bank, you should be able to measure a town's viability through a stress test.

Black Hat thinking is all about practical, realistic identification of problems, pitfalls and reasons why a process wouldn't work. It deals with the forces that could turn Kennett to the dark side, a town that is not a good place to raise a child. One like Mos Eisley (*Star Wars*), where "the Force" isn't very strong and, as Obi-Wan Kenobi warned Luke Skywalker, "You will never find a more wretched hive of scum and villainy."

Using this Black Hat thinking, we have highlighted some red flags. An issue like income inequality in our economic system is one we will have to deal with, but addressing the tax code is not within the scope of our thinking. We are not focused on why we can't do something, but on what might get in the way and how we can continue to work to achieve success. The question of "What's wrong with this picture?" is a healthy one; it makes you consider plan B and helps you prepare for the heavy seas that may occur in the future. After all, life is what happens while you're busy making other plans. (John Lennon)

Red Flag #1: How do we maintain and replenish the pool of volunteers that makes Kennett work? We documented over 2,000 volunteers who support the nonprofits in Kennett, and that doesn't even include the volunteers who support Boy Scouts, Little League, the environmental programs, the Kennett Run, the Mushroom Festival, or the churches and service clubs. This shows that it really takes a village to raise a child and you need everyone to take part in the process. The value of these volunteers is almost priceless because it's not just that they provide free leadership and labor, but they also include the passion for making these programs work. It is a rule of thumb that board members are chosen to bring one or more of three things to a board: wisdom, wealth or work. Board members sharing their work, wisdom and wealth will be even more important as the need for volunteers grow and the barriers to time and resources increase.

There are a number of headwinds to keep us from meeting our goals recruiting volunteers. With more single-family households and a reduction in the middle class, there is less bandwidth in terms of people, time and availability to volunteer. We see it in other towns, where keeping up with just supporting your own family is all that can really be expected of most in the community. We saw how the outstanding students actually had the self-awareness to feel guilty that they had to spend all their energy on their own successes, rather than their precious time with friends and family.

Each organization will need to be conscious of the care and development of their volunteers. A leadership development program for volunteers, a program to transition outstanding volunteers to the board, a progression plan for the members of the board and a sense of how leadership will be transferred is essential to the organization's success. We see this implemented in Kennett with programs from the United Way and Chester County Community Foundation that are providing development opportunities for board members. There is a whole school of thought around the care and feeding of volunteers that Joan addressed in another chapter. We see nonprofits replacing volunteers with paid employees and being unable to fill board seats.

Red Flag #2: How can we maintain the revenue streams that are the mother's milk of these organizations? There is very little federal and state money, so we rely on United Way, churches, businesses, foundations and grants. Each organization must develop their own funding strategy. The good news is there is more money going to foundations, wealthy benefactors and organizations, which should provide more opportunities for grants and well-constructed programs. But almost everything else, including local, state and federal support along with United Way funding, is shrinking as the needs grow.

Red Flag #3: How can we deal with the inequality that is structurally embedded into our economy and the various ways in which it manifests itself? This is a complex set of issues that I realize won't be answered here; But, these forces have battered Kennett over the years with the rise of Walmart and the big box stores, the failure of local manufacturing with the attendant loss of good paying jobs, and Wall Street's cutting up of DuPont and MBNA for cash. Suffice to say that in the current election cycle, the young people living in their parents' basements, whose good jobs are going overseas, are all dealing with real forces that are keeping them from living the kind of life their parents had.

We have embraced an economy that is Darwinian. It does seem to work better than the alternatives, but the rich and powerful make the rules, whereby they get paid the most. The system is designed for them to be successful and keep most of what they make. We have had a very strong run in the last 120 years with every generation being better off than their parents till now. Since the 1980's we have been treading water and the wealth is going disproportionately to the top and the big steel mills and textile mills are no longer major employers. Much of the great innovation is behind us and modern technology is not labor intensive. Apple Corporation is huge—close to six times larger than DuPont was in its heyday and with significantly fewer employees. One of my goals as an industrial engineer was to make more with less, and we have been almost too successful at our work. But that is where the growth comes from and growth is what creates wealth.

Red Flag #4: There is no consensus that poor people should be provided the support to live a decent life. In fact there is a sense by some that providing poor people help makes them dependent. Thomas Jefferson put into the Declaration of Independence the pursuit of happiness as an inalienable right. So we aren't guaranteed happiness, just the chance to pursue it. Money is not what gives us happiness, but without a certain amount of it, life is much less pleasant. Social data shows that after you get to a little over $70,000 in the United States, depending on where you live, additional money does not provide more happiness. Money per se does not provide happiness; at best it allows you to do things which can foster good relationships, earn respect, and also the things you love to do. There is just no correlation with happiness and income after you hit $70k. I think we can agree on the fact that a family that is below the poverty line, living on the street, going to bed hungry at night, not getting the medical help they need, is not living a very pleasant existence.

It is our belief that we can make Kennett a decent place to live, even if a family is living in poverty, by providing the services that cover basic needs. And yes, there really is poverty. About 10% of the residents of the Borough live below the poverty line, 6% of Chester County and 12% of the state.

In 2013, the number of students in the United States public school system that were economically disadvantaged passed the milestone of 51%. That number is 42% for the Kennett Consolidated School District. The entitlements that support these kids, their parents and grandparents are under real threat. Entitlements must be part of our future. We're the richest country in the world, but we're sending kids to bed hungry. This is an example of a potential roadblock to making Kennett a great place to live for everybody. There should be a consensus that poor people will live with a roof over their heads, enough food to eat, healthcare, and a first class education for their children. That is our dream and pretty much the dream of most of the people we have interviewed and talked to. A smart safety net can make sure every kid is kindergarten ready, parents are trained for the technical work that pays a sustainable wage, health care is a given and the community invests in people instead of writing them off. These resources will pay for themselves over time and are affordable, but there is no consensus that providing them is for the best.

Red Flag #5: The slow economic growth rate seems to be the new normal. We have come back from the Great Recession, but the only thing breaking records is the stock market. Don't forget the decreases in wages for lower income earners, or the stagnant middle income earnings. The year 2015 was great, but we still aren't where we were at the turn of the 21st century.

If you're interested in this concern read Robert Gordon's book, <u>The Death of Innovation, The End of Growth</u>. I would recommend his Ted Talk because, if he is only partly right, our ability to have success in this area of improving people's lives through wealth creation is not going to get easier. In a nutshell, he talks about four major winds in our face that will affect the money Kennett will have to reinvest in the community:

1. **Demographics:** We had a real kick to creating income when women began to enter the labor force in the 1970s as families improved their incomes. And now we are losing the baby boomers to retirement and a lot of people with good paying adult incomes are now living on fixed incomes and social security.
2. **Education:** As an economy, the United States is graduating 15% less people who start college than the Canadians; our students start their adult lives with a trillion dollars of debt.
3. **Debt:** Both college debt and national debt as a percent of Gross Domestic Product (GDP) is growing unsustainably.
4. **Inequality:** The growth in income is not distributed evenly. The growth rate of income for the bottom 80% is lower than the top 20%, and the top 20% is lower than the top 1%,

So Gordon's simple math demonstrates that these head winds will be offsetting at least half the growth that comes from the innovations that come from the economy. And then we are going to be hard pressed to replicate the inventions of the past 50 years. In addition, much of the innovation will involve doing away with current jobs, like truck driving, reading x-rays, and mushroom picking.

There are predictions, for example from the *Atlantic Monthly*, that project a future where, in our grandkids' lifetime, there will only be real jobs for a fifth of the US population. We certainly can't expect to double the standard of living every generation, which is what the economy has been doing. So my guess is that a 1% growth rate in wealth creation on average is very realistic, which is thought of as being anemic, though it is not negative like it has been in the last decade. This means we will have to provide a larger and larger segment of the population support when lack of work forces them into poverty.

Red Flag #6: How can we sustain the high quality of experienced and capable Kennett leadership that we have had in the past? It is hard to visualize another generation of Lufts, Karkosaks, Thompsons and Newtons. That may just be me thinking of the good ol' days, but they don't call it the Greatest Generation for nothing. We certainly can get good leadership, and we have a number of inspired professionals. We will just have to pay attention and provide the vision and training for great leadership. And, if one sees that potential in a young person, nurture it.

A Path Forward

**"We do not learn from experience –
we learn from reflecting on experience."**
— John Dewey, American philosopher and psychologist —

━━━◆◇◆━━━

So What? A Path Forward
(collaborative thoughts from Joan and Bob)

When Joan and I started this project, we did it with a fairly high level of humility. As my father used to remind me from time to time, I have a lot of reasons to be humble. Our primary role in this effort was to listen. We were experts at being from Kennett, a place that we know and love and this is Kennett's story. It speaks for itself through the men, women and young people who get out of bed every morning to live their lives and make Kennett better every day. After listening to nearly fifty people tell us about their successes and failures, we began to develop a point of view, best described by "Get the kids right!" So many of the people we interviewed really wanted to get the kids right. To make sure they became all that they could be. If we got that right, so much else would fall into place. Along with that realization, we are learning that the story is much deeper and broader than this, and that the current state has implications for the future.

When I tackle a writing project, I always try to channel my 11th grade English teacher, Grace Merrick, who believed that I always had something worth saying, albeit something spelled poorly and with relatively atrocious grammar. This is one of many reasons why I became an engineer. She would always challenge her students and I can hear her saying things like, "So what?" and "So, now what did you learn?" Well, we learned a few things during this look at the people and processes of Kennett.

Here is what we think that we should do next. The recommendations attempt to capture the white spaces where we think our community could do better. Yet, we are quick to say, keep paddling, keep our heads up and keep doing what we are doing so well. At the same time, keeping in mind, the old physics law of entropy. If we don't keep putting energy into the system, into Kennett, it will break down.

I repeat that, while these are our thoughts for "a path forward," they are organically coming out of the community. This is not Joan and Bob telling you this is what you should do to help Kennett or your own community. This is just our attempt to say, "From where we stand, this is what we see. What do you see? What are you going to do about it?" We have learned that it is important to have a passion for the mission you are serving or the life change that you represent. We are available to help as you think about how to improve your community and make it a great place to raise a child. Remember Dr. Emmett Brown and Marty McFly in *Back to the Future*? In our future, we have to "get the kids right."

Early Childhood: The child represents the major focus of what Kennett is all about. We believe that the foundation of the child is the family. The problem is that not all families have the resources and capability to provide their child what they need. And even some of us who do have a great deal of resources at hand still have a rough time of it. There are only two solutions to this dilemma. Plan A, provide the resources as a community to help a young child develop the capability to succeed in school and eventually function as a contributing member of society. Parents are an essential element in a child's success, so parents need to be provided the tools that keep them actively involved in their child's development throughout their school years. Plan B, do nothing and let the children fail and become a drag on society, or possibly sterilize the parents until they can pass a test indicating they are able to raise a child. This plan has some implementation issues, not to mention moral and constitutional ones.

The support that families receive varies state by state, with some coming from federal Head Start funds, but the United States spends less on early childhood education than other modern societies. Almost all of our investment comes from individual families. This leaves large numbers of kids not ready for kindergarten. I asked a Texas kindergarten teacher, who also taught in Kennett, how they do it in her state. She said, "There are two years of early childhood education for the poverty level kids and to be kindergarten-ready the child needs to be able to count up to one hundred; be ready to start reading words and know the shape of the state of Texas."

To make up for the gap in early childhood education means you have to provide four to six years of education in the first three years of school or they go through school falling behind, not getting a full education and are much more likely to not even finish high school. In Kennett, about one third of the incoming at-risk kids are receiving the pre-school they need. Keep in mind that a number of these kids are learning a new language at the same time they learn to read, write and do math. The Kennett school district has instituted an all-day kindergarten as a first step.

Tick-Tock, Head Start, Migrant Head Start, Family Literacy Program and the Family Center are all programs that attempt to tackle this issue, but they could all double in size and we still would have kids falling through the cracks.

The superintendent of schools is making great inroads by having meetings with immigrant families and focusing on getting them to understand how important education is in our society, and the results are promising. Instead of fighting to have their kids leave school to get a job and raise a family, which is their experience, they are beginning to fight for their kids to do well in school and go onto college and or professional training.

Early childhood education is important because when it is not present, children are much less likely to fulfill their potential. Getting every child into early education requires public support and benefits from parental involvement.

Volunteers: We have addressed how important it is to maintain our culture of volunteerism and that each active member of the community should know what they have a passion for and spend some of their time helping and building skills that can be useful and enabling. It takes over 2,000 volunteers to run these organizations around Kennett and the turnover is fairly high. That doesn't include the service clubs and churches, which also have volunteers and continual recruitment. The future requires that we keep adding volunteers. Paid employees are replacing some of the volunteers. This may be a thing of the future, but it is expensive and money is becoming harder to come by.

The volunteers tend to be Baby Boomers who come from a tradition of volunteering more than the Gen-X and Millennial generations. We are discovering that millennials don't do work the way Baby Boomers do. That don't like to plan too far in advance. For example, there was a need for volunteers at a Saturday morning farmer's market booth and an email went out six weeks ahead to get volunteers. No responses were received. At the Thursday night meeting of the group, two days before the event, the plea went out that we needed volunteers to man the booth and one of the young members of the group got on his smart phone, tweeted out the need and by the end of the meeting had five people who were available to work the booth. We are going to have to learn how to work differently with the next generations, but there is still work to be done figuring out the best practices to do that. In the meantime, there will be a lot of trial and error, and some organizations will be successful and some not.

Growing our volunteer pool is integral to running the programs that support the families that are raising their kids in Kennett. Doing that in a sustainable way requires outreach, competent volunteer management and understanding how different generations interact with the role of the volunteer.

Collaborations: In the past, we have had the good fortune to build standalone organizations that could focus on a specific area of a community need. Today, the middle class is dwindling, needs are expanding, and the resources available just don't cut it. Our 'standalone' organization is part of a larger system, and we can leverage the resources in the larger system by learning to collaborate with all the other organizations that compose it. Understanding one's uniqueness as a program, then drawing on other programs to fill in the gaps to meet a client's spectrum of needs will be the managing process of the future. This is a fundamental change that requires no more "stove piping" if we are going to maximize our resources.

We have learned about a model that the United Way organization has applied in another community that leverages this process. A plan is developed to provide $350,000 to early childhood over the next three years. This requires the current receivers of that funding to collaborate with the other agencies to make one application that covers all of the agencies. This way, with reduced budgets, they can continue to maximize services by reducing overhead instead of the direct support to the clients.

It also is not just the cost of executive directors and staff that put a stress on stove piped nonprofit budgets, but the resources associated with volunteers and board members. One of the leaders of a homeless shelter in Wilmington, Delaware talks about half of the nonprofits folding in the next decade because there just aren't enough qualified people to lead their boards.

The KACS organization is expanding their facilities so they can include services for their clients such as legal aid and food stamps. This provides high quality office space with easy access for their clients at minimal cost. Adding these different services into one space is not easy. People have their own ideas about the best way to do things, their own identity as professionals, habits, sense of space, faith issues, and even social norms. In spite of all the benefits we get from our kindergarten days, we still don't like to share. It is becoming more evident that for a community to stay healthy, agencies are going to have to compromise, collaborate and even merge.

Adequately fund United Way: With the southern Chester County area needs, the minimum target that we should reach with our United Way of Southern Chester County contributions is around $1,000,000 for 100,000 people. Ten dollars a person doesn't sound like much, but we missed it by 30% this year.

The reason that giving to United Way is so important is there are at least thirty-one agencies that service just the borough of Kennett Square. They provide a broad dynamic support to the community, and United Way is the managing process that makes it all work. No individual in the community can keep up with all of the community needs, which is the reason that United Way was started and continues to serve the whole community. Allocation committees diligently learn about the ways needs are being met by the nonprofits and then assign resources to where they will do the most good.

The winds of change are pushing against United Way and that kind of giving. They lost five members of their board with the downsizing of DuPont this year and giving was down over 25% as people were laid off or forced to retire. The culture of giving to an organization that doesn't directly benefit you doesn't come easily. I remember when I was starting out as a young engineer with a family and my supervisor came around and canvassed me for United Way in Virginia. My reaction was, "Absolutely not! I have better things to do with my money." My boss, Roy Adams, sat me down and said, "We live in this town and we need to give back to it, and this is a way that you can do that. Plus, DuPont is big on United Way and commits each year with the promise that employees will participate." As a result, while I never saw an individual's career affected because they didn't give to United Way. I also never saw anyone not give to the United Way. I guess it became part of the culture. The approach was not subtle, but it got me giving and forty-five years later I am a believer and was a United Way Tocqueville Society member till I left DuPont.

Southern Chester County took a major hit when 5,200 people employed by DuPont lost their jobs in Wilmington, Delaware, just 6 miles away from the county border. While boosting the local United Way donations to the yearly million dollars level won't solve the whole problem, because none of Kennett's agencies get more than a quarter of their funds from United Way, it is a base that they depend on. When After-The-Bell heard they were down 30% from their United Way request, they had to go out and do emergency fund raising. Nonprofits don't have that kind of cushion in their budgets. They are so efficient because they are running on shoestrings. If After-The-Bell can't pay for the busses to take the kids home, the kids can't come. That is the difference that United Way donations make in the community.

The village has a lot of "heroes" but United Way is the glue that holds a lot of it together, and we need to let them keep doing their job. That means building value for giving holistically to the region and providing the additional revenue to keep the lights on in the agencies that do the most good.

Relationships vs. Technology: Facebook and Snapchat can't take the place of real personal relationships. This recommendation, coming from two tip-of-the-spear Baby Boomers (Joan and I are the oldest baby boomers), may sound a little dodgy, but we believe we need venues to meet and discuss the changes we want to make. We need to build trust to build the village that helps raise a child.

Interactions like bridging, board meetings, volunteering at the food cupboard or teaching a course at After-The-Bell are necessary to build the infrastructure of knowledgeable and effective leaders and workers in a healthy Kennett community. In my career at DuPont, I watched it become a global company where a team that did anything substantial needed representation from Asia, Europe and, later, South America. These virtual teams couldn't be co-located because there wasn't time or money. But, putting them together in an actual physical location was what one Hewlett Packard executive called the closest thing to "pixie dust" to getting a team to work well and accomplish their goals on time. It was always essential that the members knew each other and had a good feel for their team members' capabilities and mind set. There is no better way to get to know each other than face-to-face meetings. Building knowledge and trust within the team was crucial to its success. The same is true about today's community. Most rich people don't know any poor people and vice versa. We need processes and systems to break down these barriers.

It is not that social media doesn't have a place in building a healthy community. Technology is invaluable for communication. How did we ever get anything done without email, the cloud and cell phones? And yes, a meeting on Skype works with a busy team; technology is necessary but not sufficient.

As we reflect on the interviews for the many Kennett community efforts, we can see that a Facebook page is no substitute for a working group with the right skills and knowledge of each other. We need mechanisms to bring people together, address issues, build teams and develop and execute plans.

Preventing Poverty: The key to preventing poverty is providing sustainable employment, jobs that pay $20 an hour with benefits. To this end we need more facilitators. That would be men and women who play matchmaker and provide direction as to what kind of education and experience will make individuals fit an employer's needs. And then help develop the flow of workers to the employers.

There are some job placement programs in the community, and there are a couple things we know. There certainly are not enough good jobs to go around and there are good jobs that aren't being filled. Plus there are not enough coaches and mentors helping people succeed at this critical process of career building.

Let's reduce that gap, fill the good jobs and upgrade individuals to better ones. The larger mushroom farms have a professional progression from picker to supervisor to manager. That requires a lot of on-the-job training and development. When organizations are farsighted enough to invest in their employees, they see the money returned many times over.

Communicate the Kennett story: The Kennett story needs to be shared. It is about creating goodness. It is about what it takes to build a village where a child can thrive. It tells what works and what doesn't work so well. It is about processes and best practices, experts, novices and volunteers making their way through life in the light of a community that has been a decent place to live since before Bayard Taylor wrote his novel in 1866, more than 150 years ago.

If the story is shared, and heard, I can't help but believe that we will see progress. People will understand how they fit in to different processes and see the fruits of their labors. We will drop the work that isn't working and build on the work that is. It will be easier for the United Way to raise their money and more of the incoming kids will hit the ground running when they enter kindergarten.

We will do our best to share these stories, but you need to share your story as well, whether it is about southern Chester County, Pennsylvania, another state or another country. Communication is one of the keys to solving the problem of how to make a community a great place to live and raise a family. When you see something that is working, say something!

Celebrate our diversity: In 2001, Mabel Thompson, a Kennett resident who knew Dr. Martin Luther King Jr. personally, formed the initial MLK CommUNITY Breakfast Committee, a committee which continues to meet to this day. Their mission is to revitalize Dr. Martin Luther King Jr.'s dream of peace and harmony among all people. The annual breakfast draws a cross-section of the community, filling the room with over three hundred in attendance. A social justice message is given by a speaker who challenges the community to address issues that may be preventing the black community and minority groups from reaching their inalienable rights both nationally and locally. These messages need to be extended throughout the year with many opportunities for the majority population to dialogue and become educated about these injustices.

Beyond our Cinco de Mayo and Día de los Muertos celebrations, we also need to come to grips with supporting a national immigration policy that accepts that undocumented workers staff our country. We need to address the eight hundred pound gorilla in the room. It was addressed decades ago, when Ronald Reagan was president, but we didn't get to the root causes. We have to address this as a nation; our dysfunctional political systems and immigration policies need to be addressed.

It manifests itself in so many ways. There are three big issues that we recognize through our interviews. First, the children of undocumented workers can't get the loans they need to further their education beyond high school. Even though most migrant parents only have a sixth grade education or less, they have dreams for their children, and the current situation limits how far their child can go in their education. Think of the interview with Christian Cordova, who was born three months after his family came to the United States and is currently at Harvard. Just a few months separates him from one of the best educations in the world and the real possibility that he might not have even finished high school. These kids who aren't citizens, through no fault of their own, don't have that opportunity. A number of them receive scholarship awards at graduation for outstanding performance, but don't get to apply them because they don't have access to Pell grants to cover the total cost of higher education. That's not including all the other federal and state programs that encourage an educated electorate. The parents of these children have it even worse. Second, the families live in fear of deportation, even though they are supporting our town's economy. We tend to recognize this in the background, but not in the pervasive way it is presenting itself. These families may have lived here for ten years, and the kids only know the United States as home. They also have children who were born here and are citizens, so, if they're deported, they face the decision of breaking up their family and leaving them with relatives so that they can still have a better future. We are deporting a half million people a year and some are clamoring to throw 11 million out.

The last and most appalling problem involves health care coverage and workman's compensation. During the time of writing this book, there were two examples of a breadwinner of a family working in a mushroom house being injured on the job. The results were uniform and swift. The individuals were fired. They had no workman's compensation and no health care. The hospital bills pile up, the families lost their cash flow and within a short time they had to deal with the threat of being out on the street. Who is going to help them?

It is time to get beyond politics and fix this problem. I believe if it wasn't for the tragedy of 9/11, George Bush would have dealt with it 15 years ago, but we don't have that excuse today. Make sure your congressional representatives know that they are part of the solution or part of the problem, and you are watching.

It's not STEM, it's STEAM: Recently a group of residents have formed a Kennett Arts Alliance. The idea started with residents, who were inspired to take on the mission of promoting visual, performing, music, craft and art classes and exhibits in the broader community. During their community engagement, it became known that both Kennett and Unionville Schools have emphasized Science, Technology, Engineering and Math (STEM) which results in less of an emphasis on the arts. STEM is needed in today's world economy, and the only place the kids are going to get it is in the schools. But research has shown that weaving arts (STEAM) into everything education does, boosts academic achievement and promotes creativity. Art has long been recognized as an important part of a well-rounded education, but when it comes down to setting budget priorities, the arts rarely rise to the top.

When I was in 9th grade, I was a member of the Science Fiction Club. We read all the great science fiction books and shared the amazing ideas about the future and other worlds that they created. Today, I still try to "grock" life and am rarely without my towel. And then, just last week one of our most gifted Hispanic students, currently a sophomore at Penn State majoring in architectural engineering, was having a rough time. He spent sixteen hours in the classroom on a design project, learning how to draw. In his field, drawing is absolutely necessary. If he had more art at Kennett, he would have been better prepared for engineering. The Kennett Library has developed a visioning team to solicit ideas from the community to determine the best design for a new library building. This has been the arena for the Kennett Arts Alliance to speak to the need for the community to provide the art opportunities that the schools may not be able to provide and to offer programming that includes integration of all the disciplines through a "maker space." As schools come to grips with limited resources many are dropping sports, music and theatre. This is very short-sighted, and we need to provide our children a well-rounded education.

The School of the Woods: Sir Robert Baden-Powell used the phrase "scouting was a school of the woods." As scout leaders and individuals who love the outdoors, we think the outdoors can be and should be part of "shaping our future one child at a time." Getting out in nature is a practice that we need to be intentional about in providing the best environment for our kids, and scouting is just one of the ways to do that. The book, <u>Last Child in the Woods: Saving Our Children from Nature Deficit Disorder</u> by Richard Louv, is a strong statement about how our children are missing out on the lessons of nature, and how this deprivation also affects their healthy development. Community youth programs have opportunities to add both arts and nature dimension to their outreach, and many are already doing this. Promoting the arts and getting out in nature are not new ideas, but as our overall society, Kennett is also at risk in losing this focus and our children missing out on the learning that helps develop their fullest potential.

Execute the plan: The stress test says having an executable plan is a big part of a successful community. We are just now publishing a land use plan for Kennett, put together for both the borough and the Kennett Township. Bricks and mortar, sidewalks and stores, homes and businesses, schools and nonprofits are what make up a town and how they work together defines the culture and spirit of the town. I know there are people who believe that the invisible hand of market forces that Adam Smith wrote about in his opus <u>An Inquiry into the Nature and Causes of the Wealth of Nations</u> (1776) will take care of this, but I've seen that work differently. That's how you get a 7/11 next to a home next to a gas station next to a school. We need a plan with thoughtful zoning laws. One can't fight Mother Nature, so the market forces must be taken into consideration. The city can't build senior citizen housing that will not be filled or pay stores to go in where the foot traffic won't support them. But more than anything, the community must own the plan. In Kennett, understand the plan that the consultants have presented, make it your own with changes and tweaks and stay involved in this community evolution. Find out what your community's plan is and how well it is being implemented. As Yoda said in *Star Wars*, "Do or do not, there is no try."

Reflections

"I know the price of success: dedication, hard work, and unremitting devotion to the things you want to see happen."

— Frank Lloyd Wright, American architect & designer —

Reflections
Bob George

As Joan and I looked over the many interviews we conducted over the past year with Kennett citizens, we were able to follow a track that begged questions and responses. We both have been influenced by Charlie Krone, who passed away while bringing this project together. Charlie taught DuPont and my old boss Bob Kasey, who then taught me most of what I know about organization development. Krone's obituary read in part:

> *"Charlie pioneered many of the founding concepts in the field of organization development, integrating several disciplines to formulate principles and processes for self-actualization, self-realization and systemic thinking. As a consultant he dedicated himself to making the world a better place through applying vision and creativity to developing organizations where people could simultaneously have a meaningful work life, contribute to the success of their business, and develop to their full professional and spiritual potential."*

Bob Kasey translated it to Creative Grandparenting (today it is called CGI) and the mentoring program that serves Delaware's schools and provides Kennett the mentoring model. It has trained well over 6,000 mentors to work in the classrooms with young kids. I think you can see the imprint of organization development on this work. You were rarely in a room with Charlie where he wasn't the smartest person in the room, though Charlie suffered fools much better than most. And he always had tremendous value for the right question. So we have been asking ourselves whether or not we have been asking the right questions, and the tool of The Five Whys came up as a way of getting to the heart of Kennett's success. The Five Whys tool gets to the root cause of an issue. When we apply The Five Whys to our inquiry, "Why is Kennett so great?," we may sound like the annoying child who continues to ask questions. Please bear with us as we peel back the onion to attempt to identify the core of Kennett's success.

1. Why is Kennett great? Because our book process of listening to the citizens of Kennett leads us to believe that the key to the success of Kennett is the child. If you can take care of the children, the good life will follow.

2. So why are the children successful? The key to the child's success is education provided by the school system and the community programs that support the child and their families.

3. Why is Kennett's education and community programs successful? Because the schools, in concert with the after-school programs, do a great job of teaching and supporting the student to help each reach his or her potential.

4. Why do the schools and after-school programs do a great job of teaching to each student? Because they focus on leadership, teachers, curriculum and tutoring, and strongly encourage the active participation of the parents.

5. Why does the school system and community have such great programs? Because the administration, teachers and community know how to teach, innovate, continually improve their practices, work with the families/community and care deeply about achieving the success of each child. With the commitment and investment of KCSD and the community, these programs continue to be adequately resourced.

Now, how the schools are financially resourced today is a discussion that creates more heat than light. It starts out with the total cost. It's not cheap to educate any kid, let alone one who doesn't show up ready to be taught. Paying for transportation ($1,000+ per kid, including private school kids), the special-education kids can cost $85,000 and teachers, administration and buildings comes to almost $20,000 per student. Now one could argue that not educating the kids adequately would threaten our whole democracy and national security. Luckily, it is pretty much agreed that our kids need to be educated, and that it is best done by "the village," so to speak. I have a sister-in-law who was on the school board in Montana where the number of kids that are home-schooled is higher than the national average of 3%. I asked her how they did, as many would come into the high schools later in their educational journey, and she allowed that many do well in a number of areas, but they don't do very well in geography. It is just very hard for one parent or tutor to be all things educationally to a child. Being a teacher is a professional career, much like being an engineer or accountant. We need to respect the profession, recognize how important it is to the future of our country, and pay accordingly.

Of course, we use taxes to pay for these costs. Most of the money comes from property taxes (approximately $5,358 per home) and a little over 1% local tax on income. While Pennsylvania is one of the more user-friendly states for retirees as it doesn't tax pensions and social security, there is still anger from the aging population at property taxes going up over $150 per year. And that is just within Kennett where there are large homes to keep the taxes relatively low for the lower middle class. In the urban areas, there isn't the real estate and industrial investment to support schools with disadvantaged students that are resource intensive. There is a case to be made that the money is backward, it is going to the mainline suburban schools of Philadelphia, and not to the resource challenged communities. Even the "mink and manure" schools around us that have virtually unlimited resources are serving a fairly homogenous school population of self-motivated kids or at least kids that have all the resources they need to succeed.

The reason why this is such a big deal, as Ta-Nehisi Coates said in his letter to his son in the book, Between the World and Me, is that 60% of the black kids who don't finish high school will end up incarcerated. When you look at the $30,000 a year it costs to incarcerate those kids, how could it not be a good idea to invest in the resources needed to provide a decent education that leads to a career? Pay me now, or pay me latter.

∞

I went back to Dr. Larry Bosley, the superintendent of the KCSD for 15 years before retiring in 1999, and asked him if the answers to The Five Whys indicate Kennett's success.

He said, "I agree that Kennett's success starts with the kids, and that we are very fortunate to have a community that can provide resources to the district. But I see what is going on around the country with kids who grew up and were not raised by a family or school system that taught them the ways of our community. You look at the Philadelphia school district, and it is just too big. I would break it up into 15 to 20 districts and give each district the freedom to do what needs to be done. Leadership is why schools do well; leadership from the superintendent, the principals, the administration, the teachers, the school board, the parents and the community. Kennett could have all the problems of Philadelphia if it didn't provide the kids the experience of *being raised*."

For Dr. Bosley, it was a binary discussion. He had the financial resources he needed and was able to pay teachers competitively and execute his plan for a school of academic excellence. He talked about how in Philadelphia all the best students were siphoned off to magnet schools such as Central, Masterman, or the High School for the Creative Arts. This takes away from the regular schools. Kennett loses some of the good students to the private schools in Wilmington or West Chester, but not that many, as their parents can choose a more diverse and still academically rigorous education while saving sometimes more than $120,000 per child over 12 years by attending Kennett schools.

Dr. Bosley talked about how there were so many different values in the air it wasn't easy to deal with all the change that was going on. He said, "In fact, I would rather work with the parents than with the students because the parents can have much more of a cultural impact than the school. When I was superintendent, I would have my own table in the cafeteria. If I wasn't at one of the other buildings, I would have lunch and the kids would come over to me and we would talk. Kids can really understand why you are doing something if you explain it to them. They are remarkably sophisticated in their insights."

Dr. Bosley gave me an example about how the teachers would come with their set of values and it would clash with the kids. He said, "In the 1960s I was an assistant principal, which has a lot of the disciplinary duties. And all of a sudden most of the black kids started coming to school wearing granny glasses. It was a style thing I guess. The principal got complaints from the teachers that they didn't like it and one kid was sent home. It didn't bother me, and I didn't see how it could be justified to send someone home for it so I ignored it and said the teacher could handle that Parent/Teacher conference. You can't be arbitrary. You need to understand your core values and reinforce them."

∞

You can see how cultures can clash, and the important thing is to have common core values to share. I see that a number of families are overwhelmed by life. They are working two and a half jobs to make ends meet and sometimes they just want the school to take care of the kids. Schools can support the child, but the equation works best when the parents support the school, as well. We work hard to encourage the parents to take responsibility for their kids. If they want them to be successful, then it is important that they are part of the equation. The schools can take the lead if the parents aren't able. After all, the English aristocracy has been raising their kids in boarding schools for centuries, although that is a different level of resource availability. The very best high schools in the United States and Europe are boarding schools – schools such as Le Rosey, Eaton, Rugby, Phillips, and Lawrenceville.

So what are the core values that create great education? Dr. Bosley said, "One of my core beliefs as an administrator was that everything we did had to be with the kids in mind. The teachers and administration shouldn't make decisions that make their job easier if it doesn't help the kids. It's all about the kids. When I observe a teacher in the classroom and sit down with them afterward for feedback, I ask them two questions. What are you trying to accomplish? Did you accomplish it? If you can't answer these questions, you aren't teaching. Dr. Tomasetti, the current superintendent of the KCSD, said his core value is respect; people should respect one another, and all our decisions and actions should be based on that premise. Dr. Tomasetti lives that belief with periodic meetings with the Spanish-speaking parents to explain to them the value of a good education in their children's lives.

One area that addresses school values is my personal story regarding the dress code. In the spring of my senior year (1964) at Kennett High School, my best friend, Steve Loeffler, came to school dressed in what I can only call formal Bermuda dress. He was the best-dressed student or adult that had come through the halls all year. But the coat and tie, dress shoes and high socks included Bermuda shorts, and he was sent home. It was a rule, no shorts. I told that story to the previous superintendent, Dr. Karkosak, and he told me that when he came to Kennett during the 1990s, shorts were already part of the dress code. And then he went to the local Mass on Sunday and found people coming to church in shorts. I guess you have to change with the times. Was this what the Nobel Laureate Bob Dylan meant when he wrote and sang, *"The times they are a changing"*?

∞

Dr. Bosley sees the current funding process for Kennett as adequate to ensure the level of quality of the education provided will continue if the mix of students doesn't change. But, he points out that it is not just about money. We need to continue to have the highly educated families contributing their diverse insights to the student body, like those from the large international firms and universities in the area. The change agents that brought the rigorous high quality educational experience to Kennett were the exceptional parents on the school board that knew what they wanted for their kids. Dr. Al Luft, Dr. Gene Bennett, Sandy Lee, Alan Hovde and others had a vision of taking the school from a place to get an education to a great place to get a great education. That meant more AP classes and more resources.

Dr. Bosley, who went into real estate after retiring from KCSD, has other worries, as well. "I worry that some of the kids whose families suffer from poverty don't have a work ethic. I have a number of Section 8 apartments/houses and many of the residents are in generational poverty, and I question where can they find hope. This is a factor that we, the town and gown, need to address together."

He feels the partnership with the school and the community is in good shape now. The school is communicating well with the town and, much like the students, when the town understands why we are doing something they are very understanding. But it wasn't always this way.

He tells this story. "When I arrived during the late 70s, they had a plan in place to spend a lot of money to upgrade the school, put in a very large auditorium where the front steps are now and add air conditioning. The school really needed the upgrades as nothing had been done for a long time, but there hadn't been much communication to the town about the need for repairing the infrastructure and bringing the maintenance up-to-date. The taxes had been low and a bond issue had to go forward. There was a major open house to explain all that was going to be done and it didn't go well. In the end, an individual filed suit against the school and because a suit was pending the school wasn't able to incur additional debt and construction had to stop. The court eventually threw out the suit, but there was a lot of damage done to reputations and trust. I became the new face of the school district and was told to hire good people to run the day-to-day work because the school board wanted him out in the community, communicating the vision of excellence that the school board had for the school."

In discussing the infrastructure that makes each school work, Dr. Bosley said, "I see that the key to each school is the principal who sets the tone. If someone comes to me and has a complaint about the school, I always say, 'Have you talked to the principal?', and sometimes they say, 'I'm afraid they will take it out on my kid.' And I say, 'If that happens, you come to see me.'"

I would also be remiss if I didn't include Dr. Karkosak's desire to include the community in the education process with his leadership in developing an education foundation. The example that was presented to us by Pennsylvania when we looked into how one would work, was a central Pennsylvania school that was using the foundation to resource teachers with materials for the classrooms that weren't covered by the school. But we saw much bigger opportunities, such as:

- A way to create innovation in the classroom with teacher grants.
- Recognition of great teaching and the best teachers.
- Support of the transition to new programs such as robotics, football, and STEM.
- Recognition of student excellence and provide financial awards and incentives to graduating seniors as they move on to their next level of education.
- A mechanism for the community to participate in this very important education process.

Then this leads to a discussion of why the family support for the kid's education is not always there. So many families are under-resourced as the economy and society are not designed to help under-served people. You can see that Kennett takes care of many of these needs better than most, with programs for the kids after school, a vibrant food cupboard to keep them fed, and a rich supportive community and police force.

You can see the reason for the poverty. The entry level jobs just don't sustain a family. The 10% of the country that doesn't have a high school degree don't even have an opportunity to move into one of the sustainable jobs. And those with a high school degree aren't much better off with the demise of the blue color well-paying manufacturing jobs. And at one of DuPont's plants in Ohio, where the graduating seniors were tested, 1/3 of them couldn't pass the test for incoming employees. But the issue is much deeper. Even if we were able to provide everyone a college education, there just aren't enough good jobs to go around. That doesn't mean we wouldn't move the wealth needle if we started focusing on the needs of the good jobs that aren't being served by the current work force. If we can provide the training and skill development to these workers, we can reduce poverty. This also doesn't address the issues that the current economy is increasing income inequality and that long-term growth for the United States may be at 1% if we do very well.

And, we all know that money isn't everything, and Kennett can still be a great place to live for all levels of income. From the insights of Dr. Bosley, you can see the mindset that is always looking to improve the school district; one that is caring deeply about the achievement of each child while assuring adequate funding. This mindset establishes a great foundation for a community in which everyone can work and live.

∞

Another question is how are we going to stay informed regarding what is happening in Kennett? What is working and not working and what can we do about it?

Historically, Kennett had great newspaper coverage. We even got the weekly paper when we went off to college. But the only model for the modern newspaper seems to be one of having wealthy people own the paper and just take the losses. That is not a sustainable model. *The Kennett News and Advertiser* (1877-1982) and Mr. Richard G. Taylor's paper was printed through my youth and everyone subscribed. We enjoyed staying up with the community and the around-town section so we could get all the gossip, but also how the town and schools where doing, along with who was leading and who was getting into trouble.

There was a transition time when Jamie Blaine (1986-2000) owned the paper. I believe he spent more on resources than the paper could sustain and eventually it had to be picked up by a company that has an active website, Facebook account, Twitter feed and Instagram.

I don't envy the modern journalist, with all the pressure to tweet and blog and get stuff out without the editorial support that the old papers had. The cover page of a recent version, now called *The Kennett Paper*, had an article touting the huge tax increase that Unionville was getting. You had to go into the article rather deeply to see that it was 3% and about $200 per house. I'm sure that helps sell newspapers, but it doesn't help the school board sell their budget.

I've heard about how frustrated the current editor of *The Kennett Paper* is with a dozen stories to cover and not enough resources. John Oliver, during his HBO program "Last Week Tonight with John Oliver," recently focused on the subject of "journalism". He referenced the lack of resources available to investigative journalists, which ultimately result in advantages being taken by crooked politicians. I am more worried about an uninformed electorate, as newspapers and electronic media are our primary sources of information for current events, and it seems voters assume the politicians are corrupt. According to the Oliver report, from

2004 to 2014, newspapers grew online revenue by $2 billion dollars, but they lost $30 billion in print revenues. This is money that could have been spent on salaries of those professionals who are keeping the public informed with both the good and bad happenings within the community.

The current coverage of Kennett and Chester County is done by a fraction of the resources that were available to the local, county and Philadelphia papers just twenty-five years ago. And there are no easy fixes for this, at least John Oliver didn't have any. He was more the canary in the coal mine. But Kennett is a community that might be able to shine more of a light on the local goings-on. If we see it as our paper and our community, we can provide the paper with press releases that give insight to what we are doing and why. We can write letters that call them on a one-sided article or even about goings-on that are not being reported on. It needs to be our job to tell our story and not let it get lost in the cacophony of the daily events. Let's make it a little harder on those corrupt politicians and more importantly let's understand and celebrate what the leaders of our town are doing. For instance, our mayor is unpaid, as are the borough council members. They are expected to show up for meetings and events, even on Saturdays, dressed for success. Will the millennials be willing to do this in 15 years?

∞

In September of 2015, as a representative of the Kennett Food Cupboard, I went to a national conference in Cincinnati that addressed the challenges of poverty. I was focused on food, but quickly realized that the challenge was much bigger and keeping our population from going to bed hungry was just the tip of the iceberg. Still, food is a big part of the opportunity that we have. In fact, adequate food supply is a global problem and while at DuPont we developed a global food security index.

One of my first insights to food insecurity was a discussion with my 10th grade Sunday school teacher, Dr. Harry Cates. He was serving as Delaware's director of social services in the late 1970s. He was one of DuPont's great scientists and businessmen, and was loaned to the new governor, Pete DuPont, when the governor asked the DuPont Company for some executive leadership help. Harry was frustrated. He had been working for a company that was at the top of its form, and state administrative organizations were a work in progress. He lamented that the only real success of LBJ's war on poverty, that included a boost from Nixon's belief, was that the United States should be ashamed to have so much of the population going hungry. But Harry felt we should celebrate our successes. And in the 1970s, food relief grew 500%. And we had pretty much done away with hunger with food stamps and school meals. But he felt the rest of the Gordian knot of poverty went pretty much untouched.

The problem is we did not hold our gains. The USDA reported that 14% of American households were food insecure during at least some of 2014. Households experiencing very low food security was at 5.6%, and this is six years after the great recession. Today foodbanks are more active than ever.

USDA's labels describe ranges of food security.

Food Security

- High food security: no reported indications of food-access problems or limitations.
- Marginal food security: one or two reported indications – typically of anxiety over food sufficiency or shortage of food in the house. Little or no indication of changes in diets or food intake.

Food Insecurity

- Low food security: reports of reduced quality, variety, or desirability of diet. Little or no indication of reduced food intake.
- Very low food security: reports of multiple indications of disrupted eating patterns and reduced food intake.

Though hunger is the 800-pound gorilla in the room of America, there are a lot more things we can do in Kennett around food than just stock a pantry and wait for families to come by once a month and pick up a week's worth of food.

The first area of support is to make sure that the families are not going hungry, and they are getting the government support they are entitled to through the food stamp program. With cutbacks and issues with the limited availability of food stamps, they rarely cover a family for the whole month, which is a major reason why KACS is so important. In 2012, almost 48 million American households were food insecure, and they were getting about $134/month of assistance. One of the reasons the clients of KACS appreciate the agency so much is that KACS works to help ensure that the families are getting the support they are entitled to. We still feel we can do a better job by partnering with the federal agencies and encouraging our clients to spread the word to their friends and families to make sure they don't go hungry.

Almost half of our clients are immigrants and offering them a half pound of kale is likely not going to be included in their meal plan. So it is important that we provide them insights into how to prepare the food that we are offering. And by providing cooking classes, we have the ability to do a number of things. It is not just expanding their menus to include different vegetables, fruits and meats, but it can give insights on how to prepare those dishes. One of the food cupboards had a large number of potatoes dropped off and to the surprise of everyone no one was taking any. After asking around, the answer seemed to be that they didn't know how to prepare potatoes. When they were told to just peel, cut, and boil them, they asked, "How do you cut them?" It seemed that plastic knives from Wendy's fast food restaurant was their knife of choice. So paring knives were made available to help skin and cut up the potatoes. As new dishes were developed for the cooking classes, there was a canvas of the participants of what equipment they had in their homes and each week they were sent home with a new recipe and a new gadget to help them execute the dish. Then the classes got into what is healthy and how much. So meals are designed to not only taste good but to be good for you. This gets into what it means to eat healthy and the need for five fruits and vegetables a day.

Our clients are much different than the general population and in many cases, they are more likely to have diabetes and be obese. It takes more than a few cooking classes to deal with these issues, but we can partner with the YMCA to provide access to exercise equipment and help them with dieting and building a healthy life style.

There is also the financial aspect of food. Healthcare, housing and food are probably the three biggest expenses of a family. There are many things a family can do to make the food dollar go farther. In the cooking class, one can show how much cheaper it is to build meals around a roast chicken than buying the parts. Where you buy your food and the quantities you buy can have a big difference in the quality and quantity of food you get. Just having a plan on what you are going to spend and how far your food dollar will go can make a big difference.

∞

The most surprising poverty conference presentation for me was by two university researchers who discussed the benefits of families coming together for dinner from an occupational health stand point. In my experience this always seemed to be a standard family event, but it seems that it isn't. When a family is close to the poverty line, and the husband is working two jobs and the wife and older kids all have their own jobs, getting together every night for a meal is a real extravagance. So this occupational health project was to develop a course for families to teach them time management, how to make an evening meal attractive and the benefits of having time together as a family, all something that middle class people take for granted.

There are significant programs to make sure that eligible American citizens are covered for their health care through Medicaid, their employer, or on the health exchanges. But it seems we forget about how important our dental care can be. Kids are brought to a dentist for the first time, if they are lucky, in elementary school. The great strength of the American dental system is preventive care, but no one is pushing these children to brush their teeth. Now the Food Cupboard is giving out toothbrushes provided by local dentists and getting families into emergency dental care. And the good news is, a new LCH dental program is on the horizon.

There is a world of chemistry and biology around food that our clients have never seen. So courses on the chemistry and biology of food can be a tremendous learning program to teach useful science to individuals who have never seen a science course. Life in the 21st century without a rudimentary knowledge of science, can be a tremendous disadvantage. Imagine observing the world with a much diminished insight on how things work.

∞

Joan has commented that many of the Latino clients she visited in their homes during her public health nursing years were not overweight when they came to this country. But, with the purchase of fast foods and joining our American lifestyle, obesity and diabetes has grown. Our community has just touched the tip of the iceberg with promoting community gardens and learning how to provide for one's own food insecurity. The migrants who frequent our food cupboards have the Mexican experience of planting gardens in their country, "putting up" fruits and vegetables for the winter months and knowing how to stretch a meal. We need to find ways to encourage and build on these strengths. Some may say that with the long hours working in the mushroom houses, they don't have time, but in reality, this process could draw on the youth and extended family and friends to take on gardening and food preparation roles. I've heard that food cupboards don't exist in Mexico. The family spirit of sharing resources with each other and living off the land are essential to this population. While we are living out our American paradigm of feeding the poor, we need to explore ways to learn how the migrant has survived in his/her country without a food cupboard and learn ways to develop these processes.

Regular physical exercise is another factor that affects weight gain. Joan tells the story of how one of her clients returned to Mexico for six weeks. She walked to the store every day to purchase food for her family's daily meals and lost 25 pounds. In our area, the stores are not close to homes, so clients are driving cars everywhere and missing the natural walking that balances diet with exercise. Providing opportunities for exercise for all community members would be a great support. The Kennett Area YMCA has offered scholarships for low-income residents to take advantage of the YMCA facility. One sees more diversity every time one opens the YMCA doors, but again, this is only a small number compared to what is needed.

It seems everyone has a relative who happens to drink a little too much, and providing classes on how to manage alcohol and deal with alcoholism can make a major contribution to improving a family's functioning capability.

And, last but not least, there is nothing that brings a community together like sharing their recipes. We are thinking that after this book, we may come out with the KACS cookbook, where we gather the best recipes from the community and share them.

Data

"Practice of true community involves responsibilities and actions that do not come naturally to us."

— Jerry Bridges, evangelical Christian author —

Kennett By The Numbers

by Joan Holliday and Bob George

The story of Kennett, we are hoping, is one that a lot of communities can identify with. The question of how to distribute limited resources, set priorities and continue making that village a better place to live and raise a family is being answered every day. There is no one answer, it is a process and a mindset, and we're hoping this book will offer some insights for you and your community. To further that end, here are some basics about our town and community:

In the book, <u>Kennett Square Yesterday: A History of the Borough of Kennett Square in County of Chester in the Commonwealth of Pennsylvania</u> (1982), the name Kennett is attributed to Francis Smith, who took up 500 acres at the mouth of Pocopson Creek in 1686. He came from Devizes in Witshire, England, where there is a village named Kennet on the Kennet River. Joseph Musgrave was the initial believer in the town Kennett Square, as it was first mentioned in an application for a tavern license in 1765. The tavern location was on the northeast corner of State and Union Streets.

On September 9, 1777, the Baron Wilhelm Von Knyphausen and 5,000 Hessian troops arrived in Kennett and camped in the northwest corner of the borough. On September 10th, British soldiers, Lord Cornwallis and General Sir William Howe arrived and camped at the current location of the Kennett High School. The next day they split up and Von Knyphausen went to meet General George Washington and his troops, and started the Battle of the Brandywine at Anvil Tavern.

There was a large contingent of Quakers and the Society of Friends, and the area was against slavery. It was part of the Underground Railroad. In 1853, Kennett was "founded" and held elections in 1855.

Geographically, when we talk about Kennett, we are referring to several town characteristics. We start with the commercial center, the Borough of Kennett Square. This is the square-shaped square mile (1.07 square miles, to be exact) that defines the borough's borders. This population of 6,176 from the US census is surrounded by Kennett Township (15.6 sq. miles) and New Garden Township (16.2 sq. miles). The population of this area is a little under 20,000. Then there is southern Chester County, which goes west to Oxford and east to the Delaware County line. It is what is covered by our United Way of Southern Chester County. This total population is close to 100,000. The southern border of the township is the Delaware state line. This creates some potentially interesting purchasing habits, as Delaware has no sales tax and more liberal liquor laws. We are west-southwest of Philadelphia, about a 40-mile drive from the city's downtown. Philadelphia is the largest metropolitan area, but you must forgive us for thinking that we are in the center of the universe, with deer and foxes walking through the bucolic setting of our back yards. If you drive 135 miles to the north you are in the Big Apple-NYC, going south the same distance, you have passed Baltimore and DC, the nation's capital. Senator Biden, for 30 years, commuted to work by Amtrak as a senator from his house just ten miles south of us.

∞

Demographically, we have been a community of immigrants for over 100 years, which I guess is also true of the country. In the borough, according to the US census the two largest ethnicities are Hispanic (48.8% of the population) and white (42.8% of the population). In Kennett Township, the Hispanic population drops precipitously to 10.5% while the Caucasian proportion jumps to 84.2%. The African-American percentages drop from 7.2 in the borough to 1.8 in the township. Driving home the point that we are a community that relies heavily on immigration, 37.9% of the borough is foreign-born. That drops to 9% in the township. The national average is about 13%.

In terms of housing, the borough has 2,024 units and the township has 3,203. The median values in the borough are $226,100 and $409,100 in the township. Consider that the national average is $175,700, Pennsylvania's is $164,900 and the whole of Chester County has a median housing value of $323,600. The average number of persons living in each household is 3 in the borough and 2.38 in the township. This shows in the data on income. Median household income is $67,378 in the borough and $102,721 outside of it. When you look at the per capita income in the past twelve months, you see that in the borough it is $26,336 while in the township it is $55,601. You would need two and a half per capita incomes to reach the median income in the borough, versus less than two outside it.

Looking at education, the borough has 25% fewer high school graduates than the national average. Only 60.8% of people over 25 years old in the borough are high school graduates. 22.6% have a bachelor's degree or higher, compared to the national average of 29.3%. When you turn to the township, those numbers jump to 96% and 58.6%, respectively. Keep in mind, as we go on to look at the schools in our community, that just under half, 48.2%, of the households in the borough speak a language other than English at home.

Kennett Consolidated School District has one high school, one middle school, and three elementary schools. It covers 34.2 square miles. That is all of Kennett, borough and township, New Garden Township and a small southern bit of East Marlborough Township. Here are some of the breakdowns of the data from the Pennsylvania Department of Education (note: percentages are often rounded to nearest whole number). In total, about 4,212 students are educated in the district. Just over half of them are white, about 42% are Hispanic and the rest is primarily split pretty evenly between African American and Asian students.

Kennett High School serves around 1,282 students. In 2014, 309 students graduated and 60% of the class enrolled in four-year college programs, 19% went on to another form of higher education (e.g. community college, technical school, et cetera), 16% entered the workforce, and 1% joined the military.

∞

Unionville and Avon Grove are two nearby towns that have high schools very close to Kennett's; four and twelve miles away, respectively. Comparing demographics amongst them will highlight some of the nuances of how and why we focus on the kids.

Unionville High School is a little larger than Kennett with 1,320 students, while Avon Grove is about 40% larger with 1,811 students. Demographically, all three are very different entities. One commonality is that the makeup of the student body is about 50% male and 50% female. Kennett has, as expected, a large representation of Hispanics, with 37%. The student body at Avon Grove consists of 18% Hispanics, and at Unionville 4%. There is the expected representation of white students, 56%, 76% and 86%, respectively, as well as African-American, 4%, 2%, and 1%. Asian students at Unionville represent 8% of the students, versus Kennett and Avon Grove's 2% and 1%.

Also fitting into the pattern are the statistics around economically disadvantaged students. Kennett and Avon Grove have 36% and 21%, while Unionville has 6%. Kennett and Avon Grove have 8% and 3% of their students learning English as a second language, compared to Unionville's 1%. Mandarin and Korean would be a large part of the Unionville ESL load.

All three schools offer a similar number of advanced placement (AP) courses. Avon Grove has 17, Kennett has 18 and Unionville has 20. Unionville and Avon Grove both have 11% of the students in special education classes. Kennett has 16%.

All three have very high graduation rates. Kennett's student dropout rate is 1.2%, Avon Grove's is 0.39% and Unionville's is 0%. Of those that graduate from Kennett, Avon Grove and Unionville, 60%, 65% and 90% go on to four-year college programs, respectively. About 19% of Kennett's and 17% of Avon Grove's students go on to other higher education programs, such as community colleges or technical schools.

∞

The schools also achieve recognition from outside the district. The Kennett Middle School website states, "For the second time since 2012, Kennett Middle School was recognized by the Pennsylvania Don Eichhorn Schools: Schools to Watch program.

The Pennsylvania Schools to Watch program annually recognizes a small number of diverse, high-performing, growth-oriented middle schools that demonstrate academic excellence, developmental responsiveness to the unique challenges of early adolescence, social equity, and school structures and processes that support and sustain the path to excellence. The middle school joins a very select cadre of 31 schools in Pennsylvania and more than 370 schools across the country that have earned the distinction of being Schools to Watch; only four others are located in the Delaware Valley Region.

And, as written in the KCSD website, the Kennett High School had two awards:

1. "The Kennett Consolidated School District is proud that the Washington Post has named Kennett High School one of America's Most Challenging High Schools. In order to name its Most Challenging High Schools, the Washington Post uses a "Challenge Index." This index is based on the total number of Advanced Placement, International Baccalaureate and Cambridge tests given at the school each year, divided by the number of seniors who graduated in May or June. Schools that had as many tests in 2015 as they had graduates, and received a ratio of at least 1.00 earned a spot on the national list. Kennett High School was ranked 17th out of 39 schools that made the national list.

2. The Kennett Consolidated School District is proud that *U.S. News & World Report* has named Kennett High School one of America's Best High Schools. To produce the Best High Schools rankings, *U.S. News & World Report* teamed up with North Carolina-based RTI International, a global nonprofit social-science research firm. The comprehensive rankings methodology is based on the key principles that a great high school must serve all of its students well, not just those who are college bound, and that it must be able to produce measurable academic outcomes to show it is successfully educating its student body across a range of performance indicators."

And, from the Avon Grove High School Web Site; *U.S. News & World Report* awarded a silver ranking to Avon Grove High School which is ranked 33rd within Pennsylvania. Students have the opportunity to take Advanced Placement® course work and exams. The AP® participation rate at Avon Grove High School is 44 percent. The student body makeup is 52 percent male and 48 percent female, and the total minority enrollment is 22 percent.

And Unionville High School is no slouch. As stated on their website, Unionville-Chadds Ford School District (UCF) has been consistently recognized as one of the top ten districts in the state by *US News & World Report* since 2010. "The Street.com" ranked UCF as one of the top 20 school districts in the country. Unionville High School received national recognition, ranked among the top 2% of public high schools in the United States, according to *US News & World Report* rankings. The Washington Post ranked Unionville High School the 11th most rigorous in the state of Pennsylvania based on its AP program, and *Suburban Life Magazine* rated Unionville High School as the top suburban high school in the Philadelphia region.

US News and World Reports ranks high schools every year across the United States. In 2016 they ranked the top 676 high schools in Pennsylvania and all three of these local high schools were in the top 10%, with Unionville #8, Avon Grove #33, and Kennett #64 in the state.

Making sure the kids have all the resources they need to succeed in school is integrally related to making sure their parents, and the entire community, are working. In 2016, the Historic Kennett Square Economic Task Force retained the services of a consulting firm to perform a Kennett Region Economic Development Study. Much of the following economic and labor information stems from findings of that study, or other government databases such as the U.S. Census or the Bureau of Labor and Statistics.

There are currently about 718 businesses in Kennett Square. The data from 2012 showed 682 in the borough and 675 in Kennett Township. Just over half in the borough and a just under half in the township are owned by men. About 100 businesses in the borough and a little less than 100 in the township are minority-owned. Of the businesses in the borough, 53% employ four or fewer people, and an additional 21% employ five to nine people.

The recent trends, basically since 2009 when the area began to finally right itself after the Great Recession, have been quite good for Kennett. Unemployment dropped quickly, particularly from 2012-2013 when it went from 5.4% to 3.7%. Compare that to Chester County where the rate was still 5.3% in 2013. It was 2015 before the county caught up to Kennett. Labor force participation has also recovered greatly. Beyond a slight dip from 2010 to 2011, the number of those employed or actively seeking employment has continued to grow.

Interestingly, the number of people that live and work in the borough is comparatively small to those that work outside it. Only 227 people, in 2013, lived and worked downtown, while 2,369 people commuted outside it. The worker inflow, however, was positive as 3,295 people drove into town for work. It is worth noting that, of the people who work in the borough, relatively few are commuting from the same area. That is, 3.9% of the people who work in Kennett are coming from Philadelphia. Another 1.3% of them are coming from Wilmington. If you take out the top ten locations, 83% are coming from "other areas". The same is true to those commuting from Kennett to outside locations with 76% of the commuters work somewhere other than the top ten most common locations. This creates a lot of challenges for public transportation solutions, of which there are very few. That being said, the commute of the average person living in town is 17 minutes. Over half of commuters take less than 15 minutes to get to work. About 67% drive alone to work, 10% less than the national average.

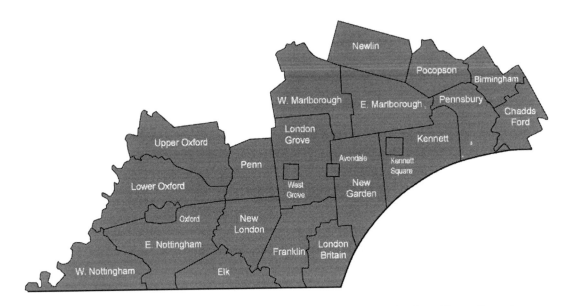

Map of Kennett and the surrounding area (courtesy of United Way of Southern Chester County)

When we look at the type of work people living in Kennett do, the two largest sectors represented are Management of Companies and Enterprises (21%) and Professional, Scientific and Technical Services (13.2%). Employment in these two sectors has grown recently, as it has in the Retail Trade sector, which has grown almost 70% since 2009. While the trends in hiring in the management and professional sectors indicate a need for relatively highly educated workers who will most likely receive good compensation, there are other factors to consider. When looking at Chester County, the Health Care and Social Assistance sector is the largest one. While the Professional, Scientific and Technical sector is a close second, the third largest is Retail Trade. Both health care and retail in large part consist of lower-paying jobs. The third to sixth largest sectors, well-paying jobs in Manufacturing, Educational Services and Finance, have seen declines in employment.

You will see on the volunteer list that we interviewed 21 organizations with a total of 2,028 volunteers that keep these organizations running smoothly.

This data sets the stage for understanding this community of southern Chester County, its resources and its poverty. The United Way has a graphic on its first web page showing 1,903 kids from ages 5 to 17 years old living in poverty in our area during 2011, well after the Great Recession. Poverty is the dark cloud hanging over the heads of a large segment of most communities. Let's hope that this story of Kennett can show how one village used its resources to address poverty and focused on shaping its future one child at a time.

Epilogue

**"The future belongs to those who believe in
the beauty of their dreams."**
— Eleanor Roosevelt, American activist and
First Lady of the United States (1933-1945) —

Epilogue
by Joan Holliday

This book was written during a 16-month period, so interviews were dispersed throughout the year. Even though some of the details that identify the number of employees, the budget, and programming may have already changed, the substance of the story and its spirit remain the same.

We acknowledge that we could have conducted many more interviews of caring groups who care for our village's children. Our hope is that we captured the critical mass and that through the stories that were told, others feel included and celebrated.

The book is personal for us. Joan's chapters come from a passionate caring about nourishing the town and keeping its values and vision. Bob's chapters come from strong beliefs about the conditions needed to keep a community sustainable and a great place to raise a child. Collaboratively, we offer the chapters on recommendations and reflections. We acknowledge that all of our comments are coming from our personal orientations, and so need to be considered in this context.

It has been an enriching experience for us. We have had many years of personal participation in the Kennett community, and yet, through the interviews, we encountered the Kennett landscape in a fresh way. Our hope is that Kennett residents will have the same experience and will continue the legacy of contributing to the town's ongoing success. To those who do not live here, the many tenets and stories that have been offered could serve as inspiration and be brought to other communities. Creating a village to raise a child is a worthy cause for all communities.

Glossary

GLOSSARY

Acronyms:

ACLU   American Civil Liberties Union

AME   African Methodist Episcopal church See also UAME.

AP   Advanced Placement (AP) is a program in the United States and Canada created by the College Board which offers college-level curricula and examinations to high school students. American colleges and universities may grant placement and course credit to students who obtain high scores on the examinations.

APEX   ASPIRA Parents for Educational Excellence

ASPIRA   National nonprofit organization devoted solely to the education and leadership development of Puerto Rican and other Latino youth.

CAMP   College Assistance Migrant Program

Carter CDC   Joseph & Sarah Carter Community Development Corporation

CCHD   Chester County Health Department

CCIU   Chester County Intermediate Unit

COAD   The COAD Group (formerly Chester County Council on Addictive Diseases

CSIU   Central Susquehanna Intermediate Unit

CTC   Communities That Care

CVIM   Community Volunteers in Medicine

DARE   Drug Abuse Resistance Education

EMS   Emergency Medical Services

EMT   Emergency Medical Technician

ESL   English as a Second Language

GED   General Educational Development tests (see GED below)

GPA   Grade Point Average

HIV/AIDS   Human Immunodeficiency Virus/Acquired Immunodeficiency Syndrome

The HOOD	The House of Original Dreams, located in Exton, PA provides education, training, and job opportunities for youth between ages 12 to 24.
ICU	Intensive Care Unit
ILA	Interactive Literacy Activities
INS	United States Immigration and Naturalization Service
IRCA	Immigration and Reform Control Act
KACS	Kennett Area Community Services
KARMA	Kennett Area Restaurant Merchant Association
KASA	Kennett After-School Association
KCSD	Kennett Consolidated School District
KEF	Kennett Education Foundation
KHS	Kennett High School
KMS	Kennett Middle School
KSRTF	Kennett Square Revitalization Task Force
KTSP	Kindergarten Transition Summer Program
LCH	La Comunidad Hispana
LEED	Leadership in Energy & Environmental Design, is a green building certification program that recognizes best-in-class building strategies and practices.
MCH	Maternal-Child Health Nurse Home Visiting Program
MCHC	Maternal and Child Health Consortium of Chester County
MDJ	Magisterial District Judge
MDTF	Municipal Drug Task Force
MEP	Migrant Education Program
MLK	Martin Luther King
MYKE	Mentoring Youth in Kennett Elementary
NCLB	Elementary and Secondary Education Act, otherwise known as "No Child Left Behind"
NFP	Nurse-Family Partnership
OSHA	Occupational Safety and Health Administration
PASA	Pennsylvania Association for Sustainable Agriculture
PAT	Parents as Teachers
PCCD	Pennsylvania Commission on Crime and Delinquency

PDC	PA Downtown Center Organization
PDE	Pennsylvania Department of Education
PIPE	Partners in Parenting Education
PSEA	Pennsylvania State Education Association
PSU	Penn State University
SAT	Scholastic Assessment Test
SPP	School Performance Profile
STEM	Science, Technology, Engineering and Math curriculum
STEAM	Science, Technology, Engineering and Math curriculum, with Arts
UAME	UAME Church – Union American Methodist Episcopal Church
USDA	United States Department of Agriculture
UWSCC	United Way of Southern Chester County
WIN	Walk In kNowledge program
YMCA	Young Men's Christian Association

NOTE*   The 2016 Federal Poverty Level Chart lists the earning level for a family of four as $24,250. The Kennett Food Cupboard increased this earning limit to $43,650—approximately 180% times the federal guideline.

About the Authors
Joan Holliday and Bob George

Joan Holliday lived in Suttons Bay, Michigan (at the little finger of the hand of the state's shape) with her parents and six siblings (one being her twin, Jean) until she attended the Mercy School of Nursing School in Detroit, Michigan in 1964. Growing up in a small town of a thousand residents, she learned the value of a village's support and membership. She received her registered nursing degree and later a Bachelor's of Science Degree in Community Health from the University of Cincinnati.

Joan is a passionate, community advocate and grassroots leader in the Kennett area, starting with her public health nursing role for thirty-two years and including her ongoing volunteer roles. She is a board member of YoungMoms, the Health and Welfare Foundation of Southern Chester County, and the Kennett Arts Alliance. Joan is a faith community nurse at St. Cornelius Catholic Church. She is the founder of the Each and All Dialogue Group, Bridging the Community, the InterGen Coalition, the Chester County Faith Community Health Ministry Network, and an author of *Path of Potential Reader* stories. Her hobbies are piano, guitar, hiking, bread-making and reflection. She is married to Bob Holliday and lives in Chadds Ford, PA. They have three children: Kim, David and Anne, and five grandchildren.

∞

Bob George is currently a principal partner at ThorntonGeorge LLC, a consulting firm that currently focuses on addressing the issues that organizations are working on to make the world better.

He came to Kennett Square, PA in the 5th grade and has lived there on and off ever since. A member of the high school class of 1964, he is now on the board of the Kennett Alumni Association. He received a Bachelor's of Science in industrial engineering from Penn State University in 1968, along with a minor in leadership and an officer's regular commission. After Vietnam, Bob followed in his father's footsteps and joined the DuPont Company as an industrial engineer in their nylon manufacturing operations in Martinsville, Virginia, during which time he also served as the chairman of the board of the Department of Social Services. His career was built on his training in industrial engineering where he improved processes and worked on benchmarking corporate processes. He was trained as a Six Sigma Black Belt and taught sales and negotiation. He contributed the benchmarking chapter to the National Safety Council's book, Safety Through Design. He led the manufacturing advisory board for engineering at Penn State, and, in 1997, was a National Science Foundation Grant recipient as an Industry Fellow in Residence at the university.

He helped start the Kennett Education Foundation and the Longwood Rotary Club. He and his wife, Jane, have four children and six grandchildren. His hobbies include reading, running, skiing, and climbing.

Made in the USA
Middletown, DE
30 March 2017